W9-BXX-766

The Art of
Card Reading at Bridge

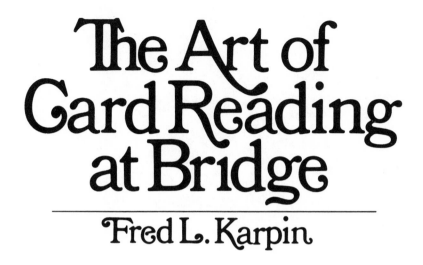

The Art of Card Reading at Bridge

Fred L. Karpin

DOVER PUBLICATIONS, INC.

NEW YORK

Copyright

Copyright © 1973 by Fred L. Karpin.
All rights reserved under Pan American and International Copyright Conventions.

Published in Canada by General Publishing Company, Ltd., 30 Lesmill Road, Don Mills, Toronto, Ontario.

This Dover edition, first published in 1982, is an unabridged and unaltered republication of the work originally published by Harper & Row Publishers, New York, in 1973.

Library of Congress Cataloging-in-Publication Data

Karpin, Fred L.
    The art of card reading at bridge.

    Reprint. Originally published 1st ed.: New York: Harper & Row, 1973.
    1. Contract bridge.   I. Title.
    [GV1282.3.K352   1982]   795.41′53   82-7277
    ISBN 0-486-21787-6 (pbk.)   AACR2

Manufactured in the United States of America
Dover Publications, Inc.
180 Varick Street
New York, N.Y. 10014

Contents

Foreword

From the moment you become a bridge devotee, counting is always with you. First, you look around to see if there is a table. When your count reaches one, you stop counting. Next you count players, to make certain that four are present. After the cards have been dealt out, you count the cards in your hand, to make sure that you have exactly thirteen.

After your hand has been sorted, you count your points. During the play and at its conclusion, you count your tricks. When the rubber has ended, you count your score. And when the evening is over, you count your winnings (or your losses, as the case might be).

The above-mentioned type of counting requires no particular skill. Its only prerequisite is a public school education through grade 2 (age 7–8). It has even been said that there are some very good bridge players who do not have the stated educational requirement, but who nevertheless have succeeded, without any outside assistance, in mastering the subject of basic counting.

But there is another type of counting at the bridge table which is known as "counting out a hand" or "card reading." By counting out a hand is meant deducing the original distribution of the hidden hands from information gained during the bidding and/or play. By card reading is meant drawing the correct inferences about the nature of an opponent's high-card holding and/or distribution, said inferences being obtained from either the bidding, the fall of the cards, or both.

Basically, card reading and counting out a hand are one and the same, although perhaps card reading would be classified as the generic, or more inclusive, term to categorize this area of counting. In this book these two terms will be used interchangeably.

A few short decades ago counting out a hand was considered by average players as being too difficult to absorb, and it was a subject that was deemed by them to be for experts only. But, in the words of Tennyson, just as "the old order changeth, yielding place to new," so counting out a hand has now become accepted and utilized as a part of the public domain, and is recognized as being not nearly so difficult as the reader might have been led to believe. Admittedly, it does require a little work and a little patience. But, in repetition, one becomes proficient very quickly in this field, after which counting out a hand tends to become ingrained. When this occurs, a person is on the way to becoming a good bridge player.

Victor Mollo, one of Europe's leading bridge authorities, puts it this way: "Learning to count out a hand is like plunging into a cold bath—difficult and a little frightening until you get into the habit. Then it comes quite easily, and leaves you with a pleasant tingling sensation when it is all over." And, may I add, from that all-important materialistic viewpoint, it reduces losses and increases winnings.

This book is devoted exclusively to the subject of card reading or counting out a hand. To those many bridge players (named herein, and nameless) whose counting exploits are presented in this text, I owe a debt of gratitude. Although they had nothing to do with the writing of this treatise, some of the counting deals that confronted them in actual combat have been assimilated into this book as illustrations of technically accurate and thoughtful play. As a result of their real-life contributions, I was spared the time and effort of creating the different types of hands required to describe many of the most important aspects of card reading. My appreciation and thanks are hereby recorded.

FRED L. KARPIN

1

How to Count
Out a Hand

There are two primary, permanent objectives in counting out a hand:

1. To determine the distribution (in the opponents' hands) of the outstanding cards of each suit, the purpose usually being to isolate one vital suit about which specific knowledge is desired.

2. To determine the certain, or probable, location of a missing key card (or key cards) in the isolated suit.

In the deal that follows, we have a simple, classic example of how one goes about isolating suits, and how, having accomplished this with absolute certainty, one is able to pinpoint the precise location of a most vital outstanding key card. Let's assume that you are the South declarer. On the previous deal you had fulfilled a four-spade contract, thus attaining that prerequisite for the winning of a rubber—namely, becoming vulnerable.

North-South vulnerable. South deals.

<pre>
                        NORTH
                     ♠ K 8 7
                     ♥ A Q 7 3
                     ♦ A J 9
                     ♣ Q 10 4
        WEST   EAST
     ♠ 9 6 3   ♠ 10 5 4 2
     ♥ 10 5 4   ♥ 8 6
     ♦ 5   ♦ Q 8 7 6 3 2
     ♣ 9 8 7 6 3 2   ♣ 5
                        SOUTH
                     ♠ A Q J
                     ♥ K J 9 2
                     ♦ K 10 4
                     ♣ A K J
</pre>

The bidding:

SOUTH	WEST	NORTH	EAST
2 NT	Pass	7 NT	Pass
Pass	Pass		

Opening lead: Nine of ♣.

After the opening club lead is made and the dummy comes into view, you are probably unhappy with what you see. You expected that when partner bid seven no-trump, thirteen tricks would be there for the taking. And all you have are twelve tricks: three spades, four hearts, two diamonds, and three clubs.

But if you think you're unhappy, cast an eye at your partner, and imagine his feelings as he sees you, with furrowed brow, examining the lay of the land. When he bid seven no-trump on his 16 high-card points, he did so because he counted on you for your guaranteed minimum of 22 high-card points. From his position, he surely figured that thirteen tricks would be there for the taking, what with your partnership possessing at least 38 out of the 40 high-card points in the deck.

As you are reflecting, your woeful-countenanced partner is probably saying to himself: "How could he have a problem? I'd wager he miscounted his points at the outset, and all he has are 18 or 19 instead of the 22 he's supposed to have. I should have listened to my grandmother when she told me never to bid a grand slam unless I was going to play it. Well, next time I'll know better—I'll bid just six no-trump."

Actually—as partner will appreciate sympathetically later on *if* you fulfill your contract—the bidding by both of you was letter-perfect. I doubt whether it will be one time in a thousand that a partnership possessing 38 high-card points does not have thirteen tricks at no-trump for the taking. But look at what happened in this deal.

Your jack of spades and jack of clubs turned out to be completely wasted cards. If each of them had been deuces, you would still have the same twelve tricks. Or, if your little two of hearts had been either the two of spades or the two of clubs, you would have four black-suit winners in whichever black suit the deuce happened to be, and a total of thirteen tricks right off the top. But fate decreed that you be dealt what you were dealt—and so you have some work to do.

You win the opening lead with, let us say, the club jack. An examination of your assets reveals that no matter how expertly or inexpertly you play, you can never win any more, nor any less, than three spade tricks, four hearts, and three clubs. So if your contract is to be fulfilled, you will have to come home with three diamond tricks.

Specifically speaking, the fulfillment of your grand-slam contract depends on finessing successfully against the diamond queen. All other avenues are closed. If you can locate that key card, a finesse against it will be routine, and you will chalk up a vulnerable grand slam. Who possesses Her Ladyship, East or West?

Let me state that any player in the world—no matter how poorly he plays—can fulfill the contract 50 percent of the time. All he has to do is to point his finger at either East or West and say: "You, my friend, have the queen of diamonds." He then proceeds to play the hand on the assumption that his pointing has been accurate—and half the time he will be right and half the time he will be wrong. But I think we all agree that this would be a heck of a way for him to play the hand, especially if his index finger is dirty.

After you capture the opening lead with your jack of clubs, you lead the club king. When it comes East's turn to play, he discards the deuce of diamonds.

Although you might not realize it at this moment, you have just come into possession of a tremendous amount of meaningful, factual information: East was dealt just one club. Since you had three clubs in your own hand originally, and three were in dummy, *West was dealt six clubs.*

Here then, at the completion of trick two, you know almost half of the cards that were dealt to West: six clubs out of thirteen cards. Even if you stopped your counting at this moment, to point your finger at East and say: "You figure to have the queen of diamonds," you would be right 63 percent of the time if you put your trust in the science of mathematics. The reason, you ask?

West has seven unknown cards, in spades, hearts, and diamonds (exclusive of six clubs) ; East has twelve unknown cards, in spades, hearts, and diamonds (exclusive of one club) . Take these nineteen unknown cards, of which one is the diamond queen, shuffle them up, give West seven of them, and give East the remaining twelve. Mathematically, 12 times out of 19 (63 percent) the diamond queen will land in East's hand.

To present this mathematical situation in "unmathematical" terms, if you take the deck of fifty-two cards, pull one out and put it face down on the table, and I ask you: "Where does the diamond queen figure to be? Is it the one that you pulled out, or is it in the pack containing the remaining fifty-one cards?," you would answer: "In the remaining fifty-one, of course." And how often would the one card you pulled out be the diamond queen? Common sense would tell you that it would be one time out of 52 because when you isolated that one card, there was exactly one chance out of (the pack of) 52 that it would be the diamond queen.

Here, then, at trick two, you have increased your chances of guessing the location of the diamond queen from 50 percent at the completion of trick one to 63 percent at the completion of trick two. And if you were not a "counter" before seeing the light in this deal, you have just become a better player. But let's go on.

Since West has seven unknown cards and East has twelve, why go through the trouble of trying to reconstruct East's remaining twelve cards? As everybody knows, since it is much easier to count to seven than it is to twelve, let's focus our exclusive attention on West's hand. Our aim, of course, will be to isolate the diamond suit, so that we can have a better idea as to the location of that vital card, the diamond queen.

What you intend to do is to play out your top spades and top hearts, observing what *West* plays as you lead out these suits. If you can ascertain precisely what West was dealt in spades and hearts (in addition to six known clubs), then you will have succeeded in isolating the diamond suit.

So you next lead, let us say, the ace of spades, the queen of spades, and then the jack of spades, which you overtake with dummy's king. You note that West, whom you are shadowing, follows suit to all three leads of spades. Nine of West's cards are now an open book: six clubs and three spades.

You next cash the ace and queen of hearts, after which you lead a low heart to your king. Having kept both of your eyes Westward, you have observed that West has followed suit to all three leads of hearts. Since you weren't watching East's plays on your heart leads, you next cash the jack of hearts. West discards a club.

You now know with absolute certainty twelve of the cards that were dealt to West, whose footsteps you have been dogging: six clubs, three hearts, and three spades. And, simultaneously, you have just proved beyond a shadow of a doubt that there is room in his hand for one diamond, at most. He might have been dealt the thirteenth spade, in which case he would have no diamonds whatsoever. Hence, since West was dealt a *maximum* of one diamond, East was dealt a *minimum* of six diamonds.

Is the light beginning to dawn? If it isn't, it will before this paragraph concludes. You next lead the four of diamonds, and West follows suit with the five-spot. You now know every one of the thirteen cards with which West started: six clubs, three spades, three hearts, and one diamond. Unless West was dealt fourteen cards, the queen of diamonds *has to be* in East's hand.

So you win the diamond lead with the board's ace, after which you lead the nine of diamonds. When East follows suit with a low diamond, you insert your ten-spot with the absolute assurance that it will win the trick. As you chalk up the score:

We	They
1500	
700	
120	
220	

and come up with a total of 2540 points in your favor (on the first deal you bid and made four spades), your material profit momentarily becomes even greater than its face value as you hear your partner comment: "Nice play, partner, nice play."

And, possibly, you speculate as to what partner might have said if you had misguessed the location of the diamond queen, thus incurring a one-trick set, with the score then reading:

We	They
	100
120	

If you reflect on these two scores, you will realize that there was a swing of more than 2500 points riding on whether you finessed successfully or you didn't. And, in the vernacular, 2500 points ain't hay, regardless of the stake of the game.

Let us now summarize the highlights of what you have thus far learned with respect to card reading or counting out a hand, as embodied in the deal you have just played. Let us do it from the very beginning, in chronological order:

1. When the dummy was put down, it was readily apparent that there were no optional lines of play available to you. You either finessed successfully for the diamond queen (victory!) or you finessed unsuccessfully (total defeat, in a material sense, and the incurring of the everlasting enmity of partner for having thrown away his money).

2. Counting out a hand begins at the moment that one of the opponents fails to follow suit, for when this happens you know exactly how that suit was divided all around the table prior to the outset of play. When an opponent fails to follow suit, you have obtained as a springboard *a fact that has been proved absolutely.*

3. Having learned, at the completion of trick two, that West had been dealt six clubs and East but one, you now forgot that East existed, and concentrated on West in order to reconstruct his original hand of thirteen cards. Why did you pick on West for your counting? Because it is a general principle of counting that when one opponent fails to follow suit, *you count his partner's hand, since you know more about the latter's hand.* As was stated, why count to twelve when it is much easier to count to seven? In other words, *count the hand which is simpler to count, the hand which has the fewer unknown cards.*

4. With the discovery that West had been dealt six clubs, you then played off your spades and hearts, watching West every step of the way. In so doing, you learned that West had been dealt three spades and three hearts.

5. When you next led a low diamond out of the South hand, and West followed suit with a low diamond, you yelled out (figuratively, of course): "Eureka!" The English translation of this Greek word is, "I have found it!" Your reference, of course, was to the diamond queen, which you then knew was in East's hand just as surely as you would have known it if East had shown you his cards.

You also learned something that will serve you well on those days when you are unable to obtain a complete and perfect count of one of the opponent's hands (and most of the time you will not be able to get a complete count, as will be observed in later chapters of this book), namely: when you are trying to locate a key card, you will play your cards on the assumption that *the opponent who is known to have the greater number of unknown cards is the one who probably has the specific card* you are looking for.

When, at the completion of trick two in the actual deal, you discovered that West had been dealt six clubs, with East having been dealt only one club, West was known to have been dealt seven unknown cards in hearts, spades, and diamonds, and East twelve unknown cards in the same three suits. Therefore East, rather than West, figured to be the possessor of the diamond queen.

In conclusion, when you are attempting to ascertain the location of a crucial card in order to finesse successfully against it, if at all possible play your other suits first (or as many of them as you can afford to play without weakening your position) to see if some clue can be obtained regarding its location. In adopting this approach, much more often than not you will obtain favorable factual information that you did not possess at the outset.

Now, gentle reader, before getting to Chapter 2, let me ask you a question: Does not the cultivation of the habit of counting figure to be more enjoyable (and more rewarding) than either (1) looking skyward, entreatingly, and supplicating the gods of chance to come to your assistance when you have a guess as to which way to finesse, or (2) cultivating the antisocial practice of peeking into an opponent's hand to see if he possesses a key card? And does not the application of counting have the additional virtues that (1) it will not disturb the gods of chance, who have more important things to do, and that (2) it will not lead to social ostracism?

2

"Counting" Practice
Pays Dividends

While in the process of writing this book, I was frequently beset by the thought: Shall I give the reader some homework at the conclusion of each chapter? After all, bridge is a competitive game, a head-to-head encounter. And in such endeavors academic knowledge is not sufficient in itself to bring about operative knowledge. Testing or rechecking in the crucible of play must follow if the techniques studied are to have any practical significance.

I finally decided against giving any homework. The major reason accounting for my decision was that the reader, in buying (or borrowing) this book, has evinced that he is keenly interested in learning about the finer points of play. I therefore assumed that he is already an active player who will be intent on applying and displaying his soon-to-be-acquired skill of card reading. Thus, I chose not to burden him with academic homework, deeming it to be unnecessary.

A second reason for my elimination of homework was this: the reader has gone to his local bookstore to purchase this book. I will collect a royalty on his purchase. In the future I will write more books. And if the potential reader feels that homework will be contained therein, it may alienate him. This I can't afford to have happen. So, being practical about the whole thing after considering it from both an objective and subjective viewpoint, I have dispensed with giving the reader any homework.

But a lingering doubt persists that perhaps I was wrong. Perhaps some immediate testing of the reader is necessary—for *his* benefit—to enable him to determine whether he has learned what he was supposed to have learned. As an argument in favor of homework, let me revert to the one deal which was the subject of Chapter 1.

It was my original intention to give the following homework at the end of Chapter 1. I was going to suggest to the reader that the next time he played bridge with his foursome he take a few minutes for practice before engaging in serious competition. I was going to recommend that the North-South cards (of the seven-no-trump contract) be kept exactly as they were. The remaining twenty-six cards (possessed by East-West) were to be reshuffled, with East and West each to receive thirteen new cards.

You, the reader, were to begin your homework by occupying the South seat and playing the grand-slam contract. Two of the other players were to sit East and West respectively (your fourth was to be assigned the duty of taking three orders for liquid refreshments).

West was to be directed not to lead a diamond (if he led that suit, you would have three diamond tricks via a free finesse). Whatever else he led would now give you the problem of trying to locate the diamond queen, using the identical type of counting approach that was the theme of the actual deal.

In your play you almost surely would not have discovered that West was dealt three spades, three hearts, one diamond, and six clubs (as in the actual deal), for this specific distribution is but one of many. You might have learned, for example, that West had been dealt three diamonds, with East having been dealt the remaining four diamonds. Had this come to pass, then four times out of seven East would figure to be the possessor of the diamond queen, and you would then have finessed against East for that key card.

Or, if you happened to learn that West had been dealt two diamonds, then you would have known at that moment that East had been dealt five diamonds. In this case, five times out of seven East would figure to have the diamond queen.

To elaborate further on this point, suppose that against your seven-no-trump contract West made the opening lead of a spade.

You would win the trick and then cash three spade tricks to complete your count of this suit. Let's assume that East and West each followed suit to three spade leads.

Let's say that you next cashed the ace, king, and queen of clubs. You note that each of the defenders follows suit to all three club leads.

Up to this point you haven't learned a thing that will help you in isolating that queen of diamonds, for each of the opponents still has exactly seven unknown cards, and it is a 50–50 proposition (as it was at the outset) as to whether East or West was dealt the diamond queen.

But then you come to the heart suit. By the time you have concluded playing a third round of hearts (or sooner), *one of the opponents will have failed to follow suit.* This has to be, for the five outstanding hearts must be divided either 5–0, 4–1, or 3–2. Let's suppose that on the third lead of hearts East fails to follow suit. Eight of East's original thirteen cards are now known to you: three spades, three clubs, and two hearts. And, simultaneously, you have just learned nine cards dealt to West: three spades, three clubs, and three hearts. Thus West has four unknown cards, while East has five unknown cards. Since any missing card figures to be in the hand that contains the greater number of unknown cards, by a vote of 5–4 East is elected as the possessor of the diamond queen.

Suppose that after you had discovered nothing (namely, that East and West each had been dealt three spades and three clubs), when you next played hearts, West failed to follow suit to the second heart lead. You would then have known seven of West's original cards: three spades, three clubs, and one heart. At the same time, you would have known ten of East's original thirteen cards: three spades, three clubs, and four hearts. With West having six unknown cards, and East having three unknown cards, six times out of nine (unknown cards) West would figure to have the queen of diamonds. And by finessing against West for Her Ladyship, you would be a winner two times out of three.

Thus, by doing the above type of homework, you would have had the actual practice of noting the failure of an opponent to follow suit, and from there proceeding to count out the opponents' hands. No matter how many millions of times you redealt the cards and gave thirteen new ones to both East and West, by the time you had cashed three spades, three clubs, and three hearts, you would have learned that one of the opponents had more unknown cards than his partner.

And so, by performing the above-described homework, you would have been on the road toward obtaining a tremendous advantage (for future application) over those players who, in a position analogous to yours, either forget to count, are too lazy to count, or simply have not learned to count. You would then really have begun to appreciate that the attempt to gain distributional information is worth the expenditure of the extra energy required to count out a hand.

If there are those readers who like to do homework, I would strongly recommend that they practice what has been presented above: that is, that they keep the North-South hands (of Chapter 1) as they were and reshuffle the East-West hands. Do this three or four times—and the lovely world of counting will have opened up for you.

The preceding paragraphs have been directed, in the main, toward those who like to do homework. In my experience this group is in the minority. I now address myself—in the main—to the majority, by presenting two more case studies of counting hands. As will be observed, the approach will be identical to that employed in the grand-slam hand of Chapter 1. In each of these two deals, the North-South hands will be identical, but the East-West hands of Deal 2 will be quite different from those East-West hands of Deal 1. In each deal you will be the South declarer (who, I must confess, lest I be accused of subterfuge, has just been tricked into doing his homework). Let's now get to work—the coffee break is over.

Deal 1

Both sides vulnerable. South deals.

```
                        NORTH
                    ♠ K 10 5
                    ♥ K 6 3
                    ♦ K 7 6
                    ♣ Q J 10 2
                        SOUTH
                    ♠ A J 6
                    ♥ A Q J
                    ♦ A Q 4
                    ♣ A 9 8 5
```

The bidding: SOUTH   WEST   NORTH   EAST
                  2 NT   Pass   6 NT   Pass
                  Pass   Pass

Opening lead: Jack of ♦.

The bidding is nothing more than a matter of definition and addition. North, looking at 12 high-card points, knows that his partnership possesses at least 34 out of the 40 high-card points in the deck (South has guaranteed 22–24). There is no necessity to employ either the Blackwood or Gerber slam conventions to check for aces: with East-West having no more than 6 high-card points between them, they cannot have either two aces (8 high-card points) or even an ace and a king (7 high-card points).

When the dummy comes into view, you count that you have nine top tricks: two spades, three hearts, three diamonds, and one club. And, of course, when this deal arose in a social game at your home, there was nobody peering over your shoulder and stating: "Look, friend, play carefully. This is a counting-out hand." So your approach to the play is a normal, unprepared one, ending with the question: Where can I get three more tricks?

By observation, the answer becomes obvious: only the club suit offers the hope for the creation of the three needed tricks.

So you win the opening diamond lead with dummy's king, after which you promptly lead the queen of clubs and finesse. The half the time that East was dealt the king of clubs, your finesse will win. If it wins, you then lead the club jack and finesse again; with the jack winning, you next lead the club ten. If this is the day when East was dealt the club king, you have just brought home your contract: two spades, three hearts, three diamonds, and four clubs. Whether you now make an extra trick by guessing which way to finesse for the spade queen becomes anticlimactic, for you have just fulfilled a vulnerable small-slam contract.

But today happens to start out on an unlucky note. When you lead the queen of clubs (at trick two), and finesse against East's hoped-for king, the finesse loses. West now comes back with the ten of diamonds, the suit he led originally. As you win the trick with your ace, *that significant happening that you have learned to look for occurs: East fails to follow suit,* discarding the three of spades.

Since you and your dummy were dealt three diamonds apiece, and East was dealt exactly one diamond, West started with six diamonds. At this point you have eleven tricks; and your only chance of making twelve tricks is to come home with three spade tricks. Who has the spade queen, East or West?

Having discovered (at trick three) that West started with six diamonds, you will now keep your eyes on West, the hand with *the fewer unknown cards,* in the attempt to reconstruct his original hand of thirteen cards. What else do you know about West's hand, in addition to his possession of six diamonds?

Well, he won trick two with the king of clubs. With clubs being fresh in your mind, you now cash your three top clubs, to complete your count of this suit. You note that West follows suit to two more club leads (he discards a diamond on the fourth club lead). You are now in possession on the factual evidence that West was dealt exactly six diamonds and exactly three clubs.

With the words of Horace Greeley ringing in your ears ("Go West, young man, go West"), you next cash your king, queen, and ace of hearts. West follows suit to all three heart leads. Twelve of West's cards are now accounted for: six diamonds, three clubs, and three hearts. The spade suit has just been isolated: West has a maximum of one card in spades.

You now lead the spade six and West follows suit with the deuce. You then turn toward East, smiling as if to say: "You, my friend, have the queen of spades just as surely as God made little green apples." You capture the spade lead with dummy's king, after which you return the spade five. East plays low, and as you triumphantly insert your jack, you reach for the scorepad to chalk up the score for a small slam bid and made. You don't even bother to look Westward to see what West plays, for you knew when you led dummy's spade five that West had been dealt six diamonds, three hearts, three clubs, and the spade deuce. The complete deal was:

```
                        NORTH
                     ♠  K 10 5
                     ♥  K 6 3
                     ♦  K 7 6
                     ♣  Q J 10 2
      WEST                                  EAST
   ♠  2                                  ♠  Q 9 8 7 4 3
   ♥  9 7 4                              ♥  10 8 5 2
   ♦  J 10 9 8 3 2                       ♦  5
   ♣  K 7 3                              ♣  6 4
                        SOUTH
                     ♠  A J 6
                     ♥  A Q J
                     ♦  A Q 4
                     ♣  A 9 8 5
```

This deal, of course, was virtually identical (in both approach and the knowledge obtained by observation and counting) to the grand-slam deal of Chapter 1. But, then, that's what homework is: repetition. If there is any point of specific dissimilarity, it would be that at the conclusion of trick three, when East failed to follow suit to the second diamond lead, you knew that West had been dealt six diamonds and one club, while East had been dealt one diamond and one club. Therefore West had six unknown cards, while East had eleven unknown cards. Hence, the spade queen figured to be in East's hand, since East had more unknown cards.

On the above deal, then, whether declarer proceeded by "feeling" (mathematical probability) or by "fact" (knowing for certain at a later stage of play) that East was the possessor of the spade queen, he would have fulfilled his contract by finessing against East for the queen of spades. But there are those other days when "feeling" ("I listened to my voices and obeyed them") runs a poor second to "fact." You will appreciate this point in just a few moments.

Deal 2

Both sides vulnerable. South deals.

```
                     NORTH
                  ♠ K 10 5
                  ♥ K 6 3
                  ♦ K 7 6
                  ♣ Q J 10 2
                     SOUTH
                  ♠ A J 6
                  ♥ A Q J
                  ♦ A Q 4
                  ♣ A 9 8 5
```

The bidding: SOUTH   WEST   NORTH   EAST
                  2 NT   Pass   6 NT   Pass
                  Pass   Pass

Opening lead: Jack of ♦.

As was stated earlier, the North-South cards above are identical to the North-South cards of Deal 1. Against your six-no-trump contract West again opens the diamond jack, which is captured by dummy's king. The queen of clubs is then led, and the finesse taken, losing to West's king. West returns a diamond, which you win with your ace as East discards the two of hearts.

Your correct feeling at this point is that East *rates* to have the queen of spades. This feeling is generated (and substantiated) by the realization that East has eleven unknown cards (exclusive of one diamond and one club) while West has but six unknown cards (exclusive of six diamonds and one club) . If these seventeen unknown cards were reshuffled, with East being given eleven new cards, while West was given the remaining six, the spade queen would figure to be in the bigger pile, namely the hand of eleven cards. But, as Gershwin once said, it ain't necessarily so. Let's continue, then, to see whether "feeling" is supported or negated by "facts."

To tricks four and five, you cash the jack and ace of clubs, with your eyes on West, the possessor of the fewer unknown cards. You observe that West follows suit to the jack of clubs and discards a diamond on the lead of the club ace. So you know that West was dealt exactly six diamonds and two clubs.

Saving the spade suit until the end, you now swing over to the third suit, hearts, to see how many hearts West had originally. When you cash the ace of hearts, lo and behold, West discards a diamond!

Here then, at the completion of trick six, you know with absolute certainty the precise distribution of West's original thirteen cards: six diamonds, two clubs, no hearts whatever—hence, five spades.

You were dealt three spades, your dummy was dealt three spades, and West was dealt five spades. Therefore East had to have been dealt the remaining two spades in the deck.

Take these seven spades, shuffle them up well, and give West five of them and East his two. Who figures to have been given the queen? West, of course. And he will have it five times out of seven.

Thus it comes to pass that after cashing the club ten, the king and queen of hearts, and the spade ace, you lead the six of spades out of the South hand. When West follows suit with the four-spot, you insert dummy's ten. This is the complete deal:

NORTH
♠ K 10 5
♥ K 6 3
♦ K 7 6
♣ Q J 10 2

WEST
♠ Q 9 8 4 3
♥ —
♦ J 10 9 8 3 2
♣ K 3

EAST
♠ 7 2
♥ 10 9 8 7 5 4 2
♦ 5
♣ 7 6 4

SOUTH
♠ A J 6
♥ A Q J
♦ A Q 4
♣ A 9 8 5

Of course, when you took the percentage play of finessing against West for the spade queen, there was no guarantee that the finesse would win. There will be days when East's two spades happen to be the Q x. But there will be many more days—precisely five days out of seven—when East's two spades will be the x x.

Again, there was no guarantee that the spade finesse would win in the above deal. But, then, in bridge you seldom get guarantees. What you did in finessing against West was to pit the percentage play against the alternative play that confronted you at the outset: a 50–50 finesse in the blind against either East or West.

In other words—and to conclude—with the 5–2 division being revealed, five times out of seven the queen figures to be in the hand holding five spades. At the start, you had a 50 percent chance —or 3½ out of 7—of guessing who possessed the spade queen. Would you not (and you would if you aspire to be a winner) rather avail yourself of a line of play that offers success five times out of seven (71 percent) as opposed to one that offers success 3½ times out of 7 (50 percent) ?

In Chapter 3 there will be presented and analyzed six real-life counting deals that arose in top-level games. So pull up a chair and sit behind South, who will be the declarer in each of the deals. Having been introduced to counting out a hand, and having done your homework like a good boy or girl, you should encounter no difficulties in following our declarers' thought processes as they wend their respective ways to ultimate victory.

3

Counting Out Hands
in Top-Echelon Circles

If there are those who think that the specific type of counting-out hands presented in Chapters 1 and 2 never actually come up in real life, they are very, very wrong. Admittedly, small-slam and grand-slam contracts (which are all we have viewed thus far) arise relatively infrequently when compared to part-score and game contracts, and when these slam contracts are arrived at, quite often they will be "lay down," with success requiring nothing more than the simple, straightforward ability to cash one's tricks.

But there is no doubt that slam hands necessitating counting out come up often enough to warrant the student's giving them more attention than just a casual, passing look-see. Actually, the counting of each and every hand that arises, no matter how simple the play may appear to be, is a habit worth cultivating. Of course, not all hands lend themselves to counting, and in many deals the habitual counter will have expended his energy in vain. However, during the course of any afternoon's or evening's play, deals will arise where the habitual counter will strike a bonanza, while the noncounter (guesser, if you will) will fall by the wayside.

Within this chapter there are presented and analyzed six deals in which counting out a hand was mandatory if the correct line of play was to be found. In the first four of these deals, counting out *guaranteed* the success of the contract. In Deals 5 and 6 a lucky guess would have been required if counting out had not been employed.

These six deals all arose in either World Championship play, National Championship play, top-level duplicate games, or high-stake rubber-bridge games. Each South declarer was one of our nation's top-ranking players. The thought processes and the approaches of these six South declarers are well worth examining, and earmarking for future reference and practical application.

Deal 1

During the past decade one of our nation's finest bridge pairs has been the duo of Arthur Robinson and Robert Jordan, both of Philadelphia. In the World Bridge Olympiad of 1968, when this deal arose, Robinson, North, and Jordan, South, had no difficulty in arriving at a grand-slam contract. In the play Jordan gave a neat demonstration of his counting ability.

Both sides vulnerable. West deals.

```
                          NORTH
                        ♠ 9 4 2
                        ♥ K Q 7
                        ♦ A 10 4 2
                        ♣ A 5 2
        WEST                                    EAST
     ♠ 8 6 5 3                              ♠ J 10 7
     ♥ J 10 9 6 5                           ♥ 8 3 2
     ♦ Q 7 6                                ♦ 9
     ♣ 9                                    ♣ 10 8 7 6 4 3
                          SOUTH
                        ♠ A K Q
                        ♥ A 4
                        ♦ K J 8 5 3
                        ♣ K Q J
```

The bidding:	WEST	NORTH	EAST	SOUTH
	Pass	1 ♣	Pass	1 ♦
	Pass	2 ♦	Pass	4 NT
	Pass	5 ♥	Pass	5 NT
	Pass	6 ♦	Pass	7 NT
	Pass	Pass	Pass	

Opening lead: Jack of ♥.

Upon learning, via Blackwood, that North had two aces and one king, Jordan bid the grand slam in no-trump. It was good that he did, for at a seven-diamond contract he probably would have gone down, since he would not have had the clairvoyance to have known that West possessed the guarded queen of diamonds. At no-trump he had no difficulty in determining the location of that key card.

After he had won the opening lead with his ace of hearts, it was rather obvious that the success of the grand-slam contract depended entirely on bringing home the diamond suit without the loss of a trick. Of course, the sole question was (or, rather, would be) whether to cash the ace and king of diamonds, hoping to fell the queen, or whether to finesse against one of the opponents for that card.

Upon capturing the opening heart lead with his ace, Jordan next cashed the king and queen of hearts, discarding a diamond from his own hand on the third heart lead. He noted, of course, that both opponents followed suit to these three heart leads.

Then came three spade leads, with everybody following suit. He next cashed the ace and king of clubs—and struck gold, for West discarded a heart on the second club lead. Thus Jordan knew at this moment that East had been dealt six clubs, in addition to three hearts and three spades. So East had, at most, one diamond.

When Jordan now laid down the diamond king, East followed suit with the nine-spot. All of East's original thirteen cards were now accounted for. Then came a low diamond from the South hand, with dummy's ten being inserted. Thirteen tricks were now there for the taking.

Deal 2

To the bridge-playing masses, Sam Stayman is perhaps best known as the originator of the Stayman Convention. But among bridgedom's elite, he is recognized also as being one of the game's finest players. In this deal we have an example of Stayman at work (if counting can be classified as work). The hand came up in the National Championships of 1951.

Both sides vulnerable. South deals.

NORTH
♠ A 7
♥ Q 8 4
♦ A Q 2
♣ A Q 10 9 3

WEST
♠ J 10 9 6 4 3
♥ J 9 7 3
♦ 5 3
♣ 2

EAST
♠ 8 2
♥ 6 5
♦ J 9 8 7 6
♣ J 8 7 5

SOUTH
♠ K Q 5
♥ A K 10 2
♦ K 10 4
♣ K 6 4

The bidding:

SOUTH	WEST	NORTH	EAST
1 ♥	Pass	3 ♣	Pass
4 ♣	Pass	4 ♦	Pass
4 NT	Pass	5 ♠	Pass
7 NT	Pass	Pass	Pass

Opening lead: Jack of ♠.

I imagine that most of our nation's bridge players, upon viewing the dummy after the opening spade lead had been made, would
have settled back in their chairs, saying to themselves: "All is for
the best in this best of all possible worlds." They would then have
tended to play automatically, figuring that either the heart suit or
the club suit would provide them with their thirteenth trick. And,
frankly, even if they played mechanically, they would be tremendous favorites to fulfill the grand-slam contract. But on this day—
as on some other days—the favorite would be a loser.

Stayman also recognized that, despite having only twelve sure
winners, the contract appeared to be a cinch. But, having traveled
this road before, he appreciated that appearances can sometimes be
deceiving.

Upon winning the opening lead with dummy's ace of spades,
Stayman next cashed the king and queen of spades, discarding a

club from dummy on the latter lead. When East discarded a diamond on the third spade lead, Stayman learned that West had been dealt six spades.

He then played the ace, queen, and king of hearts, East tossing away a diamond on the third heart lead. Stayman had just found out that West had started with four hearts (in addition to six spades).

With his eyes fixed on West, he next played the king of diamonds, after which another diamond was led to the board's ace. With West following suit to both diamond leads, twelve of his original thirteen cards were now known to Stayman: six spades, four hearts, and two diamonds.

When Stayman next cashed the ace of clubs, West played the deuce. All of West's original thirteen cards were now an open book —*and the jack of clubs was not one of them.*

The ten of clubs was now led, and when East played the seven-spot, South followed with the six. With the ten capturing the trick, the grand-slam contract was now in the bag. The king of clubs, the queen of diamonds, and the queen of clubs took the last three tricks.

Will you not agree that if Stayman had not been a counter, he would have made the "correct" assumption that the five outstanding clubs figured to be divided 3–2? Had he done so, he would never have dreamed of finessing in clubs—and the slam would have flown out of the window, never to return.

Deal 3

One of the greatest players the world has ever known was the late Helen Sobel, who passed away in 1969. It should be pointed out that in the opinion of her peers she was not thought of simply as the "best woman player," but rather as one of the best players.

Helen, of course, was a counter, for without this asset one cannot rise above mediocrity in ability. In this deal we have an example of her talent of counting out a hand. The hand arose in a high-stake rubber-bridge game at New York City's Cavendish Club. As was often the case in these high-stake games, a foursome usually contained either two experts or two dubs, or one expert and three dubs. As will be evidenced when the bidding is observed, Helen's partner, sitting North, was a dub.

Both sides vulnerable. North deals.

```
                        NORTH
                    ♠ K 10 7 6
                    ♥ 9 7 4 2
                    ♦ A J 5
                    ♣ A 5
        WEST                                EAST
    ♠ 5 2                               ♠ 9 4
    ♥ 8                                 ♥ J 10 5 3
    ♦ K Q 10                            ♦ 9 8 7 6 4 2
    ♣ Q J 9 6 4 3 2                     ♣ 10
                        SOUTH
                    ♠ A Q J 8 3
                    ♥ A K Q 6
                    ♦ 3
                    ♣ K 8 7
```

The bidding:	NORTH	EAST	SOUTH	WEST
	1 ♦ (!)	Pass	2 ♠	Pass
	4 ♠ (!)	Pass	4 NT	Pass
	5 ♥	Pass	5 NT	Pass
	6 ♦	Pass	7 ♠	Pass
	Pass	Pass		

Opening lead: Queen of ♣.

North's bidding defies explanation. His opening one-diamond bid was marginal, at best; and his jump to four spades (rather than three spades) can be justified only if he believed that Helen was a goddess gifted with the ability never to make a wrong decision in either the bidding or the play.

Mrs. Sobel's ultimate bid of seven spades was based on her sense of hearing: she thought that North had a better-than-minimum opening bid (North did *jump* to four spades). I wasn't there when the hand was played, but I can easily imagine Helen saying to herself, after North had put his hand down as the dummy: "What kind of a nut do I have for a partner?"

West's queen of clubs opening lead was captured by Helen's king, after which the ace and queen of trumps were cashed, gathering in the outstanding pieces. A diamond was then led to dummy's ace, and this was followed by another diamond, South ruffing.

Next came a club to the board's ace, East discarding a diamond. Dummy's remaining diamond was now ruffed in the closed hand. Mrs. Sobel then stopped to do some counting.

With East having failed to follow suit to the second club lead, West was revealed as the possessor of seven clubs. West had also followed suit to two trump leads and three diamond leads. So he had, at most, one heart.

The ace of hearts was then cashed, West dropping the eight-spot as East followed suit with the heart three. Since all of West's original thirteen cards were now accounted for, East had to have the tripleton J 10 5 of hearts remaining in his hand.

South's last club was now ruffed in dummy, after which the four of hearts was led. When East covered with the five-spot, Mrs. Sobel inserted her six, knowing that it would win the trick. When it did, she claimed her contract.

I don't know what the stake of the game was, but I would imagine that it was somewhere between five and eight cents a point. Since a vulnerable grand slam is worth 1500 points, and a vulnerable game nets one 500 points (both sides vulnerable) , and the trick score for making seven spades is 210 points, the fulfillment of the grand slam was worth 2210 points (actually 2310 points, considering that if she had gone down a trick, she would have lost 100 points) . At the assumed minimum rate of five cents a point, that comes out to $115.50. As I think we will all agree, counting out a hand can be most remunerative—even at a tenth of a cent a point, for a killing of $2.31.

Deal 4

If we can assume that bridge players, when they pass away, all go "upstairs," where they have air-conditioning, rather than "downstairs," where there is no respite from the heat, counting out a hand will be greatly facilitated because of the conservation of one's energy if we can accept the result of this hand as conclusive evidence.

The above is by way of prologue to this deal, in which the South declarer was my good friend the late Lester Glucksman. The hand came up in a top-level duplicate game in New York City during the winter of 1952. There was no heat in the playing room, the main furnace having broken down a few hours before. All the players—except Lester—had put on their winter coats. Lester had not only not put on his coat, but he had taken off his jacket! It took him about one minute to play out this counting hand and to obtain the optimum result.

Neither side vulnerable. South deals.

```
                        NORTH
                    ♠ Q 10 4
                    ♥ Q 5 3
                    ♦ J 6 5
                    ♣ K 10 4 2
        WEST                            EAST
    ♠ 8 6 5 3 2                     ♠ 9 7
    ♥ J 7                           ♥ 9 8 6 4 2
    ♦ 9 8 7 4 2                     ♦ A 3
    ♣ 5                            ♣ J 9 7 6
                        SOUTH
                    ♠ A K J
                    ♥ A K 10
                    ♦ K Q 10
                    ♣ A Q 8 3
```

The bidding: SOUTH   WEST   NORTH   EAST
               3 NT   Pass   6 NT   Pass
               Pass   Pass

Opening lead: Nine of ♦.

East won the opening diamond lead with his ace, after which he returned a diamond, Lester taking the trick with his queen.

On the face of it, there appeared to be nothing to the play. Certainly the five outstanding clubs figured to be divided 3–2. And if West happened to have the J x x x, four club tricks would still be there for the taking, since on the cashing of the ace and queen of clubs East would fail to follow suit to the second club lead; and it would now be a routine matter to finesse against West's known jack of clubs. Thus declarer would have twelve tricks: three spades, three hearts, two diamonds, and four clubs. But there was more to the play than was visible to the naked eye—and Lester foresaw a possible pitfall. And, by envisioning it, he avoided it.

After winning trick two with his diamond queen, declarer cashed the king of diamonds, noting that East discarded a heart. This meant that West had started with five diamonds. When he next cashed the ace, king, and queen of spades, he observed that East failed to follow suit to the third spade lead. Hence West had been dealt not only five diamonds, but also five spades. He then played the ace and king of hearts, and perceived that West followed suit to both heart leads. Since twelve of West's cards were now accounted for in diamonds, spades, and hearts, there was room in West's hand for a maximum of one club.

The three of clubs to dummy's king came next, West following suit with the five-spot. As Lester won this trick with dummy's king, it became a fact that East had to have the J 9 7 of clubs remaining in his hand.

The ten of clubs was then led, East covering it with the jack, and South capturing the trick with his ace (West discarding a spade). Dummy was now entered via the queen of hearts, and the four of clubs was led. With East possessing the known 9 7 of clubs, and South sitting over him with the Q 8, it became a routine matter for declarer to win the last two tricks.

Declarer's play was cool, wasn't it?

In Deals 1, 2, 3, and 4, which have just been viewed, each of our South declarers really had nothing more than an exercise in counting. All they had to do was to sit back and observe. And in each case, when they had collected the necessary facts, they were able to pinpoint the *precise* location of a key card, either a queen or a jack. In other words, their reward for having engaged in the visual process of counting out a hand was the receipt of a guarantee that they would fulfill their respective contracts.

In Deals 5 and 6 our two declarers utilized the identical technique of counting out a hand as was applied in the preceding four deals. But their rewards were not the guarantees of success that their predecessors had secured. In Deal 5 our South declarer reached a position where he had nothing more going for him than a slightly better chance than he had at the outset. In Deal 6 a perhaps paradoxical situation came into being, in which declarer, having counted perfectly, *deliberately* elected to adopt a line of play that figured to be a losing one!

Deal 5
Neither side vulnerable. South deals.

NORTH
♠ K Q
♥ 7 5 2
♦ K 10 3
♣ Q J 8 6 4

WEST
♠ 10 8 6 5 3
♥ J 6 3
♦ 9 6 4
♣ A 5

EAST
♠ 7
♥ 10 9 8 4
♦ Q 8 7 2
♣ 10 9 7 2

SOUTH
♠ A J 9 4 2
♥ A K Q
♦ A J 5
♣ K 3

The bidding:

SOUTH	WEST	NORTH	EAST
2 NT	Pass	6 NT	Pass
Pass	Pass		

Opening lead: Five of ♠.

Let's assume that you are the South declarer. You win the opening spade lead with dummy's queen, after which you lead a low club to your king. West captures the trick with his ace, and returns another spade, which you take with dummy's king. On this trick East discards the four of hearts.

You have just come into possession of the fact that West was dealt five spades and one club. To complete your count of West's clubs, you next cash dummy's queen. Then you play the jack of clubs, discarding the nine of spades from your own hand. On this third club lead, West also discards a spade. You now know that West started with five spades and two clubs. If the six adversely held clubs had divided 3–3, there would have been no necessity for any more counting, since twelve tricks would then have been there for the taking.

The ace, king, and queen of hearts are cashed next, everybody following suit to all three heart leads. Since East had discarded a heart on the second spade lead by West (at trick three), you have just secured a perfect count of West's hand: he was dealt five spades, two clubs, three hearts—*and exactly three diamonds.*

Higher mathematics now lends a helping hand. Since West started with three diamonds, and both you and your partner were dealt three diamonds apiece, East must have started with four diamonds. This is not a situation conducive to your wagering your life on the location of the diamond queen, but the scale definitely tips toward East as the possessor of that card, for *he who has the greater number of cards of a given suit always figures to have any one specific card that you are looking for in that suit.*

So, after having cashed your top hearts, you lead a diamond to dummy's king. You then play back a diamond, and finesse your jack when East follows suit with a low diamond. You have just become a winner.

Deal 6

This final deal has become a classic one. It came up in the 1957 Masters Team-of-Four Championship. With counting out a hand serving as a foundation, the deal illustrates the psychology that is frequently employed by a master team which feels that it is either an underdog in a match or is behind so many points that it must resort to abnormal antipercentage play if victory is to be attained.

In the South seat, as the declarer, was Pedro Cabral of New York City, paired with Sallie Johnson of Connecticut. They were half of the team playing against the favorite internationalist quartet composed of Alvin Roth, Tobias Stone, John R. Crawford, and the late Sidney Silodor. At the end of the three-quarter mark, the Cabral team was 2160 points in arrears. This was the fifty-sixth, and final, deal.

North-South vulnerable. South deals.

NORTH
♠ K 7 3
♥ A J 10
♦ A K 10 3
♣ A K 2

WEST
♠ 9 6
♥ Q 9 5
♦ Q 9 8 7 4
♣ 6 5 4

EAST
♠ 5 4 2
♥ 7 4 3 2
♦ J 2
♣ 9 8 7 3

SOUTH
♠ A Q J 10 8
♥ K 8 6
♦ 6 5
♣ Q J 10

The bidding:

SOUTH	WEST	NORTH	EAST
1 ♠	Pass	2 ♦	Pass
2 ♠	Pass	4 NT	Pass
5 ♦	Pass	5 NT	Pass
6 ♦	Pass	7 ♠	Pass
Pass	Pass		

Opening lead: Six of ♣.

Upon winning the opening lead with dummy's king of clubs, Cabral cashed the king, queen, and ace of trumps. Then came a diamond to the board's ace, after which the diamond king was played. A third round of diamonds was then led, East discarding a club as South ruffed the trick. The ace and queen of clubs were cashed next, declarer noting that each of the opponents followed suit. Now came the time for counting and analysis.

East was known to have started with exactly two diamonds, since he had failed to follow suit to the third diamond lead. East had also followed suit to three trump leads and three club leads. In addition, he had discarded a club on the third diamond lead.

Thus East was known to have been dealt *precisely* four clubs, two diamonds, and three spades. Hence he had exactly four hearts.

Since dummy and South each had three hearts, West had to have the remaining three hearts.

Since West had but three hearts, and East had four hearts, Cabral fully realized that the percentage play was to finesse against East for the heart queen, since four times out of seven East figured to possess that all-important card.

But Cabral also appreciated the fact that his team was behind, and he figured that when the deal would be replayed, his most capable opponents, holding the North-South cards, would also arrive at a grand-slam contract. Further, he knew that the other South declarer would also discover that East had been dealt four hearts and West but three, and that the other South declarer (Alvin Roth) would, as the percentage play, finesse against East for the heart queen.

So Cabral, trying to create a swing to recoup the points that his team was behind, deliberately took the antipercentage play of finessing against *West* for the queen of hearts. As luck would have it, the finesse worked, and he scored 2310 points (counting the 100 honors).

When the deal was replayed, Alvin Roth and Tobias Stone did arrive at the grand-slam contract. As Cabral had hoped for, and surmised, Roth finessed against East for the heart queen—and went down.

As a result of this final deal, the Cabral team, which had been 2160 points in arrears at the end of the third quarter, won the match by the slender margin of 180 points, having gained a total of 2340 points in the fourth quarter.

4

From Simple Hands
to Less Simple

In retrospect, the deals that have been discussed in the three preceding chapters have been nothing more than basic exercises in counting by observation. All that the various declarers were required to do was to sit back and observe. What they were looking for as they observed was for one of the opponents to fail to follow suit. And when the failure to follow suit was revealed, our declarers were able to use this knowledge as a foundation upon which to assemble facts relevant to the other two suits; and, having done this, they were able to isolate the fourth suit.

When all the accumulated data had been collected and studied, the different declarers were able either to pinpoint the *precise* location of a key queen or jack or to acquire a percentage-play knowledge (hitherto unknown) as to where that key card rated to be.

But again our declarers didn't have to work too hard—they lived a relatively passive life, as it were. In the four deals that constitute this chapter it's a horse of another color. In each of these deals the South declarers either had to *create* actively a position that enabled them to obtain a count of one of the opponents' hands, or, having obtained a count, they had to come up with an expert play to take advantage of their knowledge.

Thus, as will be observed, these declarers really had to work hard for their rewards: the fulfillment of their respective contracts.

Deal 1

In this deal South arrived at a small-slam contract which, in the post-mortem analysis, was revealed to be not a difficult one to handle properly. I think the above statement will be concurred in by everyone—after South's play has been observed. Actually, winning play necessitated nothing more than applying a "little thing" that the counter had stored in his arsenal of winning techniques. Yet this "little thing," which is possessed by all bridge players, would not have been evoked by the noncounter, who, instead, would have tended to rely on pure guesswork.

East-West vulnerable. South deals.

NORTH
♠ K 9 5 2
♥ K J 8
♦ J 10 4
♣ 6 5 3

SOUTH
♠ A Q J 10 6
♥ A 10 4
♦ A K Q
♣ A J

The bidding:

SOUTH	WEST	NORTH	EAST
2 ♠	Pass	3 ♠	Pass
6 ♠	Pass	Pass	Pass

Opening lead: King of ♣.

Let's assume that you are occupying the South seat. When the deal was actually played, the South declarer was Barry Crane of Hollywood, California.

As soon as the opening lead is made and you survey your assets, it becomes apparent that you have two potential losers, one in clubs and one in hearts. You realize immediately that the loss of a club trick is inevitable, and, simultaneously, that the sole hope of fulfilling the slam rests squarely on your ability to ferret out the location of the heart queen and then to finesse successfully against that card.

After you capture the opening club lead with your ace, you cash the king, ace, and queen of trumps, noting that West follows suit to all three rounds, while East follows suit to just one round, discarding two low hearts on the second and third trump leads. Then come three rounds of diamonds, with the observation being made that both opponents follow suit to all three rounds.

Where are you now? Do you have any clue—or an inkling of a clue—as to whether East or West possesses the heart queen? Well, you might say that East is the favorite to have that crucial card, since West was dealt three spades, three diamonds, and one club (leaving him with six unknown cards), while East was dealt one club, one spade, and three diamonds (leaving him with eight unknown cards). As an approximation, you are ahead of those bridge players who have not learned to do any serious counting. But, really, you don't have any strong feeling that East has the heart queen, do you? What next?

Since the loss of a club trick is inevitable, why not lead your jack of clubs at this point (as our actual declarer did), giving the defenders the trick? Perhaps they will then provide you with some information.

So you lead the jack of clubs, which West takes with the queen. West plays back the high ten of clubs, which you ruff. *On this trick East discards a low heart.*

West's hand should now be an open book to you. West was known to have started with three trumps and three diamonds, and with East having failed to follow suit to the third club lead, West is now revealed as the possessor of six clubs. Thus twelve of West's original thirteen cards have been accounted for.

Your next play is the four of hearts to the board's king, West following suit with the deuce. Dummy's jack of hearts is then returned, and whether East covers or doesn't cover with the queen, you have just brought home your contract by avoiding the loss of a heart trick. These were the four hands:

NORTH
♠ K 9 5 2
♥ K J 8
♦ J 10 4
♣ 6 5 3

WEST
♠ 8 4 3
♥ 2
♦ 9 7 5
♣ K Q 10 9 7 2

EAST
♠ 7
♥ Q 9 7 6 5 3
♦ 8 6 3 2
♣ 8 4

SOUTH
♠ A Q J 10 6
♥ A 10 4
♦ A K Q
♣ A J

Two questions might be raised by the reader:

1. What if East *had* followed suit to the third club lead? Well, in this case you would have known nothing more than that East was dealt one spade, three diamonds, and three clubs (six unknown cards); and that West was dealt three spades, three diamonds, and three clubs (four unknown cards). On percentage (as contrasted to the guarantee you actually did receive), you would finesse against East for the heart queen.

2. What if West had opened, let us say, a trump originally against your six-spade contract. How would you then have proceeded in your play? The answer is: in exactly the same fashion as you did, by drawing trumps and cashing your three diamonds. Then would come the ace of clubs, followed by the jack of clubs. The same position actually achieved would now be reached, with West leading a third club, East failing to follow suit.

It should be pointed out, perhaps naïvely, perhaps not, that when West was thrown into the lead with his club queen, he really had no choice but to exit with the ten of clubs. If, instead, he led a heart, you would make three heart tricks via a free finesse. And if West returned a diamond instead (if he had had one), you would have trumped this lead in dummy while simultaneously discarding the four of hearts from the South hand.

In the preceding deal there was introduced for the first time an illustration of a general type of play known in expert circles as "rectifying the count." By definition, this phrase usually refers to the process of deliberately conceding a trick to the opponents in order to obtain a greater opportunity of reaching a position where you might be able to gain information relative to the distribution of the opponents' cards. "Rectifying the count" also refers to other types of situations, such as the preparation for a squeeze, with which we are not concerned in this book.

In Deal 2, which follows, we have another illustration where the rectification of the count was essential for declarer to enhance his chances of obtaining a better count of an opponent's hand. Through its application, our South declarer came to a sure-thing ending.

Deal 2

Neither side vulnerable. South deals.

```
                        NORTH
                     ♠ K 6 4 2
                     ♥ K J 7
                     ♦ K Q
                     ♣ K 10 9 3
      WEST                                    EAST
   ♠ J 10 7 5                               ♠ Q 8
   ♥ 9 4                                    ♥ 8 6 5 3 2
   ♦ 9 8 7 5 3 2                            ♦ 10 4
   ♣ 6                                      ♣ Q 7 5 4
                        SOUTH
                     ♠ A 9 3
                     ♥ A Q 10
                     ♦ A J 6
                     ♣ A J 8 2
```

The bidding:

SOUTH	WEST	NORTH	EAST
1 ♣	Pass	1 ♠	Pass
2 NT	Pass	6 NT	Pass
Pass	Pass		

Opening lead: Nine of ♦.

Upon winning the opening lead with the diamond queen, declarer perceived that no matter how brilliantly he played, he could never come to more than twelve tricks: two spades, three hearts, three diamonds, and four clubs. Of greater importance, however, was the fact that unless he could bring home four club tricks, he would go down to defeat. And the bringing home of four club tricks required locating the club queen.

With the aim of getting a count of the defenders' distribution (via a rectification of the count), at trick two declarer led a low spade off dummy. When East followed suit with the eight-spot, South put up his nine (with, of course, no expectation of winning the trick). The trick was captured by West's ten.

West made the safe exit of a diamond, dummy's king winning. The king of spades was cashed next, and this was followed by a spade to South's ace. When East discarded a heart on this latter lead, West was known to have started with four spades originally.

South now cashed the ace of diamonds, on which he tossed away dummy's remaining spade. On this trick East discarded another heart. At this point things really started to shape up, for with East having been dealt exactly two spades and two diamonds, West was known to have started with four spades and six diamonds. When declarer next cashed his king, queen, and ace of hearts, West failed to follow suit to the third heart lead, discarding a diamond thereon.

Declarer's count of West's original thirteen cards was now complete and accurate: West had been dealt exactly four spades, six diamonds, and two hearts. The club suit had been isolated: West had started with just one club.

The deuce of clubs was then led to the board's king, West followed suit with the six-spot. Now came the ten of clubs. When East followed with the five, South played the eight. Then came a third club lead, and East's remaining Q 7 was ambushed by South's A J.

And so declarer, with the timely assistance of rectification, ended up with two spades, three hearts, three diamonds, and four clubs. In all systems of mathematics, this adds up to twelve tricks.

In Deal 3, which follows, we have our first illustration of the counting out of a below-slam contract! As we go along, more and more below-slam deals will be introduced and analyzed, since counting out a hand is an all-occasion technique.

Embodied in this deal are three major themes of play: (1) the "hold-up" play, which refers to the refusal—for some valid reason—to win a trick; (2) the rectifying of the count; and (3), the straightforward counting out of an opponent's hand. With the practical application of all three of the above, declarer was able to guarantee the fulfillment of a contract which otherwise probably would have been lost.

Both sides vulnerable. South deals.

```
                        NORTH
                     ♠ A 7 4
                     ♥ 7 6 3
                     ♦ A 10 5
                     ♣ A K 10 2
       WEST                             EAST
    ♠ 10 2                          ♠ Q J 9 6 3
    ♥ K J 9 5 4                     ♥ Q 10
    ♦ 8 2                           ♦ Q J 9 4
    ♣ J 9 8 4                       ♣ 6 3
                        SOUTH
                     ♠ K 8 5
                     ♥ A 8 2
                     ♦ K 7 6 3
                     ♣ Q 7 5
```

The bidding:

SOUTH	WEST	NORTH	EAST
Pass	Pass	1 ♣	Pass
2 NT	Pass	3 NT	Pass
Pass	Pass		

Opening lead: Five of ♥.

The bidding was eminently proper. When South, who had passed originally, jumped to two no-trump, he showed a balanced hand with protection in each of the unbid suits, and around 12 high-card points (he could not have had 13, for if he had, he would have opened the bidding). North's raise to 3 NT was, of course, automatic.

East put up the queen on West's opening lead of the heart five, and South, employing the hold-up play, permitted the queen to win. East returned the heart ten, and once again South declined to take his ace. West overtook the ten with the jack, after which he returned a third heart, South winning with the ace. On this trick East discarded the spade three. At the completion of trick three, South had learned that West had been dealt five hearts, and East but two. South also learned something that he didn't enjoy: that if West regains the lead, he will cash two heart tricks. Thus South's play is geared to keeping the "dangerous" West hand out of the lead.

Declarer realized that his prospects of coming home with nine tricks were pretty good. If the six outstanding clubs are divided 3-3, or if the jack of clubs is either a singleton or a doubleton, then dummy's ten of clubs will be promoted into declarer's game-going trick. Or, if the six missing diamonds are divided 3-3 (except if West has the Q J x), then South's fourth diamond will yield him his ninth trick.

In clubs, there is nothing to create or build up. Either South has four club tricks right now, or he doesn't. So the club suit can wait, to serve as a last resort.

Since the creation of a winner out of South's fourth diamond necessitates the prior concession of a diamond trick, South promptly gets to work on the diamond suit. At trick four, he leads a low diamond. When West follows suit with the deuce, dummy's ten-spot is inserted. The diamond play is made, basically, to establish South's fourth diamond, which would come about if the adversely held diamonds were divided 3-3. In losing this diamond trick to *East,* South remains on safe ground, since East is known to possess no hearts.

East captures the ten with his jack, and returns the queen of spades. South now employs the rectification-of-the-count play: he allows East's queen of spades to win the trick. The wisdom of South's play will become apparent in just a moment. East then leads another spade, North's ace capturing the trick.

The ace of diamonds is cashed next, and this is followed by a diamond to declarer's king. On the latter trick West discards a heart. The diamond suit has just been eliminated as a source of declarer's game-going trick—but, as a by-product, meaningful information has been garnered: East was dealt four diamonds, and West two diamonds.

The king of spades is now cashed, West discarding another heart—and the full truth is revealed: West was dealt *five* hearts (which you knew at trick three), *two* spades, and *two* diamonds (West had failed to follow to the third round of either of these suits). Therefore *West had been dealt exactly four clubs,* no more and no less. And, quite naturally, East had been dealt two clubs.

The five of clubs is now led to dummy's ace, after which a club is returned to South's queen. At this point West is known to have the J 9 of clubs remaining. So when South next leads his remaining club, and West follows suit with the nine, South puts up dummy's ten with the guaranteed assurance that the ten-spot will win the trick. When it does, declarer has his ninth trick.

In Deal 4, which is next to pass in review, three major types of plays were put to use by declarer: the finesse, counting out a hand, and the end play. This is our first venture into the end play, which is the putting of an opponent into the lead at a time favorable to declarer, and forcing that opponent to lead a suit which gives declarer a trick that he could not or might not have made under his own power.

In this prefatory deal which merely introduces the end play, the emphasis is not on the end play. The emphasis remains on the basic subject: namely, counting out a hand. But it should be noted—although only in passing—that through counting out a hand many gratifying and materially rewarding objectives other than the isolation of a suit can be accomplished. One of these objectives is (or, rather, will soon become) the end play.

Deal 4

Neither side vulnerable. South deals.

```
                        NORTH
                      ♠ 10 9
                      ♥ A 6 4 2
                      ♦ K 7 5 4
                      ♣ 7 4 3
        WEST                                EAST
      ♠ 7 6 5                             ♠ Q 4 3 2
      ♥ J 10 9 8 5                        ♥ 3
      ♦ 8 2                               ♦ J 10 9 3
      ♣ K J 8                             ♣ 10 9 6 5
                        SOUTH
                      ♠ A K J 8
                      ♥ K Q 7
                      ♦ A Q 6
                      ♣ A Q 2
```

The bidding:	SOUTH	WEST	NORTH	EAST
	3 NT	Pass	6 NT	Pass
	Pass	Pass		

Opening lead: Jack of ♥.

North's jump to six no-trump was on the aggressive side. A better bid would have been five no-trump, a vigorous invitation to South for the latter to bid the slam if he had more than his minimum (26 or 27 points, rather than 25). With his actual hand, South would have declined the invitation.

As can be observed, six no-trump was a precarious contract—but, as the Bard of Avon once remarked, all's well that ends well.

West's opening heart lead was taken by dummy's ace, after which the ten of spades was laid down and the finesse taken. When the ten-spot had won the trick after everybody had followed with low spades, the nine of spades was led, with the trick being won by South's jack. Declarer now had eleven sure winners.

As declarer appraised the situation, if the six adversely held hearts were divided 3–3 originally, or the missing six diamonds were divided 3–3, the board's fourth card in the favorably divided suit would yield South his slam-going trick. Or, if neither of these possibilities materialized, there would always be available, as a last resort, the 50–50 club finesse.

Actually, as can be observed by looking at the diagramed hand, none of these possibilities would have come to fruition. Nevertheless, South fulfilled his contract without any help from the defenders.

After cashing his four spade winners, on the fourth of which West discarded a heart (dummy discarded a club), South played the king and queen of hearts. With East failing to follow suit to the king of hearts, the heart suit had just been eliminated as a source of South's twelfth trick. But, simultaneously, South came into possession of the knowledge that West had been dealt five hearts (and three spades, which South had learned about earlier).

Next came the ace, queen, and king of diamonds. West discarded the club eight on the third diamond lead.

It might now appear (to the casual observer) that declarer had to resort to the club finesse at this point. If he had done so, he would have gone down. But he had been watching the opponents' discards very closely, and he knew that West had no spades and no diamonds left. And West, who had started with five hearts, had only one heart left, since he had discarded a heart (on the fourth spade lead) and had followed suit to three heart leads.

So South next led dummy's fourth heart, putting West into the lead (South discarding the club deuce). West's two remaining cards were the K J of clubs. South's last two cards were the A Q of clubs. West was on lead. And, for West, as with this chapter, it was the end.

5

Second Sight
with Card Reading

In all the deals contained in the four preceding chapters, declarer proceeded strictly on his own resources in counting out the distribution of the opponents' cards. His counting out was based exclusively on his *sense of sight,* plus the facts of simple arithmetic: each suit has thirteen cards, and each player started with thirteen cards in his hand.

Now, for the first time, he will begin to apply another of his senses, *the sense of hearing.* This sense comes into practical application when his opponents have entered the auction, either by having opened the bidding, made an overcall, or doubled (either for takeout or for penalties). In entering into the bidding arena, the defenders frequently provide declarer with tangible clues which he can use to his advantage.

In this chapter there are presented nine deals in which the defenders-to-be participated in the bidding. And in each case, declarer, who was tuned in to what was being transmitted, received valuable information that enabled him to fulfill a contract which would not or might not otherwise have been brought home successfully.

Deal 1, which follows, might well be described as the perfect card reading hand of all time. After the opening lead had been made by West, and the dummy was put down, our South declarer knew with absolute certainty every one of the high cards in East's hand. By utilizing this knowledge, he came up with a line of play that he would not have dreamed of if East had not opened the bidding.

Both sides vulnerable. East deals.

NORTH
♠ 10 9 8
♥ K 6 4
♦ A 5 4 2
♣ K J 9

WEST
♠ 5
♥ J 10 9 5 3
♦ 9 7 3
♣ 10 8 7 2

EAST
♠ K 6 3
♥ A Q 7
♦ K Q 10 8
♣ Q 6 3

SOUTH
♠ A Q J 7 4 2
♥ 8 2
♦ J 6
♣ A 5 4

The bidding:

EAST	SOUTH	WEST	NORTH
1 NT	2 ♠	Pass	3 ♠
Pass	4 ♠	Pass	Pass
Pass			

Opening lead: Jack of ♥.

When the dummy came into view after West had opened the heart jack, the thought flashed immediately through South's mind: East had every other outstanding high card in the deck! This thought arose out of the realization that East, who had opened the bidding with one no-trump, guaranteed 16–18 high-card points. And since North and South had 23 high-card points between them, and West had the heart jack, East *had to have* the remaining 16 points in the deck.

West's jack of hearts won the opening lead when everybody followed suit with low hearts. On West's next heart lead, a low heart was again played from dummy, and East's queen captured the trick. East then laid down the heart ace, which South ruffed.

A diamond was led next to the board's ace, after which the spade ten was played, and the finesse taken against East's king. When the finesse proved successful (as it had to be), the spade nine was played. It won the trick when East and South followed with low spades.

Now came the jack of clubs, and when East covered with the queen, South won the trick with his ace (if East had not covered, the jack would have won the trick). After the ace of trumps had picked up East's king, South led the four of clubs. With West following suit with the seven-spot, dummy's nine was inserted. When it won the trick, declarer conceded a diamond, and claimed his contract.

If East had not opened the bidding, South almost surely would have gone down, for he then would have played the club suit in normal fashion—that is, by cashing the ace and then leading a low club, finessing against *West's* hoped-for queen. And 50 percent of the time the jack would have won the trick.

As is evident, however, on this particular deal the "normal" way of taking the finesse couldn't ever be the winning play, for East was known to have the club queen as part of his one-no-trump opening bid. Hence the "normal" play had to be dispensed with, for card reading had demonstrated that the normal way of finessing would lose. Thus declarer, in desperation perhaps, really had no alternative but to utilize the play known as the "backwards finesse": leading the jack initially—and hoping that *West* possessed the *ten* of clubs.

If one were to take the club suit in the above deal *out of context,* the chance of South making three club tricks as he actually played the hand would be only one out of four, according to our mathematicians. That is, half the time East would have the club *queen,* and half the time he wouldn't. And half the time West would have the club *ten*—and half the time he wouldn't. For South to have made three club tricks (as he played the hand) required *both* of two 50–50 chances being successful: that East have the club queen *and* that West have the club ten.

Thus, as South actually played the hand, he gave himself only a 25 percent chance of bringing home three club tricks. But, as will be concurred in by all, even only one chance out of four is better than no chance out of four, since West just couldn't have the club queen.

In Deal 2 we have another example of the "backwards finesse" in action. As in Deal 1, our South declarer's application of this "mathematically inferior" play arose out of the appreciation that the normal way of finessing would have been a losing play. And, once again, had there been no defensive bidding, South would surely have gone down, since he would not have voluntarily chosen a play which offered a 25 percent chance of success when he had a 50 percent play available to him.

Deal 2

For practice, let's assume that *you* are the South declarer.

East-West vulnerable. West deals.

NORTH
♠ K J 5
♥ Q 7 4 3
♦ J 6 4
♣ A 9 8

SOUTH
♠ A Q 10
♥ K J 10 9 8
♦ 5 2
♣ K J 6

The bidding:

WEST	NORTH	EAST	SOUTH
1 ♦	Pass	Pass	1 ♥
Pass	2 ♥	Pass	3 ♥
Pass	4 ♥	Pass	Pass
Pass			

Opening lead: King of ♦.

Against your four-heart contract West opens the diamond king, after which he cashes the diamond ace. To trick three he leads the diamond queen, which you ruff as East follows suit with the ten of diamonds.

You then lead the jack of hearts, which *East* captures with the ace, West following suit. East plays back a heart. You win the trick with your ten as West discards a diamond. You next cash the king of hearts, picking up East's last trump. On this trick West tosses away another diamond.

Deferring the tackling of the club suit, you then play the king, ace, and queen of spades, noting that everybody around the table follows suit to all three leads. The crucial issue is now at hand: how do you play the club suit?

Let's assemble the knowledge we have obtained to date from both the bidding and the play. East, who has been revealed as the possessor of the ace of hearts, had passed his partner's opening bid of one diamond. Surely if East had possessed the queen of clubs —which would have given him a hand of 6 high-card points—he would not have passed. Therefore, almost surely, West rates to have the club queen.

I say "almost surely" because this might have been the day when East, having a pessimistic feeling, decided to take a chance on incurring his partner's displeasure by passing (which would have been the case if West happened to have possessed a 20-point hand). And yet this just couldn't have been the day that East masterminded the situation, for there is confirming proof that West was dealt the queen of clubs.

A vulnerable West had opened the bidding with one diamond. And what did West have for his opening bid? Five diamonds headed by the ace, king, and queen (A K Q x x) ; a singleton heart; and three miserable little spades (perhaps he also had a miserable fourth spade). Surely without the queen of clubs West would not have had the slightest semblance of an opening bid. It's just dollars to doughnuts that the club queen reposes in West's hand.

So, after cashing your three top spades, you lead the jack of clubs, which West covers with the queen, and you win the trick with dummy's ace. Whatever happens from here on, you know that you've played the hand properly up to this point, for if you had led a low club off dummy initially and made the normal play of finessing your jack, you would have gone down, losing the setting trick to West's queen. But victory is not yours yet.

You next lead the nine of clubs, and East follows with the three-spot. With an outward appearance of nonchalance, you follow suit with the six-spot, finessing against East's hoped-for ten. West follows suit with the club four. Mission accomplished. The complete deal was:

NORTH
♠ K J 5
♥ Q 7 4 3
♦ J 6 4
♣ A 9 8

WEST
♠ 9 7 4 2
♥ 6
♦ A K Q 9 8
♣ Q 7 4

EAST
♠ 8 6 3
♥ A 5 2
♦ 10 7 3
♣ 10 5 3 2

SOUTH
♠ A Q 10
♥ K J 10 9 8
♦ 5 2
♣ K J 6

May I offer you my congratulations for your play of the hand? It's nice to see that your card reading is beginning to show.

To digress ever so slightly for just a moment, it is my opinion that if one were able to put his finger on the exact point where the average player undergoes a qualitative change and starts up the road leading to the development of a good bridge player, that point would be where the average player is no longer immersed solely in his own cards, and simultaneously he begins to pay close attention to the bidding of the opponents and the clues contained therein.

In Deal 3 we have a good example of a declarer's attunement to what one opponent was telling his partner. As a result, he fulfilled a contract which otherwise he might have lost.

Deal 3

East-West vulnerable. South deals.

NORTH
♠ K 9 6 5
♥ J
♦ K 10 9 3
♣ Q 10 8 3

WEST
♠ 4
♥ K Q 10 9 8 6
♦ 8 7
♣ A K 7 5

EAST
♠ Q 7 3 2
♥ 7 5 4 2
♦ 6 5 2
♣ 9 4

SOUTH
♠ A J 10 8
♥ A 3
♦ A Q J 4
♣ J 6 2

The bidding:

SOUTH	WEST	NORTH	EAST
1 ♦	1 ♥	2 ♦	Pass
2 ♠	3 ♥	4 ♠	Pass
Pass	Pass		

Opening lead: King of ♣.

On West's opening lead of the club king, East initiated a "high-low" come-on signal by playing the nine. When West next led the ace of clubs, East completed his signal by dropping the four. To trick three West led the club seven, East ruffing.

East now came back with a heart, declarer winning the trick with his ace. Since East had ruffed a club, there were just four trumps remaining in the opponents' hands at this point, and the normal play appeared to be to cash the ace and king, hoping to fell the queen. As can be observed, this would have been the losing play—and, of possibly greater importance as far as the future was concerned, it would have been an antipercentage play.

As a fact, gathered through declarer's sense of sight, West was known to have been dealt *exactly* four clubs. Through the application of declarer's sense of hearing, West was just about certain to have no fewer than six hearts: vulnerable, he had overcalled not only with one heart, but subsequently with three hearts, missing both the ace and jack of hearts.

Thus West was dealt a *maximum of three cards* in both diamonds and spades (if he had seven hearts, then he would have but two cards in spades and diamonds). East, on the other hand, was dealt a *minimum of seven cards* in spades and diamonds, since East was known to have started with precisely two clubs and no more than four hearts (West had at least six hearts).

And so declarer, having read the first four chapters of this book, was in good shape, percentage-wise. East had been dealt seven unknown cards in spades and diamonds; West had been dealt three unknown cards in these two suits. Since any missing key card figures to be in the hand containing the greater number of unknown cards, East rated to have the spade queen.

So, after winning his ace of hearts at trick four, South led the jack of spades (to entice West, if he held the queen, to "cover an honor with an honor"). When West followed suit with the four-spot, South overtook the jack with the board's king. He then led the nine of spades, and when East played the seven, South played his eight. With the nine winning, declarer was home. A spade to his ace then felled East's queen, and South's losing heart was ruffed with dummy's last trump.

Oh, yes, I agree that, in theory, West could have been void of diamonds, and could have been the possessor of the Q x x of spades. But percentage is percentage is percentage, and seven times out of ten East figured to have been dealt the queen of spades.

It is conceivable that some readers might come to an erroneous conclusion about one of the points contained in this deal, specifically West's overcall. They might say that if only West had kept his big mouth shut (or just a little shut), he would not have told South how to play the trump suit. Going from the specific to the general, they might conclude that one shouldn't be so free with his overcalls, and thus avoid imparting significant information to declarer.

While it is true that in the above deal West's two overcalls aided declarer, more often than not sound overcalls will produce beneficial yields to the overcalling side. Bridge is a bidder's game. In the words of the late Sidney Silodor, world-renowned internationalist:

Silence may be an excellent virtue in a woman, but it is a highly debatable accomplishment in a bridge player. If you sit quietly by, with your thirteen cards clutched tightly in your hot little hands, be resigned to having the opposition bid around you, over you, and through you. In short, silence breeds defeat. You haven't a ghost of a chance! The modern-day players bid much too well for you to grow fat on their errors.

Within this chapter—the three preceding deals and the six to follow—it is true that the defenders' bidding guided declarer to the winning solution. But before we get through with this book, the reader will perceive how the worm turns (as in real life), and through the medium of defensive bidding an apparently guaranteed declarer's contract becomes doomed to defeat.

An opening bid of three, four, or five in a suit is, of course, known to all as being a preemptive bid. The "preempt" is defensive in purpose. The preemptive bidder hopes that opponents with strong hands will find it difficult to bid accurately with the auction having started at such a high level.

The preemptive opening bid—judiciously applied—will accomplish its objectives more often than not. But at times it can result in catastrophic consequences (as can a perfectly sound opening bid, overcall, or takeout double).

In an identical sense, a preemptive jump overcall—e.g., 1 ♥ by North, *3 ♣ by East;* 2 ♠ by North, *4 ♦ by East,* and so forth— even though conforming in every respect to the requirements prescribed for the bid, can turn out badly for the wielder's side. As a case in point, observe what happened in the deal that follows.

Deal 4
North-South vulnerable. South deals.

NORTH
- ♠ Q 7
- ♥ J 10 5
- ♦ A 10 8 4 2
- ♣ 8 5 3

WEST
- ♠ 9 6 5
- ♥ 8 6 3
- ♦ —
- ♣ A Q J 10 9 6 4

EAST
- ♠ J 8 4 3 2
- ♥ 9
- ♦ J 9 5 3
- ♣ K 7 2

SOUTH
- ♠ A K 10
- ♥ A K Q 7 4 2
- ♦ K Q 7 6
- ♣ —

The bidding:

SOUTH	WEST	NORTH	EAST
2 ♥	4 ♣	4 ♦	Pass
5 ♣	Pass	5 ♥	Pass
7 ♥	Pass	Pass	Pass

Opening lead: Ace of ♣.

After ruffing the opening club lead, declarer cashed his three top trumps, gathering in the adversely held pieces. He then played the spade ace—and now stopped to examine the situation at hand.

There was no question in declarer's mind that West rated to have seven or eight clubs for his preemptive jump overcall—after all, that was what East expected West to have, and (theoretically) one partner does not lie to the other. However, there did exist the outside possibility that West might have only six clubs.

West had followed to three trump leads and also to South's lead of the ace of spades. Therefore South knew for sure that West was dealt no fewer than six clubs, three hearts, and one spade, for a total of ten cards. *Thus it was impossible for West to possess the four outstanding diamonds.*

I think that it is apparent to all that as the above thoughts were circulating through declarer's mind, they were motivated by the question as to how he was going to play the diamond suit. Being a pessimist (through previously encountered bitter experiences in analogous situations), he was worried that one of the adversaries might have all four of the missing diamonds. And he had just learned that the only opponent who *might* have the four missing diamonds was *East*.

In the abstract, the normal tendency in the above situation would be to lead the king, thereby trapping West if the latter possessed the J 9 5 3. But, since it had just been proved that West could not have the four outstanding diamonds, declarer's play had to be designed to guard against East's possible possession of these four cards.

After cashing the spade ace at trick five, declarer led the six of diamonds to dummy's ace. He was rewarded for his analysis when West discarded a club. The ten of diamonds was returned next, East covered with the jack, and declarer took the trick with his king.

The board was then reentered via the spade queen, and the eight of diamonds was led. East had the doubleton 9 5 remaining, while South possessed the Q 7. East was trapped, with no escape. Thus, by dint of rational, flawless card reading, declarer fulfilled his grand-slam contract.

In the absence of a bid from partner, the standard defender's lead against no-trump contracts is the fourth-from-the-highest in one's longest suit (if partner has bid a suit, he expects you to lead it). Experience has demonstrated that this standard lead pays dividends more often than not—but, at times, it can be most revealing to declarer, and, as a result, costly to the defenders.

In Deal 5, a delayed fourth-from-the-highest lead turned out badly for the leader, for it enabled a counting declarer to reconstruct the distribution of the thirteen cards that had been dealt to his opponent.

Deal 5
Neither side vulnerable. North deals.

                            NORTH
                          ♠ 3 2
                          ♥ A 6
                          ♦ K 9 4
                          ♣ A K J 9 7 3
        WEST   EAST
     ♠ K 5   ♠ A Q 8 6 4
     ♥ K 10 8 4 3   ♥ Q 9 5 2
     ♦ J 6 5   ♦ 10 7 3
     ♣ Q 10 8   ♣ 5
                            SOUTH
                          ♠ J 10 9 7
                          ♥ J 7
                          ♦ A Q 8 2
                          ♣ 6 4 2

The bidding: NORTH   EAST   SOUTH   WEST
                 1 ♣   1 ♠   1 NT   Pass
                 3 NT   Pass   Pass   Pass

Opening lead: King of ♠.

West dutifully opened the spade king against South's three-no-
trump contract, after which he led his remaining spade, East's
queen winning. It was apparent to East (as it was to declarer) that
West had no more spades, since if he had held the tripleton K x x,
he would have led his third highest initially, and not the king. So
East knew that South still had the doubleton J 10 remaining—and
for East to cash the spade ace would result in promoting South's
jack into a winner.

At trick three East shifted to the deuce of hearts, which was
covered by South's jack and West's king. The trick was captured
by dummy's ace. Since South knew that East was an honest man,
he assumed that East was leading his fourth-highest heart. And
since it was the deuce that had been led, East had to have exactly
four hearts (he had, by definition, three higher hearts, and there
are none lower).

After next cashing the ace of clubs, declarer led the king of diamonds, then cashed the ace of diamonds and the queen of diamonds, noting that East followed suit to all three diamond leads. Thus East was known to have been dealt five spades (fact), three diamonds (fact), one club (fact), and four hearts (assumption, based on "faith").

And so all of East's original thirteen cards were accounted for—and the club queen was not one of them. After cashing his thirteenth diamond (South having observed that each opponent had followed suit to all three immediately preceding diamond leads), South next led a club and finessed dummy's jack. When it won the trick, South ended up with eleven winners: six clubs, four diamonds, and one heart. Had he cashed the king of clubs, hoping to fell the queen (instead of finessing the jack), he would have gone down.

One of the most potent weapons possessed by the opponents of the open bidder is the takeout, or informative, double. Actually, without the employment of this bid, the defenders would forever be fighting a losing cause. But, as with all defensive bids, there are times when the information conveyed to partner by the bid is picked up and utilized by the opening bidder to the latter's advantage. Such was the case in Deal 6, which follows. Had West been gifted with ESP, he would have abstained from the bidding. And, had he done so, declarer would probably have gone down at his game contract.

Deal 6

Both sides vulnerable. South deals.

NORTH
♠ J 9 7 5
♥ K J 10 3
♦ Q 7 4 2
♣ A

WEST
♠ 2
♥ A 8 6
♦ A J 9 6
♣ K 8 6 5 2

EAST
♠ K 10 4
♥ 9 7 2
♦ K 10 3
♣ 9 7 4 3

SOUTH
♠ A Q 8 6 3
♥ Q 5 4
♦ 8 5
♣ Q J 10

The bidding:	SOUTH	WEST	NORTH	EAST
	1 ♠	Double	Redouble	Pass
	Pass	2 ♣	4 ♠	Pass
	Pass	Pass		

Opening lead: Five of ♣.

South's opening bid of one spade was nothing to write home about, but then (I have been told) South hadn't had an opening bid for two hours, and in these circumstances he felt that his hand was close enough. If the final result can serve as the criterion, South was justified in making his bid.

After capturing the opening lead with dummy's ace of clubs, declarer took time out to study the situation at hand.

West's takeout double denoted the (theoretical) ability to play at either hearts, diamonds, or clubs. That is, presumably he had support for each of the unbid suits. And, almost surely, West did not possess the A K of diamonds, for if he did, he would have led the king of diamonds, rather than the blind (and dangerous) lead of a low club away from his (presumed) king. Thus West's high cards in the three unbid suits figured to be the ace of hearts, the ace (or king) of diamonds, the jack of diamonds, and the king of clubs.

Since West's point-count assets totaled a maximum of only 12 high-card points, declarer reasoned that West figured to have some distributional assets to compensate for his high-card deficiency. In all probability West was short of spades, with probably a singleton in that suit, if not a void. Declarer now proceeded to play the hand on the assumption that East had either three or four spades (trumps).

At trick two the jack of spades was led, covered by East's king, and won by South's ace. West followed suit with the spade deuce.

The queen of clubs was led next, West put up the king, and dummy ruffed with the nine-spot. The five of spades was then led, East following suit with the four. On this trick declarer played his six-spot, finessing against East's presumed ten. The queen of spades now felled East's ten. Declarer's only losers were two diamonds and a heart.

Had West not bid, declarer's first spade lead off dummy would probably have been a low one, with his queen being finessed successfully. But East, with the doubleton K 10 still remaining in this case, now couldn't be prevented from eventually winning a trump trick.

Thus West's takeout double, and declarer's correct interpretation of the high-card and distributional strength of West's hand, pinpointed the way to the winning solution.

In Deal 7, which is next to parade in review, we have another example of a takeout double that led to the doubler's demise. And again the doubler cannot be criticized. When one is telling his partner something, there is always the attendant calculated risk that the opponents will make greater use of the information conveyed than will the speaker's partner.

Deal 7

Neither side vulnerable. South deals.

NORTH
♠ Q 10 9
♥ 9 6
♦ J 10 6 2
♣ K Q 7 4

WEST
♠ 7 3
♥ K J 3
♦ A K Q 7
♣ J 10 9 8

EAST
♠ 6 4 2
♥ 10 8 7 5 4 2
♦ 9 5
♣ 6 3

SOUTH
♠ A K J 8 5
♥ A Q
♦ 8 4 3
♣ A 5 2

The bidding:

SOUTH	WEST	NORTH	EAST
1 ♠	Double	2 ♠	Pass
4 ♠	Pass	Pass	Pass

Opening lead: King of ♦.

After cashing the king, ace, and queen of diamonds (East discarding a heart on the third diamond lead), West led his remaining diamond. East ruffed dummy's jack, and South overruffed.

The queen and ace of trumps were then cashed, gathering in the four outstanding pieces. Declarer now paused to examine the situation. This was the setup as he viewed it:

NORTH
♠ 10
♥ 9 6
♦ —
♣ K Q 7 4

SOUTH
♠ K J
♥ A Q
♦ —
♣ A 5 2

To fulfill his contract, South of course had to make the rest of the tricks. As the situation now stood, his queen of hearts was a loser.

In theory, the avoidance of the loss of a heart trick could be accomplished in one of two ways: (1) if the six adversely held clubs were divided 3–3, then on dummy's fourth club South could discard his heart queen; (2) if East had the king of hearts, then South could finesse successfully against that card. South immediately eliminated the heart finesse as a possibility, for the following reason.

West had made a takeout double, announcing the equivalent of an opening bid (or better), with (presumably) some "stuff" in each of the unbid suits. By observation, West was known to have started with the A K Q x of diamonds, and two small spades (trumps). In clubs, West couldn't possibly have more than the jack, since North and South had between them the ace, king, and queen. For West's takeout double, he just had to have the king of hearts.

Declarer's next lead was the king of trumps, upon which West discarded the four of hearts, while East tossed away a low heart. Then came declarer's last trump, West tossing away the jack of hearts, with dummy discarding the heart six. This was now the position, with South on lead:

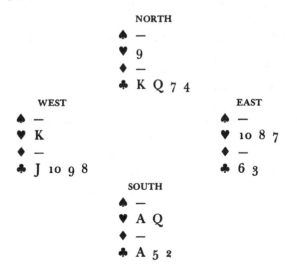

NORTH
♠ —
♥ 9
♦ —
♣ K Q 7 4

WEST
♠ —
♥ K
♦ —
♣ J 10 9 8

EAST
♠ —
♥ 10 8 7
♦ —
♣ 6 3

SOUTH
♠ —
♥ A Q
♦ —
♣ A 5 2

South now cashed the ace of clubs, after which he led a club to dummy's king. Then came the queen of clubs, East discarding a heart.

At this point, declarer knew West's original distribution: two spades, three hearts, four diamonds, and four clubs. There were two cards remaining in each hand—and one of West's remaining two cards was the *known* jack of clubs. The other was a heart. Since declarer "knew" that West had started with the heart king, West's remaining heart had to be the king.

So declarer now led dummy's heart and put up his ace, felling West's king. South's queen of hearts had just become his game-going trick.

If the reader will go back to the preceding diagram (with five cards left in each hand), it will be observed that West had been squeezed on the lead of declarer's last trump. When declarer led this card, West had to make a discard. If he tossed away one of his clubs, declarer would make four club tricks. So he really had no option but to discard the jack of hearts, blanking his king—and hoping that South wouldn't diagnose the true situation. But South was on the ball all the way—and he well deserved his triumph.

After the opening lead has been made, the most important weapons possessed by the defenders are the signals that they transmit to each other. These signals, correctly applied, enable them to attack and counterattack successfully.

As with defensive bidding, however, when these signals are being flashed, declarer also receives them, and, quite often, he makes greater use of them than do the defenders. This is unavoidable and is a part of the game, figuratively speaking.

However, many occasions arise where the defender—a victim of habit—gives an absolutely pointless signal, one which cannot possibly be helpful to partner but which may turn out to be useful to declarer. Such was the case in Deal 8, in which a defender sealed his own doom by telling declarer the location of a key card.

Deal 8

East-West vulnerable. South deals.

NORTH
- ♠ Q 10 8 6
- ♥ 6 4
- ♦ K Q 4 3
- ♣ 9 5 2

WEST
- ♠ 5 3 2
- ♥ K 9 7 3
- ♦ J 10 9 8 5
- ♣ 6

EAST
- ♠ 7
- ♥ J 10 8 2
- ♦ 7 2
- ♣ A K Q 10 7 4

SOUTH
- ♠ A K J 9 4
- ♥ A Q 5
- ♦ A 6
- ♣ J 8 3

The bidding:

SOUTH	WEST	NORTH	EAST
1 ♠	Pass	2 ♠	3 ♣
4 ♠	Pass	Pass	Pass

Opening lead: Six of ♣.

West's opening lead of the club six was taken by East's queen, after which the ace and king of clubs were cashed. West, having two discards to make on the second and third club leads, first threw away the *nine* of hearts, and then the three-spot.

The significance of this "high-low" signal was unmistakable to both East and South: it literally screamed for a heart lead by East. South, as he looked at his hand, was absolutely convinced that West was the possessor of the heart king.

At trick four, East shifted to the jack of hearts. Had West not given his signal, declarer would probably have finessed his queen. After all, East did figure to have the king of hearts for his vulnerable overcall at the three level, especially since he was known to have no high-card strength in either spades or diamonds. But, based on the "evidence," declarer spurned the finesse and instead played the ace of hearts. Declarer, incidentally, was fully aware of the fact that he had nine sure winners: five spades, one heart, and three diamonds (declarer's five of hearts would, of course, be discarded on dummy's queen of diamonds).

After winning his ace of hearts (at trick four), declarer played five rounds of trumps. This was the position prior to the lead of the fifth trump:

NORTH
♠ —
♥ 6
♦ K Q 4 3
♣ —

WEST
♠ —
♥ K
♦ J 10 9 8
♣ —

EAST
♠ —
♥ 10 8 2
♦ 7 2
♣ —

SOUTH
♠ J
♥ Q 5
♦ A 6
♣ —

When declarer led his jack of trumps to trick nine, West found himself in the vise of a squeeze. If he discarded a diamond, dummy's fourth diamond would become declarer's game-going trick. And if, instead, he tossed away the heart king, South's queen would be promoted into a winner.

Hoping against hope that East possessed the queen of hearts (East's lead of the jack had, in theory, denied possession of the queen), West discarded the heart king. Declarer now claimed the rest of the tricks.

As has been observed in this chapter, card reading is not a sure-thing panacea. Based on what he has heard (the opponents' bidding) and what he has seen (the defenders' plays), declarer makes inferences about the high-card and/or distributional holdings of the opponents. Within this chapter his inferences were always correct (as they really figured to be), but only because I made sure that the deals that I selected were intended to make his inferences correct.

If one reflects on this matter of card reading, there will be many occasions when declarer makes the proper inferences, and thereby arrives at a line of play that figures to make him a winner. However, due to Lady Luck, or the vagaries of chance (you name it), his chosen line of play (the superior one) fails; and, on examination, it is revealed that the alternative (inferior) line of play would have been successful. When things like this happen to you, it is demonstrated that in no competitive endeavor can one be a winner every time out.

In the next deal, the final one of this chapter, our declarer, via card reading and counting out, deduced both West's distribution and his high cards. And following the courage of his (not completely certain) convictions, he adopted a certain line of play. As it turned out, he was right. But on any given day he could have been wrong.

Let's assume that you, instead of observing our actual South's thought processes as he played the hand, have just become the South declarer.

Deal 9
Both sides vulnerable. West deals.

NORTH
♠ 7 4 3
♥ A K 10
♦ Q J 10
♣ A J 10 8

SOUTH
♠ A 8 5 2
♥ J 4 3
♦ A 8 5
♣ Q 9 6

The bidding:

WEST	NORTH	EAST	SOUTH
1 ♠	Double	Pass	1 NT
Pass	2 NT	Pass	3 NT
Pass	Pass	Pass	

Opening lead: King of ♠.

West, who has opened the bidding with one spade, leads the king of spades, which you allow to win, East following suit with the ten-spot. West then continues with the spade queen, East discards a low diamond, and you take the trick with your ace.

You then play the nine of clubs, following with dummy's eight when West plays low. The nine wins the trick. Then comes the queen of clubs, another successful finesse being taken against West's king. A third club lead is now made and dummy's jack is finessed. On this third club lead East discards another diamond. The ace of clubs is cashed next, East tossing away a low heart as you discard the five of spades. You now pause for review and analysis, to determine how you are going to attempt to make your ninth trick.

With East having failed to have followed suit to both a third round of spades *and* a third round of clubs, you now know that West started with:

♠ K Q J x x
♥ ?
♦ ?
♣ K x x x

Since a vulnerable West opened the bidding with so little strength in the black suits, he surely *rates to have* the guarded king of diamonds. And you appreciate, of course, that if you take the diamond finesse and it loses, West will cash three spade tricks to defeat you.

You next lead the jack of hearts, winning the trick with the board's king when West plays low. You now cash the ace of hearts, noting that West has followed suit to both heart leads. At this point you know eleven of West's original thirteen cards: five spades, four clubs, and two hearts.

And again the thought arises that West has opened the bidding. And you come to the conclusion that he just about has to have the guarded diamond king to justify his bid. So you next lead a spade, putting West into the lead. He wins the trick with the nine, after which he cashes two more spades. He then leads a diamond—and your dummy's jack wins the trick. You have just come home a winner.

These were the four hands:

```
                        NORTH
                     ♠ 7 4 3
                     ♥ A K 10
                     ♦ Q J 10
                     ♣ A J 10 8
     WEST                                 EAST
  ♠ K Q J 9 6                          ♠ 10
  ♥ 7 5                                ♥ Q 9 8 6 2
  ♦ K 4                                ♦ 9 7 6 3 2
  ♣ K 5 3 2                            ♣ 7 4
                        SOUTH
                     ♠ A 8 5 2
                     ♥ J 4 3
                     ♦ A 8 5
                     ♣ Q 9 6
```

Admittedly, when you elected to try for your ninth trick via an end play rather than via a diamond finesse, you had no guarantee that your line of play would win. West could have had, for example:

```
                     ♠ K Q J 9 6
                     ♥ Q 7 5
                     ♦ K
                     ♣ K 5 3 2
```

While the above is not what one would classify as a sound opening bid, it was not beyond the realm of possibility that West did possess this hand. And, if such had been the setup, then the winning play (pragmatically speaking) would have been for you to have laid down your ace of diamonds, felling West's singleton king. But surely, in your judgment, this line of play would have been inferior to the one you actually selected: the elimination of hearts from West's hand, and the thrusting of West into the lead, forcing him to lead away from his guarded diamond king.

Again, my congratulations to you for having played the hand in expert fashion. You're really moving up the ladder of ability.

6

The Felling
of Singleton Kings:
Luck, Skill—or Both?

You are sitting South, having arrived at a 7 ♠ contract, with no adverse bidding:

NORTH
- ♠ 9 8 5 2
- ♥ A K 7
- ♦ A K 4
- ♣ K Q 6

SOUTH
- ♠ A Q J 10 7 3
- ♥ Q 8 3
- ♦ 9 2
- ♣ A 5

West opens the queen of diamonds, which you capture with dummy's king. You lead the nine of spades and East follows suit with the four-spot. Do you finesse? Or do you put up your ace, hoping that West was dealt the singleton king?

If you put up the ace and catch the king, you are lucky—and unskillful. If you play low instead, hoping that East was dealt the king, you are skillful regardless of whether your finesse wins or loses. The reason will become apparent in a moment (if it is not already known to you).

The play of the ace will be the winning play *only* when East was dealt, specifically, the doubleton 6 4 (in which case West was dealt the singleton king). The play of the ace (as contrasted to the finesse) will be the losing play whenever East was dealt either the doubleton K 4 or the tripleton K 6 4. Are not two chances better than one? Is not the finesse the superior play?

The foregoing mathematical dissertation has nothing to do with either counting or card reading. It was introduced merely to serve as a specific example of what constitutes "luck" when it comes to catching a singleton king (as in the above) as distinguished from the type of "luck" that is embodied in the five card-reading deals that constitute this chapter.

Deal 1

Both sides vulnerable. West deals.

```
                        NORTH
                     ♠ A 10 7 3
                     ♥ Q 10
                     ♦ 10 8 4
                     ♣ K Q J 2
        WEST                             EAST
     ♠ 6 5 4 2                        ♠ K
     ♥ 7 3                            ♥ 8 6 5 4 2
     ♦ A K Q J 6                      ♦ 9 2
     ♣ 10 4                           ♣ 9 7 6 5 3
                        SOUTH
                     ♠ Q J 9 8
                     ♥ A K J 9
                     ♦ 7 5 3
                     ♣ A 8
```

The bidding:	WEST	NORTH	EAST	SOUTH
	Pass	Pass	Pass	1 ♠
	Pass	4 ♠	Pass	Pass
	Pass			

Opening lead: King of ♦.

To the first three tricks West cashed the king, queen, and ace of diamonds, East discarding the three of clubs on the third diamond lead. Had West but known the true state of affairs at this point, he would now have led another diamond—and East's king of spades would have taken the setting trick. But West elected to lead his seven of hearts at trick four, and South won the trick with his ace.

Declarer now led the queen of trumps, and when West followed suit with the deuce, the board's ace of trumps was put up. Great was declarer's joy when East dropped the king. From here in the sailing was smooth and pleasurable. Declarer gathered in West's three remaining trumps and claimed his contract.

That declarer was really lucky in finding East with the singleton king of trumps is rather obvious: with five trumps outstanding in the East-West hands, East certainly didn't figure to have been dealt the singleton king. Nevertheless, declarer's spurning of the trump finesse was the only correct play.

Going back to the bidding, West had not only passed originally, but had failed to overcall when South opened the bidding with one spade. At the completion of trick three (East having failed to follow suit to the third diamond lead), West was revealed as the possessor of the A K Q J x of diamonds. Surely if West had held the guarded spade king, he would have opened the bidding. And even if, perchance, he had passed with this holding, he certainly would have tried to recover from his lapse by making a two-diamond overcall. West's failure to bid, then, indicated beyond a shadow of a doubt that the spade king was not in his possession.

Thus declarer, with a little bit of luck (East's singleton king) and with a little bit of skill (the realization that the spade finesse *had to lose*), brought home a contract that a less discerning player might well have lost.

In the next deal, there is no question but that if East had had the foresight not to bid, declarer would have failed to fulfill his contract. But the fact is that he did bid (and justifiably so), and in doing so told our South declarer how to play the hand.

Both sides vulnerable. East deals.

NORTH
♠ K J 8 2
♥ K Q 9
♦ J
♣ A Q J 10 8

WEST
♠ 7 4
♥ 8 6 3
♦ A 9 2
♣ 7 5 4 3 2

EAST
♠ 6 3
♥ A J 10 4
♦ K Q 10 7 5 3
♣ K

SOUTH
♠ A Q 10 9 5
♥ 7 5 2
♦ 8 6 4
♣ 9 6

The bidding:

EAST	SOUTH	WEST	NORTH
1 ♦	Pass	Pass	Double
Pass	1 ♠	Pass	3 ♠
Pass	4 ♠	Pass	Pass
Pass			

Opening lead: Ace of ♦.

After winning the opening lead with his ace of diamonds, West, to trick two, led a low heart. When dummy's queen was put up, East won the trick with his ace and returned the jack of hearts, dummy taking the trick with the king.

The king of trumps was then cashed, after which a trump was led to South's ace. Next came the nine of clubs, upon which West played the deuce. With no visible hesitation, declarer put up dummy's ace. When East dropped the king on this trick (perhaps casting a suspicious eye at South), declarer claimed his contract.

If the actual East player happens to be reading this text, let me reassure him that South did not do any peeking into the East hand. The putting up of the dummy's ace of clubs, whether it turned out to be the winning play or the losing play, was quite logical. That declarer was lucky in catching East with the singleton king goes without saying. But let's look at what motivated declarer in his decision not to take the club finesse.

When East opened the bidding with one diamond, what response did West make? He said: PASS. Thus West had denied the possession of even six points. And what had West's opening lead been? The *ace* of diamonds. (Even with so much devaluation taking place, the ace is still worth four points.) So West just couldn't have the guarded king of clubs, for with an ace *and* a king, he would not have dreamed of passing initially.

Admittedly, with six clubs outstanding, the chances of East having been dealt the singleton king of clubs were very, very poor, to put it mildly. But any chance is better than no chance at all, for West just couldn't have the club king.

And so, once again, the combination of luck and skill brought about the optimum result.

In the 1953 National Team-of-Four Championships, when the following deal was played, our South declarer gave a neat demonstration of card reading. Sitting South was Alvin Roth of New York City. Roth has long been recognized as one of the greatest players of all time.

For practice, let's suppose that you, instead of Roth, are occupying the South seat. And he is watching you, instead of you watching him.

Both sides vulnerable. South deals.

```
                      NORTH
                  ♠ J 9 7 6 2
                  ♥ —
                  ♦ A Q J 9 5 4
                  ♣ J 4
                      SOUTH
                  ♠ A 4
                  ♥ K Q J 9 8 7 3 2
                  ♦ 10 6
                  ♣ 10
```

The bidding:

SOUTH	WEST	NORTH	EAST
1 ♥	Pass	1 ♠	Pass
2 ♥	Pass	2 ♠	Pass
4 ♥	Pass	Pass	Pass

Opening lead: King of ♣.

If the reader is looking askance at North's spade rebid, I would like to say that North was bound by the system he was playing (Roth-Stone). A bid of three diamonds instead would have been forcing to game. And if the question is raised: Why didn't North respond two diamonds initially?, the answer would be that, according to the system, a two-over-one response in a new suit would also have been forcing to game. Thus North was forced to rebid two spades, to give partner the option of passing below game.

After winning the opening lead with his club king, West leads the ace of clubs, which you ruff. You then lay down the king of trumps, West capturing the trick with his ace. West now shifts to the king of spades, which you win with your ace.

You next cash the queen and jack of trumps, West following suit to the queen, and East following suit to both the queen and jack. The outstanding trumps have now been picked up.

Your next lead is the diamond ten, upon which West plays the deuce. You reach for dummy's . . . ?

Suddenly you stop reaching and sit back to do some reflecting. Thus far West has shown up with the ace and king of clubs, the ace of hearts, and the king of spades. Why didn't he enter into the bidding with those cards? The answer, probably, is that he had no good suit to bid, and his hand was not suited to making a takeout double.

But surely, if West also possessed the king of diamonds, somewhere along the line he would have bid something with those 17 gilt-edged points. The answer suggests itself: West just couldn't have the guarded king of diamonds. After all, this is a national championship event, and West knows when he has the values for a bid. With the king of spades, the ace of hearts, the ace and king of clubs, and the king of diamonds, nothing under the sun could have restrained West from bidding.

And so you convince yourself that East must be the possessor of the diamond king—and that if you finesse against West's hoped-for king, your finesse is a cinch to lose. Is there really any alternative, you say to yourself, but to go up with dummy's ace of diamonds and hope that East was dealt the singleton king? So, unhappily perhaps, you call for the board's ace of diamonds. A very unhappy East slowly—and reluctantly—drops the king!

The complete deal was:

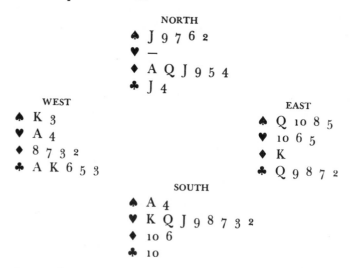

NORTH
♠ J 9 7 6 2
♥ —
♦ A Q J 9 5 4
♣ J 4

WEST
♠ K 3
♥ A 4
♦ 8 7 3 2
♣ A K 6 5 3

EAST
♠ Q 10 8 5
♥ 10 6 5
♦ K
♣ Q 9 8 7 2

SOUTH
♠ A 4
♥ K Q J 9 8 7 3 2
♦ 10 6
♣ 10

As to why West never made an overcall with his hand is un-known. But surely if his, let us say, eight of diamonds had been the king, nothing short of an earthquake could have kept him out of the bidding.

In retrospect, you really were lucky, weren't you? Of course. But think of it this way. How many of your friends would have been as "lucky" as you if they had been sitting in the South seat?

In the preceding chapter, Second Sight with Card Reading, it was demonstrated that when the defenders-to-be enter the auction, they frequently convey useful information to declarer. This is, of course, inevitable, for when one is trying to communicate with partner, the opposition will always be listening in. Thus, inherent in all bidding is the risk that the opponents will profit thereby.

But, as was also pointed out, bridge is a bidder's game—and if you aspire to be a winner, you bid when you have the prescribed values for the call which experience has demonstrated should be made. Actually, the failure to bid when you have a bid coming to you can be just as costly as bidding on submarginal values.

I don't know whether the reader has noticed it, but in the first three deals of this chapter, each declarer fulfilled his contract as a result of his interpretation of an opponent's *failure to bid!* In each case declarer was thereby enabled to deduce that the nonbidder couldn't possibly have a vital king that was outstanding. So if there still be those readers who are reluctant to bid defensively in borderline situations for fear that they might get hurt, I urge them to loosen up and speak their piece. Silence, just like aggressiveness, can breed defeat.

In Deal 4, which follows, an example of brilliant analysis is featured. It was based on the significance of the fact that one of the opponents failed to bid. In the South seat, as the declarer, was Meyer Schleifer of Los Angeles. For quite a few decades now Schleifer has been recognized as one of our nation's top-ranking players. The deal arose in a team-of-four event in San Francisco in 1952.

Both sides vulnerable. East deals.

NORTH
♠ A J 10 9
♥ 10 5 3
♦ 10 5
♣ 7 6 4 2

WEST
♠ 5 4 2
♥ 6 2
♦ Q 9 8
♣ K 10 9 8 3

EAST
♠ K
♥ A K Q J 9 8 4
♦ 7 3
♣ A Q J

SOUTH
♠ Q 8 7 6 3
♥ 7
♦ A K J 6 4 2
♣ 5

The bidding:

EAST	SOUTH	WEST	NORTH
2 ♥	3 ♦	Pass	Pass
4 ♥	4 ♠	Pass	Pass
5 ♥	Pass	Pass	5 ♠
Pass	Pass	Double	Pass
Pass	Pass		

Opening lead: Six of ♥.

For those who might be unfamiliar with this type of bidding situation, it should be pointed out that East's pass over North's five-spade bid was what is known as a "forcing pass." The pass said: "Partner, since I have opened with a strong two bid, you know that I can defeat their contract. You cannot pass. Either bid again if you feel that we can make whatever you bid, or double the opponents for penalties if you feel that that is the proper action. But don't you dare pass."

After East had won the opening lead with his king of hearts, he cashed the ace of clubs. West signaled most emphatically for a club continuation by playing the ten-spot. To trick three East led the queen of clubs, which Schleifer ruffed.

A low trump was then played out of the South hand, and when West followed suit with the deuce, dummy's ace was put up. As can be observed, East's king fell on this trick.

After the jack and ten of trumps were cashed, gathering in West's remaining pieces, the ace and king of diamonds were played. A third round of diamonds was then led, dummy ruffing as West's queen fell. All of declarer's remaining diamonds were now winners. Thus Schleifer fulfilled his doubled five-heart contract.

Why did Schleifer put up the board's ace of trumps instead of taking the finesse for the king? Here is the way he explained it:

"East had opened with a game-forcing two bid—he was known to have a powerhouse hand. Assuming that the opponents were not falsecarding when East laid down the ace of clubs at trick two, West had signaled most encouragingly with the ten. To me, West surely had the club king, especially when East continued with the *queen* of clubs at trick three. *Had West also held the guarded king of spades—in back of my spade overcall at the four-level—he surely would have taken some action over my four-spade bid.*

"But West had passed, making it virtually certain that East possessed the spade king and that a spade finesse, if taken, was bound to lose. So my only hope was that East's spade king was a singleton. Luckily, it was."

What more can be said?

The preceding two deals, although they arose in tournaments, came up in team games, where the approach is akin to that of rubber bridge. That is, the safety of one's contract is declarer's prime consideration, and one never tries for an overtrick if, in so trying, he jeopardizes his contract.

In the next deal we have an example of the difference in approach between rubber bridge (team play) and duplicate bridge. In the latter game scoring is on a relative basis, since all competing pairs play the identical deals. Thus, in duplicate bridge, one frequently jeopardizes his contract to try for an overtrick, since the overtrick can be worth its weight in gold. The hand came up in the National Open Pair Championship of 1971.

Both sides vulnerable. South deals.

```
                    NORTH
                 ♠ A J 10 9 5
                 ♥ K 7 2
                 ♦ 6 3
                 ♣ K J 7
     WEST                          EAST
  ♠ 7 6 4 3                      ♠ K
  ♥ 10 8 6                       ♥ Q 9 4 3
  ♦ A J 9 7                      ♦ K Q 10 5 2
  ♣ 3 2                          ♣ 8 6 4
                    SOUTH
                 ♠ Q 8 2
                 ♥ A J 5
                 ♦ 8 4
                 ♣ A Q 10 9 5
```

The bidding:

SOUTH	WEST	NORTH	EAST
1 ♣	Pass	1 ♠	Pass
2 ♣	Pass	5 ♣	Pass
Pass	Pass		

Opening lead: Three of ♣.

If the bidding appears inexpert, let me say that it was. But it should be appreciated that National Open Pair Championships are open to everyone, with no restrictions. As it happened, our South declarer was Jim Linhart of New York City. Jim is one of our nation's top-ranking players. His partner happened to be a novice (a pupil of Jim's, as a matter of fact).

After Jim had captured the opening trump lead with dummy's jack, he said to himself: "This is a ridiculous contract. Everybody figures to be in four spades." And he was right—actually *every* other North-South pair did arrive at a four-spade contract.

In accordance with duplicate scoring, a fulfilled four-spade contract would net the maker 620 points (trick score of 120, plus 500 for making a vulnerable game). Even if South fulfilled his five-club contract, he would have the worst score of all, since he would get only 600 points (trick score of 100, plus 500 for a vulnerable game). So South saw no sense in trying to make exactly five clubs.

At a spade contract, even if the spade finesse was unsuccessful, the North-South declarer would always make ten tricks (assuming that the opponents cashed two diamond tricks at the start), for he could get rid of his losing heart on one of dummy's high clubs. And if the spade finesse was successful, declarer would make eleven tricks. So, again, it was pointless to try for eleven tricks at South's five-club contract. Hence, abnormal play was called for.

Linhart, after winning the opening trump lead in dummy, cashed two more trumps, gathering in the adverse pieces. He then led a spade to the ace—and felled East's singleton king (if *West* had possessed the spade king, then all the declarers at a four-spade contract would make eleven tricks by finessing, thus avoiding the loss of a spade trick).

Spades were cashed next, South discarding his two diamonds on the board's fourth and fifth spades. The king of hearts was then played, after which the deuce of hearts was led, South finessing his jack successfully. He now had all thirteen tricks, for a score of 640 (trick score, 100; two overtricks, 40; and 500 for a vulnerable game).

His score beat all the other North-South scores, for every North declarer at the "correct" four-spade contract took the spade finesse, losing to East's singleton king. And against North's spade contract, each East player had led the diamond king originally, enabling the defenders to cash two diamond tricks. Thus each North-South score was 620 points.

Unquestionably, South was really "lucky" in his play. But I think we will all agree that he was most skillful in realizing what the future held in store for him if East did not possess the singleton king of spades.

7

Competitive
Bidding Situations

One of Europe's leading bridge authorities—and also one of its top-ranking players—is Victor Mollo of London. When this deal arose in a rubber-bridge game, Mollo was sitting in the South seat. In the play he demonstrated that his reputation as an excellent player of the cards was not an exaggerated one.

It is my opinion that the play of South's four-spade contract in this deal might well serve as the line of delineation between the average player and the one who has made the right turn on his way to expertise. In it there is revealed that extra something that the better player has acquired through years of experience— namely, the habitual realization that when one has obtained a meaningful clue, he does not stop and say: "Eureka! I have found it!" Instead, he continues his search for additional clues to reinforce (or negate) the initial clue. Quite often in these circumstances he ends up with a guarantee, rather than with merely a percentage play, that makes him a favorite to come up with the right play.

Before discussing Mollo's play of the hand, allow me to put you into Mollo's seat as the declarer. And, with your permission, allow me to take you by the hand and bring you to the point to which I referred as the "line of delineation." Then our hands will separate for a moment, and I will leave you to your own resources, with the question: *"Quo vadis?"* If you find yourself floundering, I promise to lead you home safely.

North-South vulnerable. West deals.

```
                    NORTH
                ♠ 7 2
                ♥ 10 8 3
                ♦ 10 7 4 3 2
                ♣ K 9 8
                    SOUTH
                ♠ A K Q J 10
                ♥ 4 2
                ♦ A 5
                ♣ A Q 10 7
```

The bidding:

WEST	NORTH	EAST	SOUTH
4 ♥	Pass	Pass	4 ♠
Pass	Pass	Pass	

Opening lead: King of ♥.

After West's king of hearts has captured the opening lead, he continues with the heart queen, East giving a high-low signal with the nine and then the five. On the next lead of the ace of hearts, East discards the diamond six, as you ruff the trick.

You then cash your three top trumps, noting that both East and West follow suit to all three leads. Since the loss of a diamond trick is inevitable, you deliberate on the way you intend to attack the club suit to make four club tricks. If you lose a club, you will of course be defeated.

And so you start reconstructing. Since East failed to follow suit to the third heart lead, West is known to have been dealt six hearts. West also followed suit to three trump leads. Thus nine of West's original thirteen cards are an open book, with his remaining four cards being unknown.

East, on the other hand, has been revealed as the possessor of just two hearts and three trumps. Therefore East has eight unknown cards in diamonds and clubs. Who has the key card, the jack of clubs? Is it East or West?

As of this moment, the evidence points rather strongly to East being the possessor of the jack of clubs: West has four unknown cards, while East has eight unknown cards. Thus, two times out of three (eight out of twelve), East rates to have been dealt the club jack.

If your thinking stops right here, you will next cash the ace of clubs, after which you will lead a club to dummy's king. You will then return the board's remaining club, and when East follows suit with a low club, you will insert your ten-spot, finessing against East's presumed jack. You will then look Westward, hopefully— and when West produces the club jack, you will become a sadder (although not, as yet, a wiser) man.

Let's go back, with Mollo, to the point where trumps had been drawn, revealing that West had started with six hearts and three trumps, while East had started with two hearts and three trumps.

It is, of course, agreed that East, rather than West, figured to have the club jack.

But what was the hurry in playing clubs at this point? Why not, instead, lead your ace of diamonds, and then follow up by playing another diamond? If you had done so (as Mollo did), you would have observed that on the ace of diamonds West would have played the diamond queen. And on your next lead of the diamond five, West would have discarded a heart.

The winning play would now become automatic, for West would have been known to have been dealt six hearts, three spades, one diamond—and *exactly* three clubs. And, of course, at the same time you would have known that East had been dealt the remaining three clubs.

From here in the winning play would have required nothing more than the energy needed to reach over to dummy to cash the king of clubs and to play another club to your ace. Next would come the queen of clubs. You would now chalk up the score for winning the game and rubber. These were the four hands:

NORTH
♠ 7 2
♥ 10 8 3
♦ 10 7 4 3 2
♣ K 9 8

WEST
♠ 6 4 3
♥ A K Q J 7 6
♦ Q
♣ J 4 2

EAST
♠ 9 8 5
♥ 9 5
♦ K J 9 8 6
♣ 6 5 3

SOUTH
♠ A K Q J 10
♥ 4 2
♦ A 5
♣ A Q 10 7

Deal 2

For those who are familiar with card reading and are accustomed to making an effort on each and every deal to count out the distribution of the opponents' cards, this deal is not an exceedingly difficult one to play correctly (although I would not say it was an easy one). But for those who forget to count (or have never learned to count), I imagine that by naturally taking the path of least resistance they would fail to fulfill the game contract arrived at by South. As will be noted, our actual South declarer acquitted himself nobly in the play.

Both sides vulnerable. West deals.

```
                        NORTH
                        ♠ J 3
                        ♥ A K 5
                        ♦ J 9 4 3 2
                        ♣ 9 5 4
        WEST                                EAST
    ♠ 9 5 2                             ♠ 7 6 4
    ♥ J 7                               ♥ Q 10 9 8 3 2
    ♦ 10                                ♦ K Q 7
    ♣ A K Q 10 7 6 2                    ♣ J
                        SOUTH
                        ♠ A K Q 10 8
                        ♥ 6 4
                        ♦ A 8 6 5
                        ♣ 8 3
```

The bidding:

WEST	NORTH	EAST	SOUTH
3 ♣	Pass	Pass	3 ♠
Pass	4 ♠	Pass	Pass
Pass			

Opening lead: King of ♣.

After winning trick one with his king of clubs, West continued with the club queen, East discarding the deuce of hearts. Next came the club ace, East discarding another low heart as South ruffed.

The ace, king, and queen of trumps then gathered in the adversely held pieces. At this point, I believe, most of our nation's players would have led the ace of diamonds and then followed up by playing another diamond. If the four outstanding diamonds were divided 2–2, this line of play would result in the fulfillment of the game contract, since only one diamond trick would be lost. In the actual setup, however, South would be defeated, since East's king and queen of diamonds would win two tricks.

Our South declarer did not adopt the above line of play, for he felt that West possibly did not possess two diamonds. In the play to the first six tricks, West had been revealed as having been dealt seven clubs and three spades (trumps). Thus West had been dealt just three red cards. And with eight hearts and four diamonds having been dealt to East and West, West did not rate to have been dealt exactly two diamonds.

What declarer did after drawing trumps was to enter dummy via the king of hearts. He noted that West followed suit with the seven of hearts (an astute West player might have diagnosed that he should have played the jack of hearts, to create the impression in South's mind that West had been dealt only one heart). Hence West was known to have just two red cards remaining—and South appreciated that West had been dealt a *maximum* of two diamonds, and that possibly West had been dealt only one diamond.

Dummy's jack of diamonds was led next. In the actual play East covered with the queen, and South's ace won the trick as West's ten fell. It now became a routine matter for declarer to lead the diamond eight and concede a diamond trick to East's king. He then claimed his contract.

If East had not covered the jack, South would have followed suit with the five. With the jack winning, all the defenders could have made from here in would have been one diamond trick.

Oh, yes, South was very lucky in catching West with the singleton ten of diamonds. But the point of his lead of the diamond jack was that it couldn't ever be the wrong play. Let us see why.

First (to repeat), if the four outstanding diamonds were divided 2–2, and West happened to capture the jack with the queen or king, when South regained the lead he would cash the diamond ace, felling the two remaining adversely held diamonds. Secondly, if West had possessed either the singleton king or singleton queen of diamonds, South couldn't ever make his contract even if the opponents had shown him their cards. If the latter setup existed, then East, opposite West's (presumed) singleton king of diamonds, would have the Q 10 7. And, in this case, if South cashed the diamond ace, felling West's king, East, with the doubleton Q 10 of diamonds remaining behind dummy's jack, would have two diamond winners.

Therefore, from declarer's position, if the adversely held diamonds were not divided 2–2, he had to indulge in the wishful thinking that West's singleton diamond was the ten. If such was the case, then by leading dummy's jack on the initial diamond lead he would entrap East's K Q 7, while simultaneously pinning West's ten. And he did just that.

It should be mentioned, perhaps naïvely, that if West were void of diamonds, or possessed the singleton seven-spot, then South was doomed to defeat, since in this setup East, with either the K Q 10 7 or the K Q 10 of diamonds, had at least two sure diamond winners.

Deal 3

This competitive card-reading deal is not a difficult one to play correctly. As a matter of fact, if the West defender had not bid at all, our South declarer would probably have adopted the identical line of play that he actually took.

The major reason for my introduction of this deal is to present an illustration of how stress and strain can be either eliminated or diminished if one is constantly attuned to the bidding of the opponents. And, simultaneously, the "all ears" player thus creates a hardship for his opponents, who begin to realize that they cannot communicate with each other without the real danger that their conversation will be utilized to the utmost by their enemy.

North-South vulnerable. West deals.

```
                        NORTH
                     ♠ Q 6
                     ♥ 9 5 3
                     ♦ 8 3 2
                     ♣ A Q 10 9 2
        WEST                                    EAST
   ♠ A J 10 9 4 2                          ♠ 7 5
   ♥ J 10                                  ♥ 8 7 6 4 2
   ♦ Q 9 7                                 ♦ K 5 4
   ♣ 5 4                                   ♣ K 7 3
                        SOUTH
                     ♠ K 8 3
                     ♥ A K Q
                     ♦ A J 10 6
                     ♣ J 8 6
```

The bidding:

WEST	NORTH	EAST	SOUTH
2 ♠	Pass	Pass	2 NT
Pass	3 NT	Pass	Pass
Pass			

Opening lead: Jack of ♠.

West's opening two-spade bid was the "weak two bid." This bid came into mass use (for tournament and duplicate players) in the 1950s, and its employment has had a beneficial result for its users. The bid, when made in first or second position, guarantees a decent suit of exactly six cards, within a hand containing 6 to 12 high-card points. The aim of the bid is twofold:

1. To preempt the opponents out of bidding space, thus forcing them to enter into the auction at either the three level or a high two level.

2. To convey to partner a precise description of the opener's hand.

The reason for the emergence of the weak two bid is a simple and logical one: the traditional, strong, forcing-to-game type of two bid arises once in a blue moon. And if one accepts this fact of

the obvious infrequency of hands that rate a strong two-bid opening, why waste a perfectly good type of bid on something that
comes up about once a month even with those who play daily?
Why not employ a better and much more frequent use for an
opening two bid? Here are three examples of the "weak" opening
two bid:

(a)	(b)	(c)
♠ x x	♠ x x	♠ A Q x x x x
♥ K Q 10 9 x x	♥ x x	♥ x x
♦ x x	♦ A K J x x x	♦ x x
♣ K x x	♣ x x x	♣ K x x
Bid 2 ♥	Bid 2 ♦	Bid 2 ♠

After West had opened the spade jack and the dummy came
into view, South knew at once exactly what West's spade holding
was: the A J 10 x x x; and, via simple arithmetic, that East had
been dealt exactly two spades.

It was also immediately apparent to declarer that he would have
to attack the club suit, and that if West held the all-important
king of clubs, then by repeated finesses the club suit would be
brought home without the loss of a trick. But if East had the club
king, precautionary measures would have to be taken to assure the
fulfillment of the contract.

Appreciating that East had been dealt precisely two spades, if
declarer won the opening spade lead with dummy's queen, he
would be in bad shape if East possessed the club king. In this case,
upon winning his king, East would return his remaining spade,
enabling West to cash five tricks in this suit.

So declarer allowed West's jack of spades to win the opening
lead. Whatever West now played back, he could not prevent declarer from fulfilling his contract. Either the ace of spades return,
or a low spade, would give declarer a spade trick, while at the
same time East's remaining spade would be removed. Thus when
East obtained the lead via the club king, he would be unable to
play back a spade. South would have his nine tricks: one spade,
three hearts, one diamond, and four clubs.

In practice, West made an excellent play when, at trick two, he
switched to the seven of diamonds, and East's king drove out

South's ace. Had East possessed the K 10 4 of diamonds (instead of the K 5 4), South's contract would have been defeated upon a diamond return by East after winning his club king.

Upon winning the diamond king with his ace, South now tried the club finesse, which lost to East's king. A diamond return then enabled West to cash the diamond queen, but all the defenders could make from here in was West's ace of spades.

As was stated, even if West had not bid, and had opened the jack of spades, declarer's correct play would have been to allow the jack to win, in an attempt to prevent the dangerous East, if he held the club king, from returning a spade later on. But with West having made his "weak" two-spade opening bid, declarer was thus spared the time and energy that he might have needed to work out the situation at hand.

Deal 4

Another "weak" bid which has been adopted by many of our better players is the "weak jump overcall." This bid, like its relative, the "weak two bid," came into vogue in the middle 1950s. Prior to that time, the jump overcall was *strong*. It would be made, for example, with this type of hand:

♠ 8 4
♥ A Q 10 9 7 5 2
♦ A K 6
♣ 5

Over an opening one-club bid, the above hand would warrant a jump overcall of two hearts, inviting partner to go on, if he had six or more points (or 1½ honor tricks). The weak jump overcall, on the other hand, denotes a poor hand containing about 8 to 10 high-card points, plus a *six-card suit* (not five and not seven). Over an opening one-diamond bid, the weak jump overcall of two hearts would be made with either of these two hands:

(1)	(2)
♠ K 2	♠ 8 5
♥ A 10 9 8 7 3	♥ Q J 9 7 6 2
♦ 7 5 4	♦ 6
♣ 9 3	♣ Q J 10 3

There are valid and cogent reasons for the use of the jump overcall to describe a weak hand rather than a strong one. First, it enables the bridge player to exercise great liberties without promising high cards. He is permitted to bid on hands with which he ordinarily would be required to pass—and this becomes a virtue if partner is not misled and the partnership remains on relatively safe ground.

Second, it results in unnatural "free bids" by the partner of the opening bidder, with the former often being goaded into this unnatural action because he knows that the weak jump overcaller has a poor hand.

Third, the bid disrupts or destroys the opponents' line of communication by depriving them of bidding space.

And fourth, it gives partner a fairly accurate picture of the pre-emptive two-bidder's hand, thus serving as both a warning and a guide to a possible sacrifice bid against the opening side's game or slam contract.

In this deal our West defender made a weak jump overcall which turned out badly for his side, for it illuminated the path for declarer's enjoyable walk to safety. Had he made a simple nonjump overcall, declarer might well have gone down at his contract.

Both sides vulnerable. South deals.

```
                        NORTH
                     ♠ 9 5 3
                     ♥ A J 10 3
                     ♦ 7
                     ♣ K Q 6 5 3
      WEST                                    EAST
  ♠ K Q J 10 8 4                          ♠ 6
  ♥ 7 2                                   ♥ K 8 5 4
  ♦ Q J 10                                ♦ K 9 8 6 5 3 2
  ♣ 9 8                                   ♣ 2
                        SOUTH
                     ♠ A 7 2
                     ♥ Q 9 6
                     ♦ A 4
                     ♣ A J 10 7 4
```

The bidding:

SOUTH	WEST	NORTH	EAST
1 ♣	2 ♠	4 ♣	Pass
5 ♣	Pass	Pass	Pass

Opening lead: King of ♠.

Before playing to West's opening lead of the king of spades, declarer paused for reflection. South's problem was whether to take the king with his ace, or, instead, to allow West's king to win the trick.

Looking ahead, South recognized that if West possessed the king of hearts, the five-club contract would be fulfilled no matter how he played the spade suit, since by repeated finesses in hearts the loss of a heart trick would be avoided. And South had no losers in either diamonds or clubs.

But if East had the heart king, then danger loomed ahead, for when East won a trick with the king, a spade return by him would enable West to cash two spade tricks.

West's jump overcall made things easy for declarer, for West, by definition, rated to have a six-card suit. Hence East had only a singleton spade. So South captured the opening spade lead with his ace, cashed the king and ace of trumps, and then led the nine of hearts, taking the finesse. East won with the king, and returned a diamond. South took his ace, and cashed dummy's hearts, on the fourth of which he discarded his deuce of spades. At the end he conceded a spade trick to West.

But let's suppose that West had overcalled with *one* spade instead of two spades. Now declarer would have a serious problem to resolve, a problem that could not be deferred. Was West overcalling on a five- or six-card suit?

If it was a six-card suit, then declarer would play the hand as he actually did. But if West had only a five-card suit, then East possessed two spades. And in this latter case, winning play would require that West be permitted to win the opening lead. When West then continued spades, East's remaining spade would be removed, as South won the trick with his ace. And when East subsequently obtained the lead with his heart king, he would have no spade to play back.

It is apparent, of course, that if declarer had made the assumption that West, for his (hypothetical) *one*-spade overcall, had a five-card suit, he would have gone down. With West, in this case, being allowed to win the opening lead with the spade king, West would continue with a spade at trick two. East would naturally capture this trick by ruffing. Eventually East's king of hearts would take the setting trick.

But, thanks to West's *two*-spade overcall, declarer *knew* that East had only one spade, and, thus, the capturing of West's opening spade lead had to be the correct play.

In Deals 3 and 4, it has been observed how (1) the weak opening two bid and (2) the weak jump overcall eliminated any problems that declarer might have had if these bids had not been made.

However, it should not be inferred from these two selected illustrations that these two "revolutionary" bids are poor calls. In the experience of our better players these two types of bids will pay dividends in the long run. Thus, just as one swallow does not make a summer, one should not say: "To heck with these bids. I'm going to toss them into the ash can. The first time I tried them, they didn't work." Just how efficient they can be will be learned when your opponents use them against you—as our experts have learned through bitter experiences.

Deal 5

It has been reiterated throughout this book that it is a moot question as to whether the bidding by the ultimate defenders is of greater assistance to the defenders or to the declarer. Again, with respect to the defenders' bidding, as embodied in Deals 3 and 4, their bidding turned out badly for them. However, in the long run, the bidding by the defenders-to-be will tend to net them a profit. Furthermore, if they never made overcalls or takeout doubles, they would forever be fighting a losing cause.

In this deal we have another illustration of a defensive bid that turned out unfortunately for the defensive side, for it literally told an astute declarer how to play his slam contract. While it might be argued—and justifiably so—that the winning play would have been found even if the West defender had had the clairvoyance to keep quiet, there can be no doubt that his bid eliminated any thoughts that our South declarer might have had about any alternative line of play.

Both sides vulnerable. South deals.

```
                        NORTH
                     ♠ A K 10 8
                     ♥ K 5 3
                     ♦ K 8 3
                     ♣ 7 5 2
        WEST                              EAST
     ♠ 9                              ♠ 4
     ♥ J 10 8                         ♥ 9 7 4 2
     ♦ A Q J 10 7 4                   ♦ 9 6 5 2
     ♣ K J 3                          ♣ 10 9 8 6
                        SOUTH
                     ♠ Q J 7 6 5 3 2
                     ♥ A Q 6
                     ♦ —
                     ♣ A Q 4
```

The bidding:

SOUTH	WEST	NORTH	EAST
1 ♠	2 ♦	3 ♠	Pass
6 ♠	Pass	Pass	Pass

Opening lead: Nine of ♠.

West made a good decision when he elected not to lead the ace of diamonds. Had he led this card, dummy's king of diamonds would have become declarer's twelfth trick.

After West's trump lead had been taken by dummy's king, declarer ruffed a diamond. The ace, queen, and king of hearts were then cashed, after which declarer ruffed a second diamond, leaving dummy with the singleton king.

A trump was next led to the board's ace. The king of diamonds was now played—and on it South discarded his four of clubs, West's ace winning the trick. Whatever West now returned, declarer's slam contract could not be defeated.

If West played back a diamond, dummy would capture the trick by ruffing, while South discarded his four of clubs. And if, instead, West chose to lead a club, South's queen of clubs would become a winner.

It is apparent that if declarer had elected to finesse his queen of clubs anywhere along the line, he would have gone down, for West would have made two club tricks. But with West having made a vulnerable overcall at the two level, not only did he figure to have the ace of diamonds, but also the king of clubs. Hence, on two counts, the taking of the club finesse could never be the right play.

Admittedly, if West had not overcalled (a pass by West would really have been an act of sheer cowardice—or ignorance), an expert declarer would have played the hand as it was actually played. The only difference would have been a matter of declarer's uncertainty about the location of the diamond ace, as contrasted with the virtual certainty that West possessed that card because of West's actual overcall. That is, when declarer, after ruffing dummy's two low diamonds, later led the diamond king, he would breathe a sigh of relief when East followed suit with a low diamond. On this lead South would discard his four of clubs (as was done in the actual deal). West, upon winning the trick with his ace, would now be end-played (as he was).

Of course, if on the lead of the diamond king East had (in theory) played the ace, South would have ruffed the trick. He would then have indulged in the wishful thinking that East, rather than West, possessed the king of clubs. But, with the overcall, declarer knew that he had a sure thing as he played the hand.

Deal 6

After the opening lead had been made in this deal, and the dummy came into view, card reading (based on the bidding) revealed to our South declarer that the East defender almost surely possessed a crucial card. Furthermore, it was also apparent to our declarer that he rated to lose a trick to that card. But, by counting out the hand, he was able to reach a position which, upon the loss of a trick to that key card, simultaneously guaranteed the success of his contract. As I am sure the reader will agree, South played the hand in truly expert fashion.

East-West vulnerable. North deals.

```
                        NORTH
                    ♠ A J 8 6
                    ♥ A J 3
                    ♦ A Q 5
                    ♣ Q 9 5
      WEST                                    EAST
  ♠ 7 4                                    ♠ 5 2
  ♥ 7 6 5 2                                ♥ 9 8 4
  ♦ J 10 8 7 3                             ♦ K 9
  ♣ 6 2                                    ♣ A K J 10 7 4
                        SOUTH
                    ♠ K Q 10 9 3
                    ♥ K Q 10
                    ♦ 6 4 2
                    ♣ 8 3
```

The bidding:

NORTH	EAST	SOUTH	WEST
1 NT	2 ♣	3 ♠	Pass
4 ♠	Pass	Pass	Pass

Opening lead: Six of ♣.

When North put his hand down as the dummy, South knew that East figured to have the diamond king, and in this case it appeared that South would have to lose two diamond tricks.

South's knowledge of this appreciation arose out of the fact that East had made a *vulnerable* overcall of North's strong one no-trump opening bid (16 to 18 high-card points). Surely, in a rubber-bridge game (which this was) East wouldn't be sticking his neck out to make a part score unless he felt that he was on safe ground. And with only 12 high-card points outstanding (North-South had 28 of the deck's 40 high-card points), East was a favorite to have all of them.

Actually, East's overcall would have been a sound one if he had a seven- or eight-card club suit, in which case he would not have needed the diamond king to justify his bid. But when a low club was played from dummy on the opening lead, and East, after winning the trick with the club ten, returned the club king, it was observed that West followed suit to the second club lead. Hence, East had only six clubs—and surely the king of diamonds.

To trick three, East led the club ace, South ruffing with the king as West discarded the three of diamonds. Trumps were next drawn in two rounds with dummy's ace and jack of trumps, after which South cashed the ace, king, and queen of hearts. Declarer then led a diamond—and put up dummy's ace, spurning the finesse.

He now returned to the South hand via the queen of trumps and led another diamond. When West followed suit with the eight-spot, dummy's queen was put up. As is evident, East captured the trick with his king. And, as is equally evident, East had just become the victim of an end play.

East, of course, had no option but to return a club, for he had nothing but clubs remaining in his hand. On this lead South discarded his remaining diamond as he ruffed the trick in dummy. The rest of the tricks belonged to him.

Let us see why declarer made his "abnormal" play in the diamond suit.

First, even if West, by some stretch of the imagination, happened to have been the possessor of the diamond king, South's contract would be assured as he played it. If, on the second diamond lead, West, with the presumed king, played low, dummy's queen would win the trick. And if, instead, West put up the king, then dummy's queen would become declarer's game-going trick, his only losers being two clubs and one diamond.

And if it was East who had the king of diamonds (which he figured to have just as surely as the sun rises and sets), then declarer knew that his contract would be fulfilled. He knew it because he had counted out East's hand: six clubs, two spades, and three hearts. Thus East had room in his hand for *only two diamonds* (he might, in theory, have had just one diamond, which would have been the case if he had been dealt four hearts).

Therefore South knew that if it came to pass that East's king captured dummy's queen on the second lead of diamonds, East would have no choice except to play back a club, giving South a "sluff and a ruff."

It should be observed that if declarer, after drawing trumps and eliminating hearts from both the North and South hands, had elected to finesse the board's diamond queen on the initial lead of this suit, he would have gone down. In this case, East, upon winning his diamond king, would have returned his remaining diamond, the nine-spot. The loss of another diamond trick, to West, would now become unavoidable.

Deal 7

Just as "a little knowledge is a dangerous thing," in the same sense a little counting can be a dangerous—and costly—thing. More specifically, many occasions arise where, in the early stages of the play, declarer obtains a partial count of the opponents' hands, a count which definitely indicates that some adversely held key card figures to be in the hand of one opponent rather than in the hand of the other. He then tends to rest on his laurels, feeling that the information now in his possession is a sufficient guide to the winning line of play.

But very often he is wrong because he did not pursue his counting a bit further; or, perhaps, because he did not expand his horizons in his quest for additional clues. And in retrospect it is revealed that complete knowledge could have been obtained, knowledge that would have negated the superficial validity of the partial knowledge obtained earlier.

The issue of partial versus complete knowledge is evidenced in this deal. As will be observed, our declarer's guide to his play was based mainly (although not exclusively) on his sense of sight, and he did not examine in greater detail the practical significance of a bid that had been made by the East defender.

North-South vulnerable. East deals.

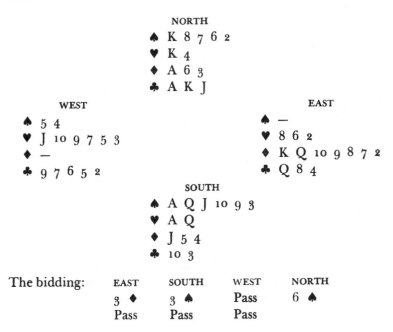

NORTH
- ♠ K 8 7 6 2
- ♥ K 4
- ♦ A 6 3
- ♣ A K J

WEST
- ♠ 5 4
- ♥ J 10 9 7 5 3
- ♦ —
- ♣ 9 7 6 5 2

EAST
- ♠ —
- ♥ 8 6 2
- ♦ K Q 10 9 8 7 2
- ♣ Q 8 4

SOUTH
- ♠ A Q J 10 9 3
- ♥ A Q
- ♦ J 5 4
- ♣ 10 3

The bidding:

EAST	SOUTH	WEST	NORTH
3 ♦	3 ♠	Pass	6 ♠
Pass	Pass	Pass	

Opening lead: Jack of ♥.

After West's opening heart lead had been captured by South's queen, declarer cashed the queen and jack of trumps, picking up West's pieces. He then led a club to dummy's ace (in the hope that perhaps East had been dealt the singleton queen). When the queen failed to drop, South reentered his own hand via the ace of hearts. He next led a club and finessed dummy's jack.

As is apparent, East captured the jack with his queen. He returned the diamond king to the board's ace. Although South was able to discard one of his diamonds on the club king, he eventually had to concede a diamond trick to East's queen. Thus he lost a slam contract that should have been fulfilled.

When West opened the jack of hearts at trick one, it was just about absolutely certain that East possessed a seven-card suit for his preemptive three-diamond opening bid. Surely if West had held a singleton diamond he would have led it automatically, since East's diamond suit might well have been headed by the ace; and if the latter were the case, then West could ruff the second diamond lead by East. Thus East should have been *known* to possess a diamond suit that was headed by the king and queen. By utilizing this knowledge, declarer could have guaranteed his slam.

But evidently South was influenced unduly by the early counting, which seemed to indicate that West possessed the club queen and that the finesse against that card was in order.

East was known to have seven diamonds and no spades, leaving him with six unknown cards in hearts and clubs. West, on the other hand, was known to possess no diamonds and exactly two spades, which meant that he had been dealt eleven unknown cards in hearts and clubs. Therefore, on probability, West, with the greater number of unknown cards, figured to be the possessor of the club queen.

If the heart-club setup were taken out of context, the taking of the club finesse would be mathematically sound. But this was only a partial clue—and an out-of-context one—and was not conclusive evidence. That evidence could have been obtained if declarer had given consideration to the fact that East was known to have both the king and queen of diamonds. Had he done so, he would have realized that the queen of clubs was really *not* the crucial card!

After drawing trumps, South should have cashed his ace of hearts, thereby eliminating hearts from both the North and South hands. Next would come the ace and king of clubs, and this would be followed by the ruffing of the club jack. The club suit would now have been eliminated from both the North and South hands.

Dummy would then be entered via the trump king, and the three of diamonds would be led toward South's jack. Of course East would win this trick with the queen—and simultaneously he would become the victim of an end play.

If East played back a heart (or, in theory, a club, if he had one), South would discard a diamond from his own hand as he ruffed the trick in dummy. The rest of the tricks would now belong to him. And if, instead, East returned a low diamond, South would put up his jack, knowing that East had been dealt both the queen and king of diamonds. With the jack winning, South would then claim his contract.

Deal 8

In this deal, intelligent card reading—plus a little bit of luck—enabled our South declarer to fulfill a contract that would have been lost had he played the hand "normally." The key to the winning line of play was obtained from the defenders' bidding.

Both sides vulnerable. East deals.

```
                        NORTH
                    ♠ 9 4 2
                    ♥ K 10 5
                    ♦ K 10
                    ♣ K Q 9 6 3
        WEST                            EAST
    ♠ 5                             ♠ A 6
    ♥ 8 6 3                         ♥ 9 7 4 2
    ♦ 9 8 6 5 4 2                   ♦ A Q J 7 3
    ♣ J 10 5                        ♣ A 8
                        SOUTH
                    ♠ K Q J 10 8 7 3
                    ♥ A Q J
                    ♦ —
                    ♣ 7 4 2
```

The bidding:	EAST	SOUTH	WEST	NORTH
	1 ♦	4 ♠	5 ♦	5 ♠
	Double	Pass	Pass	Pass

Opening lead: Nine of ♦.

Dummy's king of diamonds was played on the opening lead, East covered with the ace, and South ruffed. The king of trumps was then led, which East won with the ace, and returned the diamond queen, South ruffing. The trump queen now picked up East's remaining trump.

Next came the king, queen, and ace of hearts, after which South led his deuce of clubs. When West followed suit with the five, the board's nine was inserted. East took this trick with his ace, for the defenders' last trick. Thus South fulfilled his doubled contract.

It is apparent that if declarer had put up dummy's queen of clubs (instead of the nine), he would have gone down. In this case, East, upon winning with his ace, would have returned a club. In time West would have made another club trick.

How come declarer elected to put up dummy's nine of clubs on the initial club lead? Actually, it was his only hope. Let us see why.

First, East had opened the bidding, and he, rather than West, certainly figured to have the club ace. But what made East's possession of the club ace a certainty was East's penalty double of the five-spade contract.

From South's position, East surely would not have felt that he could defeat the five-spade contract unless he held all three of the missing aces (East was known to have no kings, since South was looking at the four kings in his own hand and dummy). Furthermore, if East had some combination of the A J or A 10 of clubs, there was nothing South could do about preventing the defenders from winning two club tricks. Therefore it had to be wrong to put up dummy's club queen on the initial club lead.

Thus, with card reading serving as a guide, and assisted by the application of analysis, South realized that his only hope of avoiding the loss of two club tricks rested in the outside chance that East had been dealt either the singleton ace of clubs or the A x (or, in theory, West's possession of, specifically, the doubleton J 10 of clubs). So South indulged in the wishful thinking that his hope was a reality—and he played the hand on the assumption that it was. On this day Lady Luck smiled kindly on him.

Deal 9

If some of tournament bridge's old-timers happen to be reading this book, the deal discussed below may seem familiar to them. And it should be. When it arose in a national championship event a few decades ago, it became a cause célèbre, with much attendant publicity. In point of fact, it resulted in South's team losing a national championship. At the completion of the play of the hand, South made a statement that was heard (and published) around the world: "How stupid can I get?"

Both sides vulnerable. East deals.

```
                        NORTH
                     ♠ 6
                     ♥ A 7
                     ♦ 10 9 5 4 2
                     ♣ K Q J 9 6
        WEST                              EAST
     ♠ —                              ♠ Q 7 5 3
     ♥ 8 4 3                          ♥ K Q J 10 9 6 2
     ♦ K Q J 7 3                      ♦ 6
     ♣ 10 8 7 3 2                     ♣ 4
                        SOUTH
                     ♠ A K J 10 9 8 4 2
                     ♥ 5
                     ♦ A 8
                     ♣ A 5
```

The bidding:

EAST	SOUTH	WEST	NORTH
3 ♥	4 ♠	Pass	5 ♥
Pass	6 ♠	Pass	Pass
Pass			

Opening lead: King of ♦.

North's five-heart call was an excellent bid. It announced not only first-round control of the adversely bid heart suit, but also a hand that had sufficient strength to undertake a slam venture if South had a sound jump to four spades. South, having full values for his bid, willingly contracted for the small slam.

After South's diamond ace had captured the opening lead, the cashing of South's ace of trumps revealed the discouraging news that East was the possessor of a sure trump trick.

It being essential to dispose of his losing diamond before East obtained the lead with the spade queen, declarer promptly went after the club suit. It was his intention to cash the ace, king, and queen of clubs and, if East had three or more clubs, the latter would be compelled to follow suit to each of the club leads. On the third club, South would discard his losing diamond.

But, as can be observed, declarer never got to play the third club, for East ruffed the second lead of this suit. In time, East made his trump queen, to hand declarer a one-trick set.

Declarer's statement, "How stupid can I get?," was quite apropos. A vulnerable East had opened the bidding with three hearts, missing the ace. Almost surely he had a seven-card suit. And it was certainly 100 percent that he had no fewer than six hearts. Also, at the completion of trick two, East was known to have been dealt four trumps. And East had followed suit to West's diamond lead at trick one. Therefore East could not possibly have started with *more than two clubs.*

Thus declarer's hope that he could cash three top clubs was an impossible dream, an enticing (and thoughtless) delusion.

What declarer should have recognized was that his sole hope of fulfilling his contract rested in the possibility that East had been dealt just one diamond, a most likely possibility, considering that East was the possessor of four spades and rated to have seven hearts. After cashing his ace of trumps at trick two, declarer should have continued with the trump king, after which the jack of trumps would be led, East's queen winning.

If East had another diamond, then declarer's defeat was inevitable from the start (in this presumed case, East had a maximum of one club). In the actual setup, whatever East played back after winning the trump queen would be captured by declarer or dummy. It would now be a routine matter for declarer to pick up East's remaining trump. He would then discard his losing diamond on the board's queen of clubs.

Deal 10

In this deal there are combined three basic ingredients of winning play: (1) the ability to count out a hand, (2) the knowledge of percentages, and (3) a working knowledge of end plays. By employing all three, our expert South declarer fulfilled his slam contract.

Neither side vulnerable. South deals.

NORTH
- ♠ Q 7
- ♥ A 9 8 5 4 3 2
- ♦ K 7 5
- ♣ 5

WEST
- ♠ J 8 6 3
- ♥ —
- ♦ J 10 9 8 4 3
- ♣ K 10 2

EAST
- ♠ K 10 9 4 2
- ♥ 7
- ♦ Q
- ♣ Q 8 7 6 4 3

SOUTH
- ♠ A 5
- ♥ K Q J 10 6
- ♦ A 6 2
- ♣ A J 9

The bidding:

SOUTH	WEST	NORTH	EAST
1 ♥	Pass	3 ♥	Pass
4 NT	Pass	5 ♦	Pass
6 ♥	Pass	Pass	Pass

Opening lead: Jack of ♦.

Dummy's king of diamonds won the opening lead, East following suit with the queen. Thus, at trick one, it was apparent that West had started with six diamonds, while East had been dealt a singleton diamond.

After the nine of trumps had picked up the outstanding trump, the five of clubs was led to South's ace. The nine of clubs was then ruffed in dummy. Declarer now returned to his own hand via the diamond ace, East discarding the deuce of spades. South then ruffed his remaining club—the jack—in dummy as West followed suit with the king. This was the position prior to the lead to trick seven:

West was known to have been dealt exactly six diamonds, and a minimum of three clubs (West might have had the club queen and falsecarded with the king). Hence West had been dealt *a maximum of four spades.* East, therefore, had been dealt a minimum of five spades.

As we all now know, whichever of the opponents has the most cards of any particular suit figures to have any one specific card in that suit. Hence, at this point, East, rather than West, figured to be the possessor of the king of spades.

Proceeding on the sound assumption that East possessed the spade king, declarer next cashed the ace of spades and followed up by leading his remaining spade. As can be observed, East's king captured this trick.

East was now end-played, since he had to return either a club or a spade. And whichever he returned (it was actually a spade), declarer would discard his losing diamond as he ruffed the trick in dummy.

If, hypothetically (on some other day), West had failed to follow to the third lead of clubs, he would have been revealed as the possessor of six diamonds, two clubs, and no hearts. He would then have been known to have started with *exactly five spades.* And East would then have been known to have been dealt *exactly four spades.*

What declarer would then have done at trick seven (see immediately preceding diagram) would have been to have led a diamond, thrusting West into the lead. If West now led another diamond, it would be ruffed in dummy, as South, when it came his turn to play, would discard his five of spades.

And if, instead, West elected to lead a low spade, dummy's

queen would be put up. It would, of course, win the trick whenever West had the spade king (as he would figure to if West had five spades originally).

Deal 11

This final deal is, in a sense, an everyday, run-of-the-mill type of hand. But it does demonstrate the fact that card reading does not always begin in the middle of the play. Speaking positively, it frequently begins right at trick one, when the opening lead is made and the dummy comes into view.

In this deal, many a player, sitting in the South seat, might well say to himself after the dummy had made its appearance: "It really makes no difference whether I win the opening lead in dummy or in my own hand." If this point of view is adopted, and declarer happens to make the wrong guess as to whether he should capture trick one in dummy or in his own hand, he loses a guaranteed vulnerable game. But if his sense of card reading rises to the fore, it will become obvious that the selection of the winning play is not an optional one.

Both sides vulnerable. South deals.

```
                    NORTH
                  ♠ K 8 4
                  ♥ K 7 5 2
                  ♦ A 5 3
                  ♣ K 4 2
     WEST                          EAST
  ♠ Q 10 2                      ♠ J 9 5 3
  ♥ A 9                         ♥ 4 3
  ♦ Q 6                         ♦ J 10 9 8 7 2
  ♣ Q J 10 9 8 3                ♣ 6
                    SOUTH
                  ♠ A 7 6
                  ♥ Q J 10 8 6
                  ♦ K 4
                  ♣ A 7 5
```

The bidding:

SOUTH	WEST	NORTH	EAST
1 ♥	2 ♣	3 ♥	Pass
4 ♥	Pass	Pass	Pass

Opening lead: Queen of ♣.

Let's suppose that South captures the opening lead with his ace of clubs. He then leads a trump, and West goes up with his ace. West returns the jack of clubs, dummy puts up the king—and East trumps. In time, declarer loses another club, plus a spade, and incurs a one-trick set. He then probably complains about his bad luck. In reality, however, he got nothing more and nothing less than what he deserved.

A vulnerable West had made a two-club overcall in a suit that was lacking the ace and king. Surely he figures to have a six-card suit. This means, of course, that East started with but one club. Furthermore, with respect to card reading, as declarer views his combined assets which contain three aces and four kings, West certainly rates to have the ace of hearts as a part of his overcall.

Declarer's worry should be that West, upon winning his trump ace at trick two, will return the club jack, and that East will trump dummy's king. If this comes to pass, declarer will end up losing *two* club tricks.

From the viewpoint of proper play, declarer should capture the opening lead with the board's king of clubs (not with his own ace). A trump will then be led, West winning the trick with his ace. West will now return a club, the deuce will be played off dummy, and East will ruff as South follows suit with the club seven. Thus declarer will not be losing a thing, since East will be ruffing a trick that West would have made later anyway. Putting it another way, by winning with the club king at trick one, declarer would be rendering East's ruff harmless.

8

Classic
Card-Reading Deals

From a technical point of view, card reading is defined as "drawing the correct inferences about the nature of an opponent's high-card holding and/or distribution, said inferences being obtained from either the bidding, the fall of the cards, or both."

But within the Halls of Mount Olympus, wherein dwell the gods (our top-flight experts, of course), card reading is expanded to include not only the physical attributes of sight and hearing but also the attribute of creativity, which embodies the sense of practical imagination (if I might be permitted to create this sixth sense).

By creativity, I refer to that faculty of an imaginative declarer to construct the adversely held cards in such a way as to enable him to come up with the only winning line of play. This technique of creativity is superimposed upon the facts secured from basic card reading. It becomes mandatory when the specific situation at hand reveals that the application of the senses of sight and hearing (as revealed by fact or inference) are not sufficient to bring about a rational solution. It then becomes necessary to create the conditions under which success will be attained. In other words, there is created a new world, a Utopian world perhaps, which must exist if defeat is to be averted. And the "constructor" then proceeds on the assumption that the ideal, imagined world is the real world.

The six classic deals presented in this chapter all arose more than fifteen years ago. But age has not diminished their sheer beauty. As a matter of fact, their grandeur has been enhanced with the passage of time and might well serve as a prototype for aspiring bridge players who are seeking to cultivate the sixth sense of creativity.

In one of these deals (Deal 5) declarer's creativity was of a perhaps paradoxical type. Instead of creating the conditions which were necessary for the fulfillment of a contract, he sought for the possible circumstances under which his contract could be defeated. He then assumed that his "creation" actually existed—and, by so doing, he discovered the only line of play that would guarantee his contract.

Deal 1

This hand arose in the National Championships of 1957. In the South seat was Charles J. Solomon of Philadelphia. Through the years Solomon has been acknowledged as one of tournament bridge's great players. In the play of this hand his technical and imaginative ability is clearly demonstrated.

North-South vulnerable. West deals.

```
                        NORTH
                    ♠ A 5 4
                    ♥ 2
                    ♦ A K 9 8 7 5 4
                    ♣ J 8
        WEST                                    EAST
    ♠ 9                                     ♠ K Q J 8 3
    ♥ 9 5 3                                 ♥ 7 6 4
    ♦ Q J 10                                ♦ 6 3 2
    ♣ A 10 9 7 6 5                          ♣ 4 3
                        SOUTH
                    ♠ 10 7 6 2
                    ♥ A K Q J 10 8
                    ♦ —
                    ♣ K Q 2
```

The bidding:

WEST	NORTH	EAST	SOUTH
3 ♣	3 ♦	3 ♠	5 ♥
Pass	6 ♦	Pass	6 ♥
Pass	Pass	Pass	

Opening lead: Nine of ♠.

West's preemptive opening three-club bid was miles away from the book requirements for the bid, but it did accomplish its objective: it drove the opponents to a very poor slam contract.

After West's nine-of-spade opening lead had been made, there was no doubt in Solomon's mind that the nine-spot was a singleton. This conclusion was arrived at through the appreciation that East, for his three-level bid, certainly figured to have a five-card suit.

It was also apparent, as Solomon gazed woefully at the dummy and his own hand, that West surely had the club ace. Armed with this knowledge of West's hand, he then proceeded to "create" the distribution of the adversely held cards that was necessary for the fulfillment of his contract. His construction was perfect—as was his highly imaginative play.

After winning the open lead with dummy's ace of spades, he cashed the board's ace and king of diamonds—upon which he discarded his king and queen of clubs. He then ruffed a diamond with his ace of hearts, after which he played three top hearts, gathering in the opponents' trumps.

He next led his deuce of clubs, and poor West had the lead with the club ace. West, with nothing but clubs remaining in his hand, had no choice except to return a club to dummy's high jack. On the board's established diamonds, South discarded his three losing spades.

In order to fulfill his contract, South had to assume that West had exactly one spade and the club ace (if West had a second spade, he would lead that card upon winning his club ace). And, of course, from declarer's point of view, the six outstanding diamonds *had to be* divided 3–3. If these circumstances existed, then by the elimination of the red suits from West's hand, West would be end-played when he was put into the lead with the club ace. And so it was.

Deal 2

A deal virtually identical in type and creativity to the preceding deal was handled most efficiently at the table by Alphonse ("Sonny") Moyse, Jr., the esteemed former publisher and editor of *The Bridge World* magazine. For years Sonny has been acknowledged by his peers as one of the finest rubber-bridge players this nation has produced. His play in this deal speaks for itself (and for his peers). The hand came up in a high-stake rubber-bridge game in 1954, at New York City's Cavendish Club.

North-South vulnerable. South deals.

NORTH
- ♠ Q 5
- ♥ 4
- ♦ A K 7 6 5 3 2
- ♣ J 7 3

WEST
- ♠ K J 10 9 8 6 3 2
- ♥ 10 3
- ♦ 8 4
- ♣ 8

EAST
- ♠ 7
- ♥ 7 6 2
- ♦ Q J 9
- ♣ K Q 10 6 4 2

SOUTH
- ♠ A 4
- ♥ A K Q J 9 8 5
- ♦ 10
- ♣ A 9 5

The bidding:

SOUTH	WEST	NORTH	EAST
2 ♥	4 ♠	5 ♦	Pass
6 ♥	Pass	Pass	Pass

Opening lead: Eight of ♣.

On West's opening club lead dummy's three-spot was played, East put up the ten, and Moyse captured the trick with his ace. He then cashed his three top trumps, after which he led his singleton diamond to dummy's ace. On the king of diamonds, which came next, Moyse tossed away his ace of spades!

A third diamond lead was then ruffed by South. Dummy's remaining diamonds were now all winners. Moyse next led his four of spades toward dummy's queen, and West was a gone goose, for after winning his spade king he had no choice but to lead another spade to dummy's queen. On the board's high diamonds South tossed away his two losing clubs.

Moyse's play, like Solomon's, was highly imaginative, but quite logical. West was a cinch to possess a seven- or eight-card spade suit headed by the king. His opening club lead looked like (and felt like) a singleton, and, from Moyse's point of view, he *created the fact* that it was a singleton. Thus, by eliminating hearts and diamonds from West's hand, while simultaneously establishing the board's diamond suit and getting rid of his own spade ace in the process, he could thrust West into the lead with the spade king. West would then have no choice but to lead a spade to dummy's high queen.

Of course, it also took some high-class imagination to perceive the necessity of discarding South's spade ace to be able to put West into the lead. As is known, however, in the classrooms within the Halls of Mount Olympus, our experts spend much time thinking about such things.

Deal 3

This deal arose in 1951, in the Indonesian Pair Championships of that year. The South declarer, who is virtually unknown to most of the bridge-playing world, was L. Spier of Holland.

In addition to depicting beauty in the thought processes of our top players, this deal also serves as an example of the fact that creativity is not confined to players in the United States. Creativity is universal.

Also in this deal, as in the two preceding ones, it will be observed that the tossing away of an ace or king (as though the world were coming to an end and nothing mattered) can well be the only right play.

Neither side vulnerable. South deals.

```
                        NORTH
                     ♠ 6 4
                     ♥ 4 2
                     ♦ J 7 5
                     ♣ A K J 8 7 5
      WEST                                    EAST
  ♠ 2                                     ♠ K Q J 10 8 7 5
  ♥ 8 7                                   ♥ 9 6 3
  ♦ Q 10 9 8 6 4 2                        ♦ —
  ♣ 10 9 6                                ♣ Q 4 3
                        SOUTH
                     ♠ A 9 3
                     ♥ A K Q J 10 5
                     ♦ A K 3
                     ♣ 2
```

The bidding:

SOUTH	WEST	NORTH	EAST
2 ♥	Pass	3 ♣	4 ♠
6 ♥	Pass	Pass	Pass

Opening lead: Two of ♠.

The opening spade lead was captured by Spier's ace, after which three rounds of trumps were played, a low club being discarded from dummy on the third trump lead. The king of diamonds was cashed next, on which East discarded a spade.

The distribution of the opponents' cards was now an open book to declarer. East surely possessed seven spades at the outset, for West's original lead had been the spade deuce. Even in Indonesia (and Holland), when one possesses two cards in partner's suit, he leads the higher of the two. Since there is no card lower than the two, West's lead had to be a singleton.

East had also followed suit to three trump leads—and had failed to follow suit to the very first diamond lead. Thus he had to have *exactly three clubs*. West, of course, had the other three outstanding clubs.

At the exact moment that East's distribution became known to

South, so did West's. The latter had started with one spade, two hearts, seven diamonds, and three clubs.

And so, counting out a hand and card reading had brought declarer to the point where all the relevant facts with respect to the original distribution of the adversely held cards had been assembled. Actually, the only thing declarer didn't know was: which of them possessed the club queen?

With the six outstanding clubs known to be divided 3–3, it was purely a 50–50 proposition as to whether East or West was the possessor of the club queen. If West had Her Ladyship, then declarer could lead his singleton club and finesse dummy's jack successfully, to bring home all thirteen tricks. But if the finesse of the jack lost to the queen (as it would have), declarer would be slaughtered, losing a club trick, two spades, and, in time, a diamond to East's queen.

But Spier, like Solomon and Moyse in Deals 1 and 2, had a sure thing going for him. After cashing his diamond king (at trick five), he led his deuce of clubs to dummy's king. He then cashed the club ace—on which he discarded his ace of diamonds! He next ruffed a club, both opponents following suit (as Spier knew they would).

Spier next simply led his three of diamonds, and West, who was known to have nothing but diamonds left in his hand, won the trick with his queen. He had no option but to lead another diamond, enabling the board's jack to win the trick. Thus Spier avoided losing any spade tricks—and, in my book (no pun intended), simultaneously entered bridgedom's Hall of Fame.

Deal 4

In 1933, on a rainy Thursday evening in Philadelphia, the club championship of the Franklin Bridge Club was being conducted. During the course of play this deal came up. It has since been recorded for posterity.

By the way, how have you, the reader, progressed with your ability to count out a hand and to do some card reading when the occasions call for it? Did I hear you say that you've come along very well? If so, I'm delighted. Would you like to try your hand at some creativity in card reading? If so, here's your opportunity.

Let's suppose that you are the South declarer in this deal.

Both sides vulnerable. South deals.

NORTH
- ♠ Q 10 6
- ♥ 6 5 3
- ♦ J 6 5 2
- ♣ K Q 7

SOUTH
- ♠ A K 2
- ♥ A K Q 10 9 7
- ♦ A K 7 4
- ♣ —

The bidding:

SOUTH	WEST	NORTH	EAST
2 ♥	Pass	3 ♥	Pass
6 ♥	Pass	Pass	Pass

Opening lead: Three of ♦.

You play the five of diamonds on West's opening lead of the three, East puts up the eight-spot, and you capture the trick with your ace. You then cash your three top trumps, West following suit to all three leads. East, after playing the four on your initial trump lead, discards the two and three of clubs on your second and third trump leads.

When you now lay down the diamond king, you receive the disheartening news that West's opening diamond lead was a singleton, for on this trick he discards the four of clubs. You now know that East still has the Q 10 of diamonds remaining over your dummy's J 6. How do you go about avoiding the loss of two diamond tricks?

Just how difficult the winning play was will be observed in a moment. I am, at this point, going to lay out the four actual hands so that you can play your slam contract in "double dummy" fashion.

NORTH
♠ Q 10 6
♥ 6 5 3
♦ J 6 5 2
♣ K Q 7

WEST
♠ J 9 5 3
♥ J 8 2
♦ 3
♣ A J 8 6 4

EAST
♠ 8 7 4
♥ 4
♦ Q 10 9 8
♣ 10 9 5 3 2

SOUTH
♠ A K 2
♥ A K Q 10 9 7
♦ A K 7 4
♣ —

It is a tough nut to crack, is it not?

At trick six South cashed his ace of spades. He then led the deuce of spades, and when West followed suit with the five, South inserted dummy's ten, finessing against West's hoped-for jack. When the ten won the trick, South laid down the king of clubs, and on it discarded his king of spades!

West, upon winning the trick with his ace, found himself in the position of being forced to lead a black suit. And whichever he led (he chose a club), dummy's queen of clubs and queen of spades would win two tricks. And on them South would discard his two losing diamonds (as he actually did).

As our declarer played the hand, he created the conditions which had to exist if the slam contract was to be fulfilled: West had to possess both the jack of spades and the ace of clubs. That South was lucky in catching West with both of these key cards goes without saying. But I think that there will be concurrence in my statement that he really deserved to be lucky for his display of ingenuity. In conclusion, all I can say with respect to South's play is one word: "Wow!"

Deal 5

This classic deal is perhaps just a shade off the beaten path of imaginative creativity, for it does not embody the creation by declarer of the conditions necessary to *fulfill* a contract. But the theme of the deal is close enough to the subject of imaginative creativity to warrant its presentation as a classic card-reading deal.

Once again, allow me to put you into the South seat, to see whether you can handle the situation as our actual South declarer did. In retrospect, it will be observed that all that is required to bring the slam contract home safely is an abnormally pessimistic frame of mind. The deal, incidentally, came up in a bridge game in 1949.

Both sides vulnerable. East deals.

```
                       NORTH
                    ♠ 7 2
                    ♥ 8 7 4
                    ♦ 6 5 3
                    ♣ A 10 8 5 3
                       SOUTH
                    ♠ A 5
                    ♥ A K Q J 10 9 2
                    ♦ A K Q
                    ♣ 9
```

The bidding:	EAST	SOUTH	WEST	NORTH
	3 ♠	4 NT	Pass	5 ♦
	Pass	5 NT	Pass	6 ♣
	Pass	6 ♥	Pass	Pass
	Pass			

Opening lead: King of ♣.

Your bidding was excellent. When you made the Blackwood call of four no-trump, you knew that even if partner had absolutely nothing, you would be safe at five hearts. And when your partner showed up with the missing ace, your hopes ran high: if partner had either of the black kings, a grand slam would be there for the taking.

However, when partner denied the possession of any kings by his six-club call, you settled for a small slam in hearts. Had this been a duplicate game, in which game honors do not count, you would, of course, have bid six no-trump. At rubber bridge, however, you correctly wanted to collect your 150 honors in hearts.

On West's opening lead of the king of clubs, you reach over to play dummy's ace—or do you? If you play it, you have just gone down, for East ruffs the ace! And eventually you will be compelled to lose a spade trick. These were the four hands:

```
                        NORTH
                    ♠  7 2
                    ♥  8 7 4
                    ♦  6 5 3
                    ♣  A 10 8 5 3
        WEST                              EAST
    ♠  8 4 3                          ♠  K Q J 10 9 6
    ♥  6 5                            ♥  3
    ♦  7                              ♦  J 10 9 8 4 2
    ♣  K Q J 7 6 4 2                  ♣  —
                        SOUTH
                    ♠  A 5
                    ♥  A K Q J 10 9 2
                    ♦  A K Q
                    ♣  9
```

On the bidding as it occurred, you certainly had no reason to know or even suspect that East would be void of clubs, and that he was prepared to ruff the opening club lead. Nevertheless, it would have been very wrong for you to have put up dummy's ace of clubs at trick one, for the play stood to lose everything—and to gain nothing, since the loss of a spade trick was inevitable.

Your dummy had come down with a very lovely "accidental" card, the *eight* of trumps. And with your possession of the six top trumps, the eight-spot could be utilized as an entry to dummy.

The correct play was made by our actual declarer, for he envisioned the theoretical possibility that East *might* conceivably be void of clubs: he allowed West's club king to capture the opening lead by playing a low club from dummy (East discarding a low diamond). When West next continued with the club queen, declarer again played a low club off the board. South ruffed this lead not with the deuce but with the nine-spot.

He then played the ace of trumps, after which he led the trump deuce to the board's eight-spot. On the preserved ace of clubs, he discarded his losing five of spades.

In effect, what declarer did in his play was to exchange a trick for a trick: instead of losing a spade trick later, he lost a club trick. But in playing the hand as he did—with extreme pessimism—he made sure that the board's ace of clubs would win a trick.

Deal 6

This final classic deal arose in the Vanderbilt Cup Championships of 1954. It features a situation in which proper card reading served as the foundation to the winning line of play. However, superimposed on this foundation was the element of psychology, the application of which enabled our South declarer to outwit our East defender.

Both sides vulnerable. East deals.

```
                        NORTH
                     ♠ Q 9
                     ♥ 5 4 2
                     ♦ A Q 8 7
                     ♣ 10 8 3 2
        WEST                              EAST
     ♠ 10 3                            ♠ A J 7 6 5 2
     ♥ A Q 10 9                        ♥ K J 3
     ♦ 10 6 5 4 2                      ♦ J 9 3
     ♣ 9 5                             ♣ K
                        SOUTH
                     ♠ K 8 4
                     ♥ 8 7 6
                     ♦ K
                     ♣ A Q J 7 6 4
```

The bidding:

EAST	SOUTH	WEST	NORTH
1 ♠	2 ♣	Pass	3 ♣
Pass	3 NT	Pass	Pass
Pass			

Opening lead: Ten of ♠.

When West opened the ten of spades, South knew that the ten-spot was either a singleton or the top card of a doubleton 10 x. He knew this because, conventionally, if West had possessed three spades headed by the ten-spot (10 x x), he would automatically have opened his third-highest spade instead of the ten. At the same time, declarer appreciated that East possessed either six or seven spades headed by the A J, depending on whether West's ten-spot was a singleton or the top of a doubleton.

With the above card reading serving as the factual foundation, declarer recognized that he could win two spade tricks for himself by putting up dummy's queen on West's opening lead of the spade ten. When East would capture this trick with his ace, South would have the doubleton K 8 remaining over East's J x. And then when he would subsequently lead the nine of spades off dummy, a guaranteed successful finesse against East's jack would give him two spade tricks.

But South knew for a fact that while he was doing his thinking prior to playing to trick one, East was also doing some thinking. East, of course, would also appreciate that West had a maximum of two spades, headed by the ten. And if dummy's queen of spades was played to the first trick, East, upon winning with his ace, might well come to the conclusion that South still had the doubleton K 8 remaining. If he came to this conclusion, East would perceive the futility of continuing the attack in spades. He would then, in all probability, shift to a heart, dummy's weak suit—and this South couldn't stand, for a shift to hearts by East figured to defeat the three-no-trump contract.

So South deliberately threw a spade trick out of the window by following suit with the board's nine of spades on West's ten. East, recognizing that he could now prevent declarer from winning two spade tricks, played the encouraging seven-spot on the trick, South's king winning.

Declarer now went into high gear. He next led the diamond king, which he overtook with the board's ace. He then played the ten of clubs—and joyfully greeted the appearance of East's king. His contracted-for nine tricks were now there for the taking: one spade, two diamonds, and six clubs.

In the post-mortem analysis of the deal (with three kibitzers participating), it was agreed that declarer played the hand in expert fashion. But the consensus was that East performed in a manner "unbecoming an expert." The issue under discussion was that if declarer was willing to throw away a spade trick (by playing dummy's nine), should East have been delighted to help him (by not playing his ace)? The answer, "No." The reason was a simple one.

East knew that South was a very good player—and that South wouldn't be tossing a trick away unless he had sound justification for so doing. As East should have analyzed the situation, South's justification for restricting himself to just one spade trick had to be that he was afraid of a shift to hearts by East.

Thus, according to the conclusion of the post-mortem tribunal, East should not have been taken in by South's apparent misplay. East should have captured the opening lead with the spade ace. He should then have shifted to the jack of hearts. The defenders would now have cashed four heart tricks, thereby sending South down to defeat.

9

Defensive Play: Counting and Card Reading

All constituted authority, in addition to every bridge player, from the top-flight expert down through the rankest neophyte, will agree that of the three departments of bridge—bidding, declarer's play, and defenders' play—the most difficult to master is defenders' play. And, going further, there is unanimous concurrence in the oft-repeated assertion that more mistakes are made in defense than in either of the other two departments of bridge. There are two major reasons accounting for this deficiency in the techniques of defense.

First, when declarer is playing out a hand, he sees the twenty-six cards that belong to him and his partner, the dummy. He knows exactly how many cards of each suit his side possesses, what the quality of the cards is, and what his specific current problems are, or what his future problems might be. In brief, he knows his *precise* strength and weakness, and is thereby enabled to deploy his resources in an intelligent manner while waging his campaign. The defenders, on the other hand, do not see each other's cards, but only the thirteen that each of them holds. Thus, the defenders' task is automatically much more difficult, since each must try to figure out, or deduce, or imagine (or guess!) what his partner is holding.

Second, it is an established fact that scientific development in the field of defense has lagged far behind the scientific development of bidding methods and techniques of declarer's play. There are relatively few guiding principles to point the way to winning defense, primarily because each situation, no matter how similar it may appear to be to some previously encountered situation, invariably has some point of dissimilarity. As a consequence, a defender is frequently on his own, because the pattern (if there is one) of defense varies greatly from deal to deal. Also, many diverse defensive situations arise where there exists no precedent to take a defender by the hand and lead him to the desired objective. In these latter situations judgment and/or imagination must operate independently of any established, governing law.

From the defenders' point of view, in order to attack and counterattack successfully, they must rely in the main on the few scientific principles that are available to them. These consist of a system of "conventional leads" and a system of "signals." With the application of these principles of standard leads and standard signals, the defenders are usually able to convey to each other the proper line of defense. It is mandatory, for their self-preservation, that each partner be continually on the alert to receive and correctly interpret whatever scientific information his partner is trying to transmit. If this approach is adopted, the natural difficulties inherent in proper defensive play can be reduced substantially, for knowledge, mutual understanding, and partnership cooperation will then tend to minimize guesswork and rugged individualism. In brief, each defender must point the way to the other, and while this will not eliminate guesswork, it will narrow the areas where guesswork will otherwise exist, thereby resulting in fewer mistakes. And, as any expert will confirm, victories are not won by being brilliant, but rather by making fewer mistakes than one's competitors.

It is perhaps paradoxical that in the field of counting and card reading, the defenders have an edge over the declarer. Quite often, from the declarer's point of view, he is handicapped in his counting and/or card reading because *neither of the opponents has bid.* In these circumstances, he must frequently deduce (or guess) what one of the defenders might possess in the way of high cards and/or distribution. And when one is in this position of conjecturing, he is quite apt to misjudge on occasion.

But each of the defenders always has factual evidence in his possession, namely *the bidding by the declarer*, for in every situation the declarer will have bid one suit, two suits, three suits, or no-trump (if declarer hasn't bid, then the wrong guy is playing the hand). This guaranteed factual evidence, in the possession of an "all-ears" defender, is possibly the most powerful weapon possessed by the defensive side.

As an example of the power of the attunement of a defender to declarer's bidding, and the practical application of the knowledge derived therefrom, observe the following deal. It arose in a national championship event some years ago.

Both sides vulnerable. North deals.

```
                       NORTH
                   ♠ 6 2
                   ♥ Q 10 6 5 2
                   ♦ A 5
                   ♣ A K 6 5
        WEST                            EAST
    ♠ 8 7 3                         ♠ Q J 5
    ♥ K                             ♥ A J 9 8 3
    ♦ 10 6 2                        ♦ 7 4
    ♣ Q J 9 8 4 2                   ♣ 10 7 3
                       SOUTH
                   ♠ A K 10 9 4
                   ♥ 7 4
                   ♦ K Q J 9 8 3
                   ♣ —
```

The bidding:

NORTH	EAST	SOUTH	WEST
1 ♥	Pass	2 ♦	Pass
2 ♥	Pass	2 ♠	Pass
3 ♣	Pass	3 ♠	Pass
4 ♦	Pass	4 NT	Pass
5 ♥	Pass	6 ♦	Pass
Pass	Pass		

Opening lead: King of ♥.

On West's opening lead of the heart king, the deuce was played from dummy. After a huddle by East that took more than two minutes, East overtook the king with his ace and returned a heart, which West ruffed for the setting trick. It is apparent that if East had allowed his partner's king to win the trick, declarer would have fulfilled his slam contract. He would have accomplished this by ruffing a third spade lead, thus establishing his two remaining spades as winners, and by discarding his remaining heart on dummy's ace of clubs.

Let us examine the thought processes of East which led to his overtaking the West's king of hearts. First, let us review the bidding, and the facts which East assembled therefrom.

After South's initial response of two diamonds, he had subsequently bid spades twice all by himself. Therefore South possessed five spades. But if South had had five diamonds and five spades, *he would have bid spades first.* Therefore South's only justification for having bid diamonds first must have been that South had six diamonds.

Thus South had room in his hand for exactly two cards in hearts and clubs, and he was known to have at least one heart, for West, had he held the tripleton K 7 4 of hearts, would have led the four of hearts and not the king. And so South had to have either two hearts (the 7 4) or one heart and one club.

As East viewed the setup, if South had one heart and one club, then the slam contract could not be defeated. That is, if South held:

♠ A K x x x
♥ x
♦ K Q J x x x
♣ x

then all the defenders could make would be one heart trick, for South would be able to establish his two low spades by cashing his ace and king and then ruffing a third spade lead. And how did East know that South would be able to accomplish this? Again, card reading provided the evidence.

South was known to have five spades. East was looking at three spades, and dummy had two spades. Thus West had to have three spades. So East knew that the six spades possessed by his partnership were divided 3–3—and that declarer would have no problem in establishing this suit by ruffing a third spade.

It was also theoretically conceivable (although highly unlikely) that South held:

♠ A 10 x x x
♥ x
♦ K Q J 10 x x
♣ x

If such were the case, then by overtaking the king of hearts with his ace, and returning the three of hearts, East would be permitting South to discard a spade on this lead, as South won the trick with the board's five-spot. After drawing trumps, declarer would then enter dummy via the king of clubs, and on the ace of clubs he would discard another spade. On the high queen of hearts he would toss away still another spade. But in this setup South would still have to lose his ten of spades to West's (presumed) king, and thus go down at his slam contract. Hence East's overtaking of the heart king with the ace could never be the cause of South's fulfilling of the slam.

After having assembled and analyzed all of the facts presented above, East came to the conclusion that the only circumstance whereby South's six-diamond contract could be defeated would be if West's king of hearts was a singleton. Having the courage of his convictions (the latter being substantiated by "facts"), it came to pass that East overtook the king with his ace and returned a heart. It was hard work for East—but highly rewarding.

The above deal, in my opinion, is an example of top-echelon card reading. The type of thinking that East displayed is not born overnight. It comes with experience, and requires not only the technical knowledge necessary to interpret the opponents' bidding correctly (i.e., that South possessed five spades, hence six diamonds), but also the ability to assemble and organize in a limited period of time all the other facts available (i.e., that West would not have led the king of hearts from a tripleton K x x). As was stated, this can be hard work. And when one has learned to think as East did, he has surely reached at least the periphery of expertise.

There is one other salient feature embodied in this deal, a feature which is recognized in all of its importance by the expert, but which is not appreciated fully by the nonexpert. This feature is the recognition that the play to the first trick is not merely the play of four cards, one by each player. As has been observed, there is the background in the bidding serving as a springboard, and, stemming from this, the practical realization of how important the play at trick one can be in determining a defender's (or a declarer's) destiny. It is an undisputed fact of life that continuing victories at the bridge table are not achieved by some fortuitous fall of the cards at tricks ten, eleven, twelve or thirteen. They are won early in the game, when the requisite strategy and tactics of the specific deal are formulated and promptly put into action.

Far more often than the nonexpert might imagine, bridge victories are won (or lost) right at the opening lead, when the defenders launch their initial attack. What happens at trick one often leads, inexorably to victory or defeat: the correct play (or lead) is made, and the defenders are en route to victory; the incorrect play is made, and defeat becomes unavoidable (e.g., the above deal).

The final deal of this prologue chapter on card reading and counting by the defenders is a simple one, although perhaps simple in retrospect only. The hand came up in the National Team-of-Four Championships of 1946. Sitting in the West seat was one of the greatest players the world has ever known, the late Helen Sobel.

Neither side vulnerable. South deals.

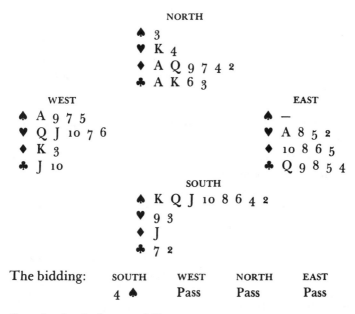

NORTH
♠ 3
♥ K 4
♦ A Q 9 7 4 2
♣ A K 6 3

WEST
♠ A 9 7 5
♥ Q J 10 7 6
♦ K 3
♣ J 10

EAST
♠ —
♥ A 8 5 2
♦ 10 8 6 5
♣ Q 9 8 5 4

SOUTH
♠ K Q J 10 8 6 4 2
♥ 9 3
♦ J
♣ 7 2

The bidding:

SOUTH	WEST	NORTH	EAST
4 ♠	Pass	Pass	Pass

Opening lead: Queen of ♥.

Dummy's king of hearts was put up on Helen's opening lead of the queen, and East captured the trick with his ace. A heart was returned, West winning with her ten-spot. She then exited with the jack of clubs, which was won by dummy's ace.

The board's singleton trump was led next, South's king being taken by West's ace, East discarding a heart. West returned the ten of clubs to dummy's king.

At this point, declarer's only problem was how to get back to the South hand to gather in West's two remaining trumps. It looked like the best way was to lead the ace of diamonds, and then ruff a second diamond lead (rather than lead a third club and trump in the South hand). As can be observed, declarer was quite right in his thinking.

And so, at trick six, dummy's ace of diamonds was cashed, South of course following suit with the jack. On this trick Helen dropped the king of diamonds! South now took time out to reanalyze the situation.

It didn't take him long to realize that the king had all the earmarks of being a singleton, and that if he now led a second diamond (as planned originally) and trumped it low, West would overruff with her nine-spot (so he thought). And if, instead, South ruffed the diamond with his ten-spot, West would discard something—and her remaining 9 7 5 of trumps would in time yield her one trump trick.

After some agonizing thinking, South decided to accept the fall of West's diamond king as the truth—namely, that it was a singleton. So South chose to lead a third club off dummy in order to get to his hand. He ruffed with the eight-spot—and West overruffed with her nine, for the setting trick.

It is obvious, of course, that if declarer had not been taken in by West's false-card of the diamond king, he would have fulfilled his contract by ruffing a second diamond lead. His remaining three high trumps would then have picked up Helen's three trumps.

Would you say that Helen Sobel's false-card of the king was a brilliant play, a cute play, or an imaginative play? Actually, it was none of these; in fact, it was a simple play for a defender who was accustomed to counting out a hand automatically.

From her seat, she knew that declarer had started with exactly eight trumps, since East had failed to follow suit to the initial trump lead off the board. And South, in the play to the first five tricks, had been revealed as the possessor of two hearts and two clubs. Thus when South followed suit with the diamond jack on the lead of dummy's ace, he was known to have nothing left in his hand but trumps.

And so the false-card of the king on dummy's diamond ace could never have been a play that would have cost anything. Extending this thought, the play of the king had everything to gain and nothing to lose.

Let us now turn our attention to Chapter 10, wherein defensive card reading and counting in action will be observed and analyzed.

10

Defense When the
Defenders Do Not Bid

In this chapter there are contained thirteen deals in which the defenders, through the employment of counting and card reading, were able to defeat declarer's game or slam contract. In none of these deals did either defender have the advantage of a bid from his partner, such as an overcall or a takeout or a penalty double. In each deal, therefore, the process of independent thinking became the first (and only) line of defense.

The defenders' counting and card reading thus had to develop, of necessity, through (1) interpreting the significance of partner's opening lead, (2) the study of dummy and the thinking defender's own hand, (3) the construction of declarer's hand to make it consistent with his bidding and, aided by the understanding of partner's lead, developing therefrom the construction of partner's hand in such a manner as to give the thinking defender the hope of defeating declarer's contract, (4) interpreting correctly a misplay that declarer made and capitalizing on that knowledge, and (5) defending in such a manner as to give declarer an incorrect picture of a defender's hand, thus leading the former to a wrong card-reading conclusion.

Deal 1

This deal arose in a rubber-bridge game many years ago. When I first saw it, I felt the urge to stand up and applaud. I hope that the reader will have the same emotions I had.

North-South vulnerable. South deals.

NORTH
♠ 8 4 3
♥ 10 8 7 2
♦ K J 6 4
♣ K 2

WEST
♠ Q 7 6 2
♥ J 6 5 4
♦ 3
♣ 9 8 7 5

EAST
♠ J 10 5
♥ A Q 9 3
♦ Q 10 2
♣ J 10 6

SOUTH
♠ A K 9
♥ K
♦ A 9 8 7 5
♣ A Q 4 3

The bidding:

SOUTH	WEST	NORTH	EAST
1 ♦	Pass	2 ♦	Pass
3 NT	Pass	Pass	Pass

Opening lead: Two of ♠.

On West's opening spade lead, East put up the ten and South captured the trick with his king. The ace of diamonds was played next, and this was followed by a low diamond, West discarding the five of clubs. Dummy's jack was inserted, and East won the trick with his queen.

At this point, the normal return by East would be to play back a spade in order to attempt to establish West's suit. Had East done this, South would have romped in with nine tricks: two spades, four diamonds, and three clubs. But East did not play back a spade at trick four. Instead, he took a rather lengthy time out to analyze the situation at hand.

From his lead of the spade deuce as his fourth-from-the-highest spade, West was known to have started with exactly four spades. And, of course, West's failure to have followed suit to South's second diamond lead stated that West had been dealt a singleton diamond.

It was just about certain that West did not have either five hearts or five clubs, since if he did he would have led from his five-card suit originally against the no-trump contract, instead of from his four-card spade suit. Therefore, East concluded, West, who had eight unknown cards in hearts and clubs, had started with exactly four hearts and four clubs.

Thus West's original distribution had to be 4–4–4–1, the single-ton being the diamond. Since East was looking at four hearts in his own hand, and four in dummy, with West known to have four hearts, declarer had to possess a singleton heart.

Upon winning his diamond queen at trick three, East laid down his ace of hearts, felling South's singleton king. He next led the three of hearts to West's jack, as South discarded a spade. A third heart led by West now entrapped the board's 10 8, and East's Q 9 of hearts won two more tricks. So South went down a trick.

It is admitted that East might have been mistaken in his recon-struction of West's original thirteen cards: that West might have had, for example, five miserable low clubs and had elected to lead from a quality-laden four-card spade suit rather than from a broken-down five-card club suit. However, this did not seem prob-able to East, since even if West did possess the latter, he would have tended to lead his longer suit and preserve his high cards in the four-card suit to serve as entries for the establishment and cashing of his hoped-to-become-established five-card suit.

And, frankly, even if on this deal East had turned out to be wrong in his analysis of the situation, he would merit a "Well done!" for his intelligent application of card reading.

Deal 2

Many years ago a famous expert had won a national champion-ship. A kibitzer, who had been sitting beside him during the three and a half hours of play during the final session, was asked later: "How did you enjoy watching him play?" She replied: "I really don't see how he won. During the twenty-six deals I watched, he did *absolutely* [the kibitzer's emphasis] nothing bril-liant."

It is a popular misconception that tournaments (and rubber-bridge games) require brilliance to be victorious. Actually, win-ners achieve their lofty position by not committing blunders, and especially by not being careless. In a word (or three), winners attain their status by continually being "on the ball."

In this deal we have an example of simple, active thinking that resulted in the defeat of South's game contract. Had our East defender played mechanically (as I believe many players might have done), declarer would have fulfilled a contract to which he was not entitled.

The card reading applied in this deal is elementary and in sharp contrast to the type employed in the preceding deal. In point of fact, however, the occasions for the employment of this type of simple, elementary card reading arise about ten times as often as the heavy, profound type depicted in Deal 1.

Both sides vulnerable. South deals.

NORTH
♠ 8 6 5 2
♥ 9 5
♦ K Q J 10 7 2
♣ K

WEST
♠ J 10
♥ A Q 4
♦ 6 4 3
♣ Q 10 7 6 2

EAST
♠ A 4
♥ J 8 7 3 2
♦ A 9
♣ 8 5 4 3

SOUTH
♠ K Q 9 7 3
♥ K 10 6
♦ 8 5
♣ A J 9

The bidding:

SOUTH	WEST	NORTH	EAST
1 ♠	Pass	2 ♦	Pass
2 ♠	Pass	3 ♠	Pass
4 ♠	Pass	Pass	Pass

Opening lead: Six of ♣.

West's opening lead of the club six was captured by dummy's king, after which the deuce of spades was led. Had East mechanically followed suit with the four-spot—either because he thought that South might have a guessing situation in the trump suit, or because East was a firm believer in the statement that aces were born to capture kings and queens, not deuces—declarer would have fulfilled his contract with ease. He would have won the trick with his king or queen, and on the ace of clubs he would have discarded one of dummy's two hearts. It would now become a routine matter for declarer to restrict his losses in the heart suit to one trick. All he would then have lost would have been one trump trick, one diamond, and one heart.

At trick two, however, when the deuce of trumps was led off the board, East promptly put up his ace. To trick three he played a heart—and there was now no way for declarer to avoid the loss of two heart tricks. A one-trick set was the result.

East's decision to rise with the trump ace was a simple, albeit well-reasoned one. On the given bidding by North-South, West would surely not have underled the ace of clubs at trick one, in the blind. Frankly, if West had made up his mind to lead clubs, and he possessed the ace, he would have led it. Thus East knew after dummy's king of clubs had captured the opening lead that South still retained the ace of clubs.

So, from East's point of view, if he played low on dummy's deuce of trumps, he would be giving South the opportunity to capture the trick. Upon so doing, South would then cash his club ace, discarding a heart from dummy.

This East couldn't afford to have happen. As he appraised the layout, his best hope of defeating declarer's contract was for the defenders to make two heart tricks—and his play made that hope a reality.

Deal 3

In this deal we have another illustration of simple, active, rather than passive, card reading. Had our East defender been a subscriber to the tenet, "They also serve who only stand and wait," he would still be waiting while declarer was pocketing the profits.

Neither side vulnerable. North deals.

NORTH
♠ 6
♥ A K Q J 8
♦ A K Q J 9
♣ 5 3

WEST
♠ K Q 10 8 3
♥ 9 6 4 3
♦ 10 4 2
♣ 7

EAST
♠ A 9 5 4 2
♥ 10 7
♦ 7 5 3
♣ K 8 2

SOUTH
♠ J 7
♥ 5 2
♦ 8 6
♣ A Q J 10 9 6 4

The bidding:

NORTH	EAST	SOUTH	WEST
2 ♥	Pass	3 ♣	Pass
3 ♦	Pass	5 ♣	Pass
6 ♣	Pass	Pass	Pass

Opening lead: King of ♠.

After West had opened the king of spades, and the dummy was put down, three facts were quickly apparent to East: (1) that West possessed the queen of spades, (2) that the defenders were not going to make any tricks in either hearts or diamonds, and (3) the defenders were en route to taking the one and only spade trick they were going to make. These facts were based on West's conventional opening lead and on routine observation.

Via card reading (or, perhaps, simply via the uncomplicated sense of hearing), South surely figured to have a seven- or eight-card club suit headed by the A Q J. If he had a worse club suit, he would have contented himself with a mere four-club rebid over three diamonds instead of making the slam-try leap to five clubs, thus announcing a really good club suit. Since East was looking at the club king in his own hand, there was no doubt in his mind about the goodness of South's club suit.

As East correctly viewed the setup, there was just one hope of defeating South's slam contract, and that was for him to make his king of trumps. As matters stood now, the king was trapped, since South, by entering dummy a couple of times via a red suit, would be able to take two successful finesses against the trump king, and thereby avoid the loss of a trump trick.

But East gave declarer no opportunity to take two finesses—and, simultaneously, East gave his partner no chance to go wrong at trick two. East unhesitatingly overtook his partner's king of spades with the ace at trick one, and returned a low spade, West's queen covering South's jack. Declarer had no choice but to trump the trick in dummy.

The board's remaining trump was then led, South finessing his queen successfully. He now had no option but to lay down his ace of trumps, hoping that East had been dealt the doubleton K x of trumps originally. When this hope failed to materialize, South exposed his cards and conceded a one-trick defeat.

It will never be known, of course, but if East had permitted his partner's king of spades to have captured the opening lead, West might conceivably have led a heart or a diamond at trick two— haven't we all seen our partners make such plays? South would then have fulfilled his contract—and East would have become the goat instead of the hero.

Deal 4

As a general principle, when one is leading in his longest suit against no-trump contracts, the partner of the leader usually returns the suit in order to assist in its establishment. Especially does this hold true when it is perfectly obvious that declarer is weak in the suit.

But every principle has its exceptions. And when logical card reading makes it perfectly obvious that it is futile to assist partner in establishing his suit, new worlds to conquer must be sought.

In this deal we have an example of the nonreturn of partner's suit. Sitting in the East seat was Alan Truscott, one of our nation's top players and the bridge editor of *The New York Times*.

Both sides vulnerable. South deals.

```
                        NORTH
                     ♠ Q 7 5
                     ♥ 6 4 2
                     ♦ A K Q J 7 2
                     ♣ 6
     WEST                                    EAST
  ♠ 9 8                                   ♠ A 10 6 4
  ♥ J 8 5                                 ♥ K Q 7
  ♦ 10 6                                  ♦ 8 5 3
  ♣ Q J 10 8 7 3                          ♣ K 9 4
                        SOUTH
                     ♠ K J 3 2
                     ♥ A 10 9 3
                     ♦ 9 4
                     ♣ A 5 2
```

The bidding:

SOUTH	WEST	NORTH	EAST
Pass	Pass	1 ♦	Pass
2 NT	Pass	3 NT	Pass
Pass	Pass		

Opening lead: Queen of ♣.

On West's opening lead of the club queen, Truscott signaled encouragement by playing the nine-spot. South played the deuce on this lead, allowing West's queen to win. To trick two, West led the club eight, East putting up his king. Once again South declined to take his ace.

The normal tendency at this point would be for East to lead his remaining club, thereby forcing South to take his ace, and simultaneously establishing West's club suit. But Truscott realized that it would be futile to do this. Here is his reasoning.

South, with his jump to two no-trump after having passed originally, indicated that he had about 12 high-card points. Dummy also had 12 high-card points. And East himself was looking at 12 high-card points. Thus West had at most 4 high-card points, of which 3 were known to be in clubs (the queen and the jack, based on West's opening lead of the club queen). Hence, if West's suit were to be established, it could never gain for the defenders, since

West couldn't ever get to cash it, for he had no outside entry.

So, at trick three, with the hope that his partner's one outside high card was the jack of hearts, Truscott shifted to the seven of hearts (the seven, rather than the king, because if declarer happened to have the A J 9 of hearts, he would tend to play the nine-spot, thus enabling West's hypothetical ten to win the trick). South followed suit with the ten, and West's jack captured the trick. West returned a heart, East's queen being taken by South's ace.

All South could now come to were eight tricks: six diamonds, one heart, and one club. When play had ended, the defenders had made two club tricks, two hearts, and the spade ace.

Had Truscott made the mechanical return of his remaining club at trick three, declarer would actually have been forced to win ten tricks. Sooner or later he would have led a spade to East's ace—and East would have had no club left to play back to his partner. Declarer would now have two spade tricks, one heart, six diamonds, and one club.

Deal 5

On a transcontinental flight some years ago, the pilot switched on the intercom and spoke to the passengers:

"Ladies and gentlemen, may I have your attention. I have two announcements to make. One is good news and the other bad. I'll give you the bad news first.

"Our radar and automatic pilot have ceased to function and we could be considered lost. And now for the good news. During the past hour, flying at thirty-eight thousand feet, we have just broken the world's speed record for commercial flights."

By analogy, with respect to the game of bridge, victories are not won by the swiftest, for speed pays no dividends when one has lost control of the situation. This deal depicts swiftness in unproductive action: our South declarer played hurriedly (and unthinkingly) to the first trick. Although he was not aware of it, at that point he had lost control of his destiny, for his swiftness enabled our East defender to put card reading to practical use.

Neither side vulnerable. South deals.

NORTH
♠ 6 4
♥ A 8 6 3
♦ K Q J 10
♣ J 9 4

WEST
♠ J 10 9 7 2
♥ K Q 9 4
♦ 7 4
♣ K 2

EAST
♠ 8 5 3
♥ J 10
♦ A 6 5 2
♣ 8 6 5 3

SOUTH
♠ A K Q
♥ 7 5 2
♦ 9 8 3
♣ A Q 10 7

The bidding:

SOUTH	WEST	NORTH	EAST
1 ♣	Pass	1 ♦	Pass
1 NT	Pass	2 NT	Pass
3 NT	Pass	Pass	Pass

Opening lead: Jack of ♠.

South promptly won the opening spade lead with his *ace*, after which he led a diamond, the trick being captured by East's ace. East now made a nice shift to the heart jack, which was permitted to win. The continuation of the heart ten was overtaken by West's queen, the trick being won by dummy's ace.

Declarer, having just eight tricks at this point, decided to take the club finesse immediately. And so he took it, losing the trick to West's king. West then cashed two heart tricks, to hand declarer a one-trick set.

Declarer committed a grievous error when he so hurriedly captured the opening spade lead with his ace, instead of with the queen. In making his play, declarer transmitted significant information to the thinking, card-reading East defender.

East knew at that moment that declarer had started with the A K Q of spades. The reason? Well, it was based, first, on East's understanding of the conventional opening lead that had been made by West.

East correctly assumed that West was making the standard opening lead in his longest suit; and the lead of the jack, while affirming the possession of the spade ten, simultaneously *denied possession of the spade queen.* If West had possessed the queen and the jack, he would automatically have led the queen, the higher of touching honors. Therefore East knew that South had the queen of spades.

Why, East asked himself, was South capturing the opening lead with the ace, when he could have won it with the queen? Surely, if South had held, let us say, the A Q or the A Q x of spades, he would have won the first trick with his queen, instead of expending the ace needlessly. The answer suggested itself at once: South must have the A K Q, in which case it wouldn't matter to him (from the viewpoint of economy) whether he took the trick with the ace, the king, or the queen.

Thus East perceived the hopelessness of returning a spade at trick three (after he had taken trick two with his ace of diamonds). Hence his shift at trick three to a heart, as a matter of having hope versus no hope.

If South had won the opening lead with his queen of spades, he might well have had a happy future. In this case, East might have assumed that West's spade suit was headed by an A J 10 or a K J 10 combination, which combinations were certainly within the realm of distinct possibility. And if East had come to this latter conclusion, he would have returned his partner's suit instead of shifting to the killing lead of the jack of hearts.

Deal 6

This deal serves to substantiate the point made in the preceding deal—namely, that speed in itself is no asset at the bridge table. As in the preceding deal, South played unthinkingly to the first trick, and thereby conveyed to the East defender a significant piece of knowledge that enabled East to defeat South's game contract. In justification of South's play, one might say that he was making an honest attempt to deceive the defenders. But, as will be observed, he picked the wrong time to do it.

Both sides vulnerable. North deals.

NORTH
♠ K 7 2
♥ 7 5
♦ 8 3
♣ K Q J 10 9 4

WEST
♠ J 10 6
♥ J 9 8 3 2
♦ A 9 7 5
♣ 3

EAST
♠ Q 9 5
♥ Q 10 6
♦ K J 10 4
♣ A 6 2

SOUTH
♠ A 8 4 3
♥ A K 4
♦ Q 6 2
♣ 8 7 5

The bidding:

NORTH	EAST	SOUTH	WEST
3 ♣	Pass	3 NT	Pass
Pass	Pass		

Opening lead: Three of ♥.

East put up the heart queen on the opening lead, and South captured the trick with his *ace*. He then led a low club, East's ace taking dummy's king. After a few moments of thought, East made what a newspaper reporter might describe as "a brilliant return": he shifted to the jack of diamonds. Before our declarer could turn around, the defenders had rattled off four diamond tricks and had sent declarer down to defeat. What motivated East to switch to the diamond suit, instead of returning a heart, the suit that his partner had led?

First, as the foundation upon which East's card reading was built, East knew that declarer had either three or four hearts. This was based on the observation that West had opened the three of hearts. If that card was West's lowest heart, then West had exactly four hearts. And if West also happened to possess the deuce of hearts, then West had started with exactly five hearts. Thus, depending on whether West had four or five hearts, declarer had either four or three hearts.

Why, East asked himself, did declarer, holding, let us say, the A x x or the A x x x of hearts, so promptly win the first heart trick? Why didn't he, instead, hold up the ace until the third lead of that suit? If he did, and East possessed the ace of clubs (a 50–50 proposition) then East would be unable to lead back a heart for West to cash his established suit. Surely South, a good player, would not have taken his heart ace at trick one unless he had justification for so doing.

Having thus reasoned, East came to the conclusion that South's justification for his immediate taking of the heart ace was that South was not at all worried about the heart suit. The only thing that could have made South so worry-free would be his possession of the heart king (in addition to the ace, of course).

However, East could have been mistaken. South might have had, for example, the A J x of hearts, in which case the winning of the first trick with the ace would be the right play. When South would next lead a club, he would indulge in the 50–50 hope that West possessed the club ace, in which case South's remaining J x of hearts would constitute a second stopper against West if the latter then chose to lead the heart king. But, whatever the result might have been in other circumstances, East could not have been faulted for having failed to make a good attempt at card reading.

With the board's established club suit staring him in the face at the completion of trick two, East correctly felt that if his side did not get four more tricks immediately, there would be no tomorrow for them. Hence his decision to shift to a diamond at trick three, with the hope that West possessed the ace of diamonds. As luck would have it, East's wishful thinking materialized.

As can be observed in retrospect, declarer made a mistake when he chose to win the opening heart lead with his ace, rather than with his king. Had he taken the trick with the king, East almost surely would have returned a heart when he captured trick two with the club ace. After all, as East would have viewed the situation, West might well have started with, for example, the A J 9 3 2 of hearts, with South possessing the K 8 4. And in this setup, South would have had no option but to win trick one with the heart king.

In conclusion, it should be mentioned (perhaps naïvely) that if East had played back a heart at trick two, declarer would have fulfilled his contract: two spades, two hearts, and five clubs.

Deal 7

In this deal, had our West defender made the normal, natural opening lead against South's game contract, he could not have been criticized from a technical point of view. Yet, had he taken refuge in the sanctuary offered gratuitously by orthodoxy, he would have been guilty of having failed to have tuned in to the opponents' bidding. But, through experience, he was aware of the necessity of the permanent attunement to the bidding of his adversaries—and the practical application of the clue contained therein resulted in the defeat of South's contract.

Both sides vulnerable. North deals.

```
                        NORTH
                     ♠ K J 2
                     ♥ Q 9 5 3
                     ♦ 9
                     ♣ A K 8 4 2
        WEST                                  EAST
     ♠ A 5 3                              ♠ 7 6
     ♥ K 7                                ♥ 8 4 2
     ♦ Q J 10 8                           ♦ A 7 6 5 4 2
     ♣ J 10 7 6                           ♣ 9 3
                        SOUTH
                     ♠ Q 10 9 8 4
                     ♥ A J 10 6
                     ♦ K 3
                     ♣ Q 5
```

The bidding:	NORTH	EAST	SOUTH	WEST
	1 ♣	Pass	1 ♠	Pass
	2 ♠	Pass	3 ♥	Pass
	4 ♥	Pass	Pass	Pass

Opening lead: Ace of ♠.

North made a nice decision when he elected to raise South to two spades on three-card support. As it turned out, however, South negated North's rebid when he chose to introduce his heart suit, and it resulted in his downfall. Over two spades, if South had bid four spades, thus concealing from the defenders that he possessed four hearts, West would have made his normal opening lead of the diamond queen—and South would then have fulfilled his contract.

Of course, according to accepted standards, West's normal opening lead should have been the diamond queen anyway, the top of a sequence of adjacent high cards. But West's ear told him that a superior lead was available. On the bidding, North-South figured to have eight spades between them, and possibly nine (although it was conceivable in theory—although not likely—that South had only four spades, and North only three). And on the bidding it sounded as though North-South had eight hearts between them. East, therefore, rated to have two spades at most, and possibly only one. Since West had only two trumps, East rated to have three. The chances of East's ruffing either the second or third lead of spades looked good to West.

Thus reasoning, West opened the ace of spades, East following with the seven-spot, and then West continued with the spade three, East completing his high-low signal by playing the six-spot. Dummy's king of spades won the second spade lead, after which the nine of trumps was led off the board and the finesse taken against East's hoped-for king. When West won this trick, he promptly returned his remaining spade, East ruffing the board's jack. The diamond ace was then cashed, for the setting trick.

West's opening lead could, of course, have turned out otherwise—one gets no guarantees in this game of bridge. Had North, instead of South, possessed the trump ace, West would have been finessed out of his king of trumps, and East would never have gotten around to trumping a spade. But even if this had happened, West would have received an "A" for his card reading and his follow-through.

Deal 8

In real life in the majority of deals, the defenders do not do any bidding. Thus the sole clue as to what a defender should lead at trick one is obtained by listening to and interpreting the bidding of his opponents. When the logical interpretation is made, the winning lead (if one exists) will be found more often than not. In this deal, as in the preceding one, we have another example of an "all ears" defender at work.

The reader will note that this deal bears a similarity to Deal 7. However, where in Deal 7 our West defender had *heard* each of his opponents bid the same suit (spades), in this deal he had to make an inference about a type of bid that was made by one of his opponents. His inference was the correct one. The result was that our defender came up with the only lead that could have defeated South's contract.

North-South vulnerable. South deals.

```
                        NORTH
                     ♠ Q 7 5
                     ♥ A J 3
                     ♦ Q J 4
                     ♣ K J 10 2
      WEST                                  EAST
   ♠ J 10 9                              ♠ 8 6 4 3 2
   ♥ 8 2                                 ♥ 9 6 5
   ♦ A 9 5 2                             ♦ 3
   ♣ A 9 6 3                             ♣ Q 8 7 4
                        SOUTH
                     ♠ A K
                     ♥ K Q 10 7 4
                     ♦ K 10 8 7 6
                     ♣ 5
```

The bidding:

SOUTH	WEST	NORTH	EAST
1 ♥	Pass	2 NT	Pass
3 ♦	Pass	3 ♥	Pass
4 ♥	Pass	Pass	Pass

Opening lead: Ace of ♦.

North's "book" response of two no-trump showed a hand containing 13 to 15 high-card points, with protection in each of the unbid suits. When South then made a three-diamond rebid, he was offering North a choice of the red suits. North indicated his preference for hearts, and South went on to game in that suit.

From West's point of view, South almost certainly had a five-card diamond suit. After all, with North's original bid denoting a very positive desire (and the ability) to play at no-trump, South would not have made a rebid that might have led to an eleven-trick minor-suit game contract if he had possessed merely a four-card suit.

Further, when North jumped to two no-trump (*before* South had bid diamonds), he announced that he had the diamond suit guarded. Hence North had to have at least the K x of diamonds, possibly the K x x, the Q J x, or the Q x x. Actually, as West card-read the bidding, North figured to have three diamonds, since there existed only one combination where North could have jumped to two no-trump with only two diamonds. That combination was, of course, the K x, since with the doubleton Q x or J x, he would not have had a positive stopper in this suit.

Based on the above application of card reading, West opened the ace of diamonds, and despite the appearance of East's unencouraging three-spot, he continued with the diamond deuce at trick two. The deuce of diamonds lead (rather than the nine) was a suit-preference play, telling East to return the lower-ranking of the two obvious suits (clubs versus spades, with the suit being led and the trump suit always being eliminated from consideration). Had West been the possessor of the spade ace instead of the club ace, he would have led the diamond nine at trick two, telling East to play back the higher-ranking of the two obvious suits (spades versus clubs).

As is apparent, East ruffed the second diamond lead, after which he dutifully returned a low club to West's ace at trick three. Upon capturing this trick with his ace, West played back another diamond, which East ruffed for the setting trick.

It is apparent that if West were not a card reader, at trick one he would have made the normal, time-honored opening lead of the jack of spades. Declarer would then have made twelve tricks by winning this opening lead with the spade king, cashing the ace and queen of trumps (noting that each opponent followed suit to both trump leads). Next would come the ace of spades, after which a trump lead to the board's jack would pick up East's last trump. On the spade queen South would discard his singleton club. The only trick that the defenders would get would be West's ace of diamonds.

Deal 9

In this deal we have another illustration of a defender who spurned the normal, orthodox opening lead because his card reading had indicated that the normal lead figured to be a losing one. The lead he actually made was truly a gorgeous one—but gorgeous only if you happen to love defenders more than you love declarers.

When this deal arose in a rubber-bridge game, this was the bidding:

NORTH	EAST	SOUTH	WEST
1 ♥	Pass	3 ♣	Pass
3 ♦	Pass	4 NT	Pass
5 ♥	Pass	7 NT	Pass
Pass	Pass		

The five-heart call was the Blackwood response showing two aces. You are sitting West, on lead against South's seven-no-trump contract. You hold:

♠ J 10 9 7
♥ 6 2
♦ K 9 8
♣ J 7 5 3

What do you lead?

The following was West's reasoning, as he related it to me:

"South's jump-shift bid of three clubs, followed by his subsequent jump to seven no-trump, certainly indicated that he had a magnificent club suit. This was confirmed by the fact that South, after finding out that North held two aces, plunged right into seven no-trump *without bothering to inquire about kings* via a five no-trump bid. Actually South bid seven no-trump all by himself, knowing nothing more than that North had thirteen points and two aces. He just couldn't count to thirteen tricks in no-trump unless he expected to produce a helluva lot of tricks in clubs.

"But South didn't know, as I did, that he was not going to bring home his club suit—my jack would prevent him from so doing. Of course, I could have made the perfectly natural lead of the jack of spades. However, if I did that, declarer might be compelled to attack the diamond suit after finding out about the club situation, and with the ace of diamonds figuring to be in dummy, the diamond finesse might be all that he needed to fulfill his contract. So . . .

"I led the nine of diamonds on the sound assumption that declarer would not risk a finesse on the very first trick unless no better play was available. And, as you can see by looking the entire deal over, this was the only opening which could have (and did) defeat the contract:

NORTH
♠ 3
♥ A J 10 9
♦ A Q J 10 2
♣ 8 6 4

WEST
♠ J 10 9 7
♥ 6 2
♦ K 9 8
♣ J 7 5 3

EAST
♠ 8 6 5 4 2
♥ 8 7 5 4 3
♦ 7 4 3
♣ —

SOUTH
♠ A K Q
♥ K Q
♦ 6 5
♣ A K Q 10 9 2

"No declarer in his right mind would have taken that diamond finesse on the opening lead when he had what looked to be six sure club tricks, four hearts, three spades, and the ace of diamonds for frosting. If I had not made the diamond lead, and had led the spade jack instead, declarer would have played the ace of clubs at trick two, and upon receiving the news that I had a sure club winner, he would have been forced to take the diamond finesse—twice. He would then have ended up with fifteen tricks: five diamonds, three spades, four hearts, and three clubs."

In the actual play, declarer put up the board's ace of diamonds at trick one, after which he led the four of clubs. When East discarded a diamond on this lead, South had become a loser. He won the trick with his ace and led a diamond. West made haste to take his king, and a lay-down grand-slam contract had incurred a one-trick set.

Deal 10

A precept that has been handed down from generation to generation ever since the feudal days of bridge is "always return your partner's suit." Generally speaking, the application of this principle will pay dividends more often than not, especially when it is apparent that partner is leading in a good suit, and by returning his suit, it will become established.

But there are no hard-and-fast rules that can serve as a guide in these circumstances, for no two situations are exactly alike. And quite often, as in this deal, a logical card-reading analysis of the available evidence will demonstrate the incorrectness of playing back partner's suit. This deal, incidentally, arose in a high-stake rubber-bridge game at New York City's Mayfair Bridge Club.

Both sides vulnerable. South deals.

```
                        NORTH
                     ♠ K J 10
                     ♥ 9 8 4
                     ♦ A 5
                     ♣ 10 9 7 3 2
        WEST                              EAST
     ♠ 7 4                             ♠ A Q 8 5 2
     ♥ J 6 5 3                         ♥ 10 7 2
     ♦ J 9 7 2                         ♦ K 8 6 4
     ♣ Q 8 5                           ♣ 4
                        SOUTH
                     ♠ 9 6 3
                     ♥ A K Q
                     ♦ Q 10 3
                     ♣ A K J 6
```

The bidding:	SOUTH	WEST	NORTH	EAST
	1 ♣	Pass	2 ♣	Pass
	2 NT	Pass	3 NT	Pass
	Pass	Pass		

Opening lead: Two of ♦.

When a low diamond was played from dummy on the opening lead, East's king won the trick. East's natural instinct was to return a diamond, driving out dummy's ace and simultaneously either establishing or developing partner's suit. But first he paused to examine the situation confronting him and to reflect on the bidding.

After North had made a weak single raise in clubs (6 to 9 points and four or more clubs), South had the perfect right to pass. Nevertheless, South had made a move toward game by bidding two no-trump. Unquestionably South had a very strong hand containing a minimum of 18 points, and very possibly 19 or 20.

As East gazed at both his hand and dummy, card reading came into play. It was rather obvious that South had no high-card strength whatsoever in spades. And surely, with that good green wherewithal being of primary consideration, South had the diamond suit fully guarded, for he would not have bid two no-trump with *two* suits completely unguarded.

So East came to the right conclusion: South had to have the diamond queen; furthermore, South had to have *exactly* three diamonds, since West's fourth-best opening lead of the diamond *deuce* announced that West had precisely four diamonds.

Thus East perceived the hopelessness of returning a diamond, since South was known to have two sure winners in this suit. After some thought, he came up with a truly inspirational lead at trick two—the five of spades!

East's hope was that West would be able to obtain the lead in either hearts or clubs, and West would then certainly return a spade. The board's remaining doubleton K J of spades would now be ambushed by East's A Q, and East would make four spade tricks.

Dummy's ten of spades won this trick, after which declarer cashed his ace and king of clubs. When the queen did not fall, South led the jack of clubs. Upon winning with the queen, West returned his remaining spade—and East-West chalked up 200 points for defeating a vulnerable South two tricks.

Deal 11

If trickery can be rightfully described as beautiful, East's defense in this deal fits that description. It came into being through the application of card reading, which indicated that South had a problem. After a while East was able to isolate and diagnose South's problem. He was then able to give South a little push—in the wrong direction.

North-South vulnerable. South deals.

NORTH
♠ K Q 10 5
♥ J 6 4
♦ K 7
♣ Q J 8 6

WEST
♠ J 4
♥ 8 7 5 2
♦ Q J 10 8 4 3
♣ 5

EAST
♠ 8 7 6 3
♥ Q 10 9
♦ 6 5
♣ 7 4 3 2

SOUTH
♠ A 9 2
♥ A K 3
♦ A 9 2
♣ A K 10 9

The bidding:

SOUTH	WEST	NORTH	EAST
2 NT	Pass	3 ♠	Pass
4 ♣	Pass	6 ♣	Pass
7 ♣	Pass	Pass	Pass

Opening lead: Queen of ♦.

After dummy's king of diamonds had won the opening lead, declarer paused for reflection. Since East had nothing better to do at the moment, he also paused for reflection, to assemble current facts for future utilization. The longer South reflected, the more East liked the situation, for if South had had thirteen tricks he would not be wasting everyone's time.

With West having opened the queen of diamonds, he was known to possess three high-card points in diamonds (he would not have led the queen unless he had the jack). North had 12 high-card points, and East was looking at 2 high-card points in his own hand. Thus 17 high-card points were accounted for, which left 23.

Since South had opened the bidding with two no-trump, he was known to have 22 to 24 high-card points. Thus the whereabouts of only one point was unknown. That one point had to be the jack of spades, since South had to have the four aces and the two kings not in evidence.

To tricks two and three, South cashed his ace and ten of trumps, West discarding a diamond on the second trump lead. Declarer next led his ace of diamonds, after which he led a third diamond and ruffed it with the board's queen of trumps. East now had a discard to make—and he thought not only of it, but of the entire situation at hand. After a few moments of contemplation, he knew that South *did not have the spade jack!*

South was known to have started with four club winners in his hand (the A K 10 9). The king and ace of diamonds had already won two tricks. And the diamond that had just been ruffed in dummy added up to seven winners. With the ace and king of hearts that South was known to possess, the total was brought up to nine tricks for declarer. If South had the jack of spades (in combination with his known ace), then together with dummy's spade holding, South had four spade winners, which would bring the total to thirteen tricks.

Again, if South had the A J or the A J x of spades, he would have finished playing the hand a long time ago. Hence South did not have the spade jack, and his problem *had to be* the determination of how he was going to play the spade suit.

And so, at trick five, when South ruffed a diamond with the board's queen of clubs, East, having a discard to make, found a gorgeous one—he underruffed with seven of trumps!

This play by East set declarer's little gray cells into action. Why, declarer asked himself, didn't East discard either a spade or a heart instead of needlessly expending a trump? The only logical answer (and bridge is a logical game) as declarer viewed it had to be that East held both the spade jack and the heart queen, and he didn't want to unguard either of them.

So declarer first cashed the ace and king of hearts (there are days when one catches a doubleton queen). The North hand was then entered via the trump jack, and the five of spades was led. When East followed suit with the deuce, declarer confidently inserted his nine-spot, finessing against East's (presumed) jack. West pounced upon the nine with the jack. That he returned a heart to East's queen to defeat declarer two tricks was anticlimactic.

If, when called upon to make a discard on the third diamond lead, East had tossed away an insignificant low spade, declarer would easily have fulfilled his contract by playing the spade suit normally. He would have first drawn East's remaining trumps and then cashed the ace and king of hearts. Next would come a spade to dummy's king, and then a spade to his ace. With the fall of West's jack, South would now enter on the scorepad all of those gorgeous numbers that one collects for making a vulnerable grand slam.

Deal 12

In this deal we have a situation analogous to the one presented in the preceding deal—namely, a deliberate, calculated plot designed to talk declarer into taking a losing finesse. The necessity for the defensive deception was born through card reading. The hand came up in the National Championships of 1957.

North-South vulnerable. North deals.

```
                        NORTH
                    ♠ 10 9
                    ♥ A J 7
                    ♦ A K Q 10 2
                    ♣ J 6 4
      WEST                                    EAST
  ♠ 6 3                                   ♠ Q J 8 7 5
  ♥ 2                                     ♥ K 8 6 4 3
  ♦ 9 8 5 3                               ♦ J 6
  ♣ 10 9 8 5 3 2                          ♣ 7
                        SOUTH
                    ♠ A K 4 2
                    ♥ Q 10 9 5
                    ♦ 7 4
                    ♣ A K Q
```

The bidding:	NORTH	EAST	SOUTH	WEST
	1 ♦	Pass	1 ♥	Pass
	2 ♦	Pass	2 ♠	Pass
	3 ♥	Pass	4 NT	Pass
	5 ♥	Pass	6 NT	Pass
	Pass	Pass		

Opening lead: Ten of ♣.

Before getting to East's defense in this hand (East is to become our hero), let us look at the play from declarer's point of view.

After winning the opening lead with his club queen, declarer led the ten of hearts, and took the finesse when West followed suit with the heart deuce. Upon capturing this trick with his king, East returned the queen of spades, South taking it with his ace. South now led a low heart to dummy's ace, West discarding the two of clubs.

The ace of diamonds was cashed next, and this was followed by the cashing of the ace and king of clubs. On these last two tricks East discarded the five and seven of spades. South then took his king of spades, East following suit with the eight-spot. Declarer now paused to take stock.

East was known to have started with five hearts (West having failed to follow suit to the second lead of this suit). East also almost certainly had five spades originally: when he won his heart king at trick two, his shift to the queen of spades at trick three guaranteed possession of the jack. When compelled to make two discards on the second and third club leads, he had tossed away the five and seven of spades. And when declarer cashed his second high spade, East had followed suit with the eight-spot. So East still retained the spade jack (the fifth spade).

Since East had followed to one club lead and one diamond lead, twelve of his original thirteen cards were known—and his thirteenth card *had to be* a diamond, since East had failed to follow suit to the second club lead by South (his thirteenth card couldn't be a spade, since West had followed suit to both spade leads).

Thus, since East was known to have started with two diamonds, West had to have been dealt the remaining four diamonds in the deck. On percentage, therefore, since West had begun with four diamonds and East with only two, West figured to have the diamond jack.

So declarer now led his remaining diamond and finessed dummy's ten-spot. When East won this trick with his jack, he cashed his jack of spades, and inflicted a two-trick set on declarer.

Should declarer have fallen for East's two spade discards (when with no pain East could have discarded a couple of low hearts which South knew that East possessed)? I really do not know. All I can say is that East was an excellent player, while South was a

notch or two below expert. Thus, perhaps, South's gullibility can
be charged to inexperience.

Let's now take a look at East's play. Holding the J x of diamonds, East knew that declarer had it in his power to bring home
five diamond tricks. He knew also that if this came to pass, declarer would fulfill his slam contract.

So East deliberately set about to create an incorrect picture for
declarer by giving the latter a perfect count of East's hand. By
tossing away his two low spades, he knew that declarer would
eventually come to the conclusion that East had started with five
spades. And, of course, declarer would know in time that East had
been dealt five hearts and one club. East, by discarding his two
spades, would thereby be informing South that East had started
with two diamonds.

Of course East could have prevented declarer from obtaining a
count by simply discarding two low hearts—but he was most
happy, willing, and able to give declarer a push in the wrong direction. And the beauty of the whole thing, from East's point of
view, was that his spade discards were on the house: they might
gain, but they couldn't ever lose.

Deal 13

In this deal there is presented a battle of counting, in which
our South declarer did a perfect job in counting out the distribution of a defender's hand. Putting the knowledge obtained to practical use, he came up with a line of play that would have surely
succeeded against 99 percent of the world's players.

Unfortunately for him, however, our West defender was also
doing the identical counting (of his partner's hand) . And he came
up with a most beautiful play to thwart declarer. West, incidentally, was Richard L. Frey, who was considered to be one of
the world's top-ranking players during the 1930s and 1940s.

East-West vulnerable. North deals.

```
                    NORTH
                 ♠ A Q 6 3
                 ♥ Q J 8
                 ♦ 9 3 2
                 ♣ A 8 4
    WEST                              EAST
 ♠ —                              ♠ 5 4 2
 ♥ 10 9 6 3 2                     ♥ 7 5
 ♦ K J 10 6 5 4                   ♦ Q
 ♣ K Q                            ♣ J 10 9 7 6 5 2
                    SOUTH
                 ♠ K J 10 9 8 7
                 ♥ A K 4
                 ♦ A 8 7
                 ♣ 3
```

The bidding:

NORTH	EAST	SOUTH	WEST
1 ♣	Pass	2 ♠	Pass
3 ♠	Pass	4 NT	Pass
5 ♥	Pass	6 ♠	Pass
Pass	Pass		

Opening lead: King of ♣.

After capturing the opening lead with the board's ace of clubs, declarer promptly led a low club and ruffed it. He next reentered dummy with the spade queen, after which he ruffed dummy's remaining club, West discarding the diamond four.

The ace and king of trumps were then cashed, picking up East's last two pieces, and leaving both dummy and declarer with one trump apiece. Now came a heart to dummy's queen, after which a heart was returned to South's ace. Declarer now stopped playing in order to do some counting.

From West's failure to follow suit to the third lead of clubs, East was known to have been dealt seven clubs. And East had followed suit to three rounds of trumps and to two rounds of hearts. Thus, twelve of East's cards were an open book to declarer.

If East's unknown thirteenth card was another heart, then declarer was doomed to lose two diamond tricks, since West would
then have started with seven diamonds consisting of the K Q J 10
x x x. The probability of West's holding these seven diamonds was
just about nil, for with them, plus his K Q of clubs, he surely
would have bid over South's two-spade response.

As declarer correctly appraised the setup, his only hope of avoiding the loss of two diamond tricks was for East's singleton diamond to be big enough to win the initial diamond lead. If this
developed, then East would be forced to play back a club, on
which South would discard his remaining low diamond while
ruffing the trick with dummy's last trump.

So declarer, after having cashed the queen and ace of hearts in
that order, led the seven of diamonds toward dummy's nine. If
Frey had put up the ten-spot—certainly the natural play when one
stops to consider that the ten would beat dummy's nine-spot—declarer would have fulfilled his contract, since East would have
been compelled to capture the trick with his queen. And, simultaneously, East would have fallen a victim to the end play just
described.

But Frey was counting right along with declarer. He knew that
his partner had started with exactly seven clubs and three trumps.
He also knew—with certainty—that his partner had been dealt exactly two hearts, for the only outstanding heart was the king. Declarer had to have this card, since dummy's queen of hearts had
captured the initial heart lead two tricks back. Thus Frey knew
that his partner had been dealt precisely one diamond.

Upon further analysis, Frey quickly came to the conclusion that
his partner's singleton diamond figured to be the queen. The reason for his conclusion was that if declarer had started with the
A Q x of diamonds, he certainly wouldn't be leading a low diamond out of his hand.

So when, at trick nine, declarer led the seven of diamonds out
of his hand, Frey did not mechanically play the ten-spot. Instead,
he put up his king—and he felled his partner's queen. Frey then
continued with the diamond jack, and declarer was compelled
eventually to lose another diamond trick to West's ten.

Incidentally, if declarer had cashed his third high heart (the
king) before playing the diamond, East would have had the op-

portunity of becoming a hero, and Frey would not have had the chance to display his "genius at work." On the third heart lead East would (we trust) have discarded his diamond queen. No matter what declarer or Frey now did from here in, declarer would be compelled to lose two diamond tricks.

11

Defense When
Both Sides Bid

As was stated earlier, in every deal the defenders have the advantage of knowing or inferring declarer's high-card strength and/or distribution because declarer has always made one or more bids. In many of these situations, through proper card reading and counting, the defenders can capitalize on this knowledge. In substantiation of this point, there were presented the thirteen deals contained in Chapter 10.

In Chapter 10 neither of the defenders ever bid on any deal, so their sole clues leading to winning defense had to be developed exclusively from their analysis of the opening lead and declarer's bidding and/or play. In this chapter, on the other hand, the defenders bid in every deal, and, as a result, a defender's knowledge of the significance of partner's bid becomes a fact that illuminates the way to the winning line of defense. It should be pointed out, however, that in all of the deals contained herein, the knowledge of declarer's hand—based on his bidding and/or play—is the foundation upon which the defenders' bidding is superimposed as a superstructure. In combination, the two form the finished edifice from which the defenders take dead aim and fire.

Deal 1
One of the most spectacular defensive card-reading deals that I have ever come across is this one. It arose in a rubber-bridge game

at New York City's Mayfair Bridge Club in 1951. The imaginative defensive play was made by Harry Fishbein, the proprietor of the club at that time. He was in the West seat.

North-South vulnerable. South deals.

NORTH
♠ J 7 6 2
♥ Q J 4
♦ K 9 3
♣ 10 6 3

WEST
♠ Q 4
♥ 6 5 3
♦ A Q J 10 6 2
♣ Q 5

EAST
♠ 10 3
♥ 10 9
♦ 8 7 5 4
♣ A K 9 7 2

SOUTH
♠ A K 9 8 5
♥ A K 8 7 2
♦ —
♣ J 8 4

The bidding:

SOUTH	WEST	NORTH	EAST
1 ♠	2 ♦	Pass	3 ♣
3 ♥	Pass	4 ♠	Pass
Pass	Pass		

Opening lead: Queen of ♣.

With his partner having bid clubs, Fishbein got off to the natural lead of the queen of clubs. When it won the trick, he continued with his remaining club, East's king winning. East now laid down his club ace, and Fishbein had a discard to make.

After a few moments of thought he came up with a discard that was really a beauty: he tossed away the ace of diamonds!

To state that East was amazed by this discard would be the understatement of the year. One thing that East learned for sure was that West did not want East to lead a diamond at trick four (West had bid diamonds, and the diamond king was in dummy).

Certainly, as East appraised the situation at hand, Fishbein did not want a heart return, no matter what his heart holding was. If he had a heart trick, he would always make it since he was behind the heart bidder. And Fishbein couldn't be void of hearts, for if he were, then declarer had been dealt eight hearts headed by the A K. The latter was an impossibility, based on the fact that South had opened the bidding with one spade and had been revealed as the possessor of three clubs. Actually, if West had wanted a heart return, he could have suggested it by discarding the deuce of diamonds, thereby disclaiming any interest in the very suit he had bid.

And so, by a process of elimination (based on deduction), East returned a fourth club—and no matter what South played to this lead, he could not prevent Fishbein's queen of trumps from being promoted into a winner, and the setting trick.

It will be observed that if Fishbein had not discarded the ace of diamonds, and if East had then played back a diamond at trick four, declarer would have ruffed. His ace and king of spades would then have gathered in the outstanding pieces. Since he had five sure heart winners, the rest of the tricks would now belong to him.

What motivated Fishbein to make his sensational discard of the diamond ace? It was his imaginative card reading, which was based on his close attention to South's bidding. South had bid spades and hearts, the latter suit at the three level, vulnerable, opposite a passing partner. Surely he rated to have at least nine cards in the major suits (or else he would have been bidding on four spades and four hearts). South had also followed suit to the first three club leads. So South rated to have one diamond, at most. And it was quite conceivable that he had no diamonds whatsoever, in which case West's ace of diamonds would never win a trick.

Furthermore, Fishbein knew that his queen of trumps would become a *sure* winner (100 percent) if he could get his partner to lead a club at trick four. Thus his discard of the diamond ace—with the faith in partner's ability to make the correct interpretation of this discard.

Deal 2

In the previous deal there was observed an example of a logical, voluntary tossing away of an ace. In this deal we have a situation that is broadly similar: the logical, voluntary *trumping* of partner's ace, despite the fact that the ace was going to win the trick. Before getting to the specifics, however, allow me to introduce a brief diversion.

Years ago, when bridge was in its infancy, the player who trumped his partner's ace was either laughed at or derided, for his wasting of a trump was considered to be a sign of incompetence or weakness of intellect. His folly usually became the talk of the town, and he was eventually ostracized by the better players.

Undoubtedly, in some cases, the trumping of partner's ace was due to ignorance or perhaps inattention—that is, the trumper didn't know that it was his partner's ace that he was trumping. But in the great majority of cases the trumping of partner's ace was done by design because card reading had indicated that it was the right play. This is one of those "right play" deals. One of our forefathers was sitting in the East seat.

Both sides vulnerable. West deals.

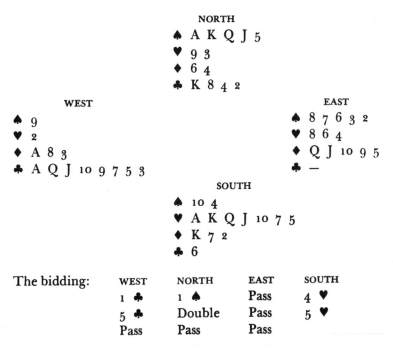

NORTH
♠ A K Q J 5
♥ 9 3
♦ 6 4
♣ K 8 4 2

WEST
♠ 9
♥ 2
♦ A 8 3
♣ A Q J 10 9 7 5 3

EAST
♠ 8 7 6 3 2
♥ 8 6 4
♦ Q J 10 9 5
♣ —

SOUTH
♠ 10 4
♥ A K Q J 10 7 5
♦ K 7 2
♣ 6

The bidding:

WEST	NORTH	EAST	SOUTH
1 ♣	1 ♠	Pass	4 ♥
5 ♣	Double	Pass	5 ♥
Pass	Pass	Pass	

Opening lead: Ace of ♣.

After West had opened the ace of clubs and the deuce was played from dummy, East paused for quite a while to survey the lay of the land. It quickly became apparent to him that South, for his leap to four hearts and his subsequent bid of five hearts over North's penalty double, had a long, solid heart suit. It became equally obvious to him that his partner, West, had no high-card strength whatsoever in spades. Thus West had done a heap of bidding for a man who had no strength at all in the major suits.

The question was, then, what did West have to justify his opening bid and his free bid of five clubs? Since the king of clubs was in evidence in dummy, and West had bid the suit as though he owned it, surely West possessed a minimum of seven clubs, and very probably eight, headed by the A Q J. And since West was known to have no high cards in either spades or hearts, he just had to have a high card in diamonds. If that card were not the ace, then South's contract figured to be unbeatable.

Even if West possessed only seven clubs—which would mean that South had two clubs—and East trumped the *second* club lead, the setting trick would have to come from West's (presumed) ace of diamonds (if South had the ace of diamonds, he would be able to get rid of his remaining diamond losers by discarding them on dummy's spades). But if West had the eight clubs he really rated to have for his vigorous bidding, then it would be essential to win two diamond tricks in order to defeat South's five-heart contract.

And so, having given full analysis to the bidding by both South and West, East arrived at the winning conclusion: he trumped his partner's ace of clubs at trick one, and returned the queen of diamonds at trick two. At the conclusion of trick three, declarer had suffered a one-trick set.

It is evident that if West's ace of clubs had not been ruffed by East at trick one, declarer would have fulfilled his contract. As a matter of fact, he would have made an overtrick if West did not cash the diamond ace at trick two, for declarer, after drawing trumps, would have discarded his three diamonds on dummy's top spades.

Deal 3

All bridge players are aware of the fact that contract bridge cannot be learned by memorizing different rules and applying each specific rule to each different situation. If it could, then anyone with a retentive memory would have the capacity to become a great bridge player. However, bridge is not a mechanical game, and the true test of a good bridge player is not his ability to memorize rules and regulations, but rather his ability to be flexible and to apply his judgment to each new situation that confronts him. This perhaps simple deal is a case in point.

Both sides vulnerable. South deals.

```
                        NORTH
                     ♠ A 9 6 4
                     ♥ 6 5
                     ♦ K 9 7 2
                     ♣ 8 7 3
        WEST                              EAST
     ♠ 8 3                             ♠ 7 5 2
     ♥ K Q 10 9 4 3                    ♥ A J 8 2
     ♦ 6 4                             ♦ 8 3
     ♣ A Q 6                           ♣ K 5 4 2
                        SOUTH
                     ♠ K Q J 10
                     ♥ 7
                     ♦ A Q J 10 5
                     ♣ J 10 9
```

The bidding:	SOUTH	WEST	NORTH	EAST
	1 ♦	1 ♥	2 ♦	2 ♥
	2 ♠	3 ♥	3 ♠	Pass
	4 ♠	Pass	Pass	Pass

Opening lead: King of ♥.

This is conjecture on my part, but I imagine that if this deal had arisen in an average game, on West's opening lead of the heart king East would have signaled for a continuation of the suit by playing the eight-spot or the jack. West would then have led a second heart, South ruffing. It would now be a routine matter for South to draw trumps and to cash five diamond tricks. He would then claim his contract, having made five trump tricks (one by ruffing a heart) and five diamonds.

But our East defender was a good player who long ago had cultivated the habit of paying close attention to the bidding that had taken place. He had heard his partner make an overcall at the one level. And he had heard him rebid his heart suit at the three level, vulnerable, on a suit that was missing the ace and jack. So East concluded that in all likelihood West possessed a six-card suit. It was conceivable, of course, that West might have had only five hearts. (But, then, one gets no guarantees in bridge.)

Thus if East signaled for a continuation by West of the heart suit, South figured to ruff the second heart lead. When that occurred, control of the situation would pass over to declarer.

As East viewed the setup, the defenders' sole hope of defeating South's four-spade contract rested in their ability to cash at least two club tricks. So, at trick one, East overtook his partner's king of hearts with the ace and promptly led the deuce of clubs. South put up the ten, and West captured the trick with his queen. After West then cashed the ace of clubs, upon which East followed suit with the five, West pondered about what to lead next.

The question in West's mind was whether he should now play his remaining club, hoping that East possessed the king; or whether, instead, he should attempt to cash his high queen of hearts. He resolved the problem correctly by leading a club, and East's king took the setting trick.

West's reason for continuing with a third club was based on faith in East's play at trick one: if East had held the tripleton A x x or the A J x of hearts, he would not have been in such a hurry to overtake West's opening lead of the heart king. And so West concluded that East had been dealt four hearts—and that, therefore, the third club lead was called for.

Deal 4

When this deal came up some years ago in the Masters Team-of-Four Championships, a bit of well-reasoned card reading by the East-West defenders resulted in the defeat of South's contract. Sitting West and East, respectively, were two of the world's top-ranking players, Waldemar von Zedtwitz and Lee Hazen, both of New York City.

Neither side vulnerable. West deals.

```
                        NORTH
                     ♠ 7 5 4
                     ♥ 8 6 3
                     ♦ A K Q J 10
                     ♣ A 5
        WEST                              EAST
     ♠ A 8 3                           ♠ 6
     ♥ A K Q 10 7                      ♥ J 9 4 2
     ♦ 9 6 5                           ♦ 4 3
     ♣ K 6                             ♣ Q J 10 8 3 2
                        SOUTH
                     ♠ K Q J 10 9 2
                     ♥ 5
                     ♦ 8 7 2
                     ♣ 9 7 4
```

The bidding:

WEST	NORTH	EAST	SOUTH
1 ♥	2 ♦	2 ♥	2 ♠
3 ♥	3 ♠	Pass	Pass
4 ♥	Pass	Pass	4 ♠
Double	Pass	Pass	Pass

Opening lead: King of ♥.

Upon winning the opening lead with his heart king, von Zedtwitz studied the situation confronting him. By perceiving his own hand and dummy, he noted that East figured to have just about absolutely nothing in the way of high-card strength. Hence he concluded that East's free raise to two hearts had to be based on four hearts and, in all probability, the queen of clubs.

And so to lead a second heart at trick two rated to be a losing play, since South would trump it. At trick two, von Zedtwitz banged down his king of clubs!

Dummy won this trick with the ace, and a trump was then led, South's jack being taken by West's ace. West now returned his remaining club to East's ten, after which the queen of clubs was laid down. As is obvious, West ruffed this lead with the trump eight, and dummy was unable to overruff. Thus declarer incurred a one-trick set.

Although West is the number-one hero of this deal, East should also share in the credit. When he won trick four with his ten of clubs, the question in his mind was whether to return a heart to West's ace (for the hoped-for setting trick), or whether, instead, he should play the queen of clubs, hoping that West had a trump big enough to beat dummy's seven-spot.

His selection of leading the club queen is easy to understand: at trick two, West had chosen not to play a second heart and had elected instead to make the gambling play of the king of clubs. Therefore West must have known that South had no more hearts. So East correctly followed West's line of defense.

But, just as there are heroes, so there are goats—and South was the goat on this deal, for he had it in his power to neutralize West's fine card reading. All South had to do at trick two, when West led the king of clubs, was to decline to capture the trick with dummy's ace. It would then have become impossible for East to have obtained the lead subsequently, and West would never have gotten around to trumping the third club lead. But, even if South had acquitted himself nobly, it would not have detracted from the defenders' imaginative defense.

Deal 5

When this deal arose in a top-level team-of-four game, both West defenders were called upon to do some card reading. At the first table, West found himself in a position where he was forced to make a guess—and he guessed wrong, thereby permitting our South declarer to fulfill his contract.

When the deal was replayed, East came up with a fine play and thereby eliminated the guess that our West defender had had to make when the deal was played originally. The result was that South's contract was defeated.

This deal, in my opinion, is a heavy one, for it involves a type of defensive thinking that can be developed only through experience in similar types of thinking.

East-West vulnerable. East deals.

NORTH

♠ K
♥ K Q 10 9
♦ A K J 5
♣ K Q 10 2

WEST

♠ Q 9 7 3 2
♥ 6
♦ 8 7 3
♣ A 9 5 4

EAST

♠ A J 10 8 4
♥ A 4
♦ Q 10 9 4 2
♣ 8

SOUTH

♠ 6 5
♥ J 8 7 5 3 2
♦ 6
♣ J 7 6 3

The bidding:

	EAST	SOUTH	WEST	NORTH
	1 ♠	Pass	2 ♠	Double
	Pass	3 ♥	3 ♠	4 ♥
	Pass	Pass	Pass	

Opening lead: Three of ♠.

The bidding was the same at both tables, as was West's open-ing lead of the spade three. At the first table, after winning the opening lead with the ace of spades, East shifted to the eight of clubs, and South followed suit with the six-spot. West now went into a brown study. The question to be resolved was whether the eight of clubs was a singleton or the top of a doubleton.

As West analyzed the situation, there was no doubt in his mind that East possessed the ace of hearts (trumps). This conclusion was arrived at by looking at his own hand and dummy. East had opened the bidding with one spade, and it was obvious that his spade holding contained, at most, the ace and jack. In diamonds, East had, at most, the queen. And in clubs he had nothing. With-out the ace of hearts, East would not have had the slightest sem-blance of an opening bid.

If East's eight of clubs was a singleton, then the winning play would be for West to win the trick with his ace, and play back a club for East to trump. Eventually East's ace of hearts would take the setting trick.

But if East's eight of clubs was part of a doubleton, then the right play for West would be the encouraging nine, allowing North to win the trick. When trumps would next be led, East would take his ace, to return his remaining club. West, upon capturing this trick with his ace, would now return a third club for East to ruff, for the setting trick.

Of course, if East had a doubleton club, and West captured East's lead of the club eight at trick two, to return a club, dummy would win the trick as East followed suit with his remaining club. Now when a trump was led, East would take his ace, but the defenders would be helpless, and East's opportunity to have trumped a club would have escaped.

After the above thoughts had flashed through West's mind, he decided to assume that East's eight of clubs was the top card of a doubleton club. So he played the nine-spot, which was taken by dummy's ten.

The king of trumps was then led off the board, and East took his ace. After trumps were later gathered in by declarer, West made his ace of clubs. Thus declarer fulfilled his contract, his only losers being to the three outstanding aces.

On the replay of the deal, East also won the opening lead with his ace of spades. But at trick two he came up with an "above the call of duty" imaginative play which, as subsequent events demonstrated, eliminated the guesswork that confronted our West defender when the deal was played originally. At trick two East cashed his ace of hearts. At trick three he led the eight of clubs.

There was now no ambiguity in West's mind, for by looking at dummy he knew that East could never again obtain the lead to play a second club (if he had one). Hence West had no choice but to hope that East's eight of clubs was a singleton. So he won the trick with his club ace, and returned a club. East's four of trumps now took the setting trick.

Deal 6

Some years ago, during a protracted losing streak at the bridge table, Chico Marx, one of the four Marx Brothers of theatrical fame, wrote to a playing-card manufacturer: "Gentlemen, are you still manufacturing aces and kings?"

Virtually all rubber-bridge players have gone through similar periods of tribulation when their opponents held all the aces and kings. Yet, even in these dire circumstances, one can occasionally alter his seemingly apparent destiny. As evidence, take a look at the East hand in this deal. Despite its worthlessness, East became the hero of the deal, for his meaningful discards formed the solid foundation which enabled West to do some crucial counting and card reading.

Neither side vulnerable. West deals.

```
                        NORTH
                     ♠ 7 4
                     ♥ J 9 3
                     ♦ J 10 9
                     ♣ Q J 10 4 2
        WEST                              EAST
     ♠ J 10 9                          ♠ 6 3
     ♥ A K Q 2                         ♥ 8 7 5
     ♦ Q 7 6                           ♦ 8 5 3 2
     ♣ K 9 3                           ♣ 8 7 6 5
                        SOUTH
                     ♠ A K Q 8 5 2
                     ♥ 10 6 4
                     ♦ A K 4
                     ♣ A
```

The bidding:

WEST	NORTH	EAST	SOUTH
1 ♥	Pass	Pass	4 ♠
Pass	Pass	Pass	

Opening lead: King of ♥.

After cashing the king, queen, and ace of hearts, West then deliberated as to whether to play the heart deuce, the remaining heart in the deck. If East possessed the trump eight, he would uppercut with this card, forcing declarer to overruff with the ace, king, or queen. In these circumstances West's jack of spades would be promoted into a winner and the setting trick. But West decided not to gamble on this lead, since, in his opinion, either the queen of diamonds or the king of clubs figured to take the setting trick. It was just as well (for his side) that he did not lead the thirteenth heart, for declarer would have ruffed it with the board's seven of trumps as South discarded the four of diamonds from his own hand. The rest of the tricks would now belong to declarer.

At trick four, West made the safe exit of the trump jack, South winning the trick with his queen. South then cashed all of his trumps. This was the position around the table prior to the lead of South's last trump:

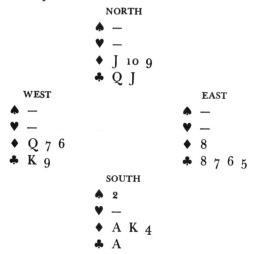

On the lead of South's deuce of trumps, West has a problem. As can be observed, if he discards the six of diamonds, South will now win three diamond tricks. And if, instead, he tosses away the nine of clubs, unguarding his king, South might have (in theory, on some other day), the A x of clubs. The club ace will then fell West's now-singleton king, thereby promoting dummy's queen into a winner.

At the table, however, our observant West had no problem, thanks to East. After East had followed suit to two trump leads, he was called upon to make three more discards on South's next three trump leads. He tossed away, in this order, the two, the three, and the five of diamonds.

From West's viewpoint, the *four* of diamonds was not in evidence—and surely if East had possessed this card, he would have discarded it (in natural order) before discarding the five of diamonds. Therefore West knew that South possessed the diamond four.

So West, at trick nine (when South led his last trump) tossed away his nine of clubs, baring his king, and eventually he won his queen of diamonds, for the setting trick. Thus East, with his worthless hand, actually took his partner by the hand and guided him to the winning line of defense.

Deal 7

Up until about a decade ago the standard opening lead from any A K x, A K x x, A K x x x combination and from any K Q x, K Q x x, etc. combination had always been the same card, the king. Quite often this lead of the king created an ambiguity that couldn't be resolved, for partner didn't know—until too late—whether the leader possessed the ace or the queen. Thus, from the viewpoint of the leader's partner, his card reading tended to degenerate into guesswork—and on a certain number of occasions he misguessed. This deal illustrates the costly result of this type of misguess.

To avoid this ambiguity, many of our better players now lead *the ace* from any A K x or A K x x combination, and *the king* from any K Q x or K Q x x combination. So when it comes the leader's partner's turn to play, he knows with certainty that the leader of the king has the queen, *but does not possess the ace,* and that the lead of an ace denotes possession of the king. The leader's partner can now intelligently give a positive or a negative signal on the leader's card, to indicate whether he wants that suit continued or not.

But there are many experts (and virtually all of our nonexperts) who still lead the king from an A K x combination and from a K Q x combination—and at times they are sorry that they haven't gone "modern." Such was the case when this deal arose in the 1971 World Championships.

Both sides vulnerable. South deals.

NORTH
♠ K Q 9
♥ K Q 8 2
♦ J 2
♣ A 8 7 3

WEST
♠ —
♥ A 5
♦ K Q 10 9 6 5 4 3
♣ J 10 4

EAST
♠ A 7 5 4
♥ 10 9 6 4 3
♦ —
♣ K 9 6 2

SOUTH
♠ J 10 8 6 3 2
♥ J 7
♦ A 8 7
♣ Q 5

The bidding:

	SOUTH	WEST	NORTH	EAST
	Pass	1 ♦	Double	1 ♥
	2 ♠	3 ♦	3 ♠	Pass
	4 ♠	Pass	Pass	Double
	Pass	Pass	Pass	

Opening lead: King of ♦.

The deuce of diamonds was played from dummy on West's opening lead of the diamond king—and East had a problem: did West have the ace or queen of diamonds?

If West had the ace, then East's correct play would be to discard on the first two diamond leads, allowing West to win the tricks. In time East would hope to win a trick with the club king, in addition to, of course, the trump ace.

However, if West's lead was from a K Q combination in diamonds, then card reading (based on an examination of his hand and dummy) clearly indicated that West had to have the heart ace for his opening bid and subsequent rebid. If the latter were the existing setup, the winning defense would be to ruff the diamond king, lead a heart to West's ace, and then ruff a second diamond. Declarer would now be down one trick for sure, and down two if East were able to win a trick with his club king.

East made the losing guess—he discarded a heart on the diamond king. South won the trick with his ace and led the jack of hearts to West's ace. West then cashed the diamond queen, after which he continued with the ten of diamonds. Dummy ruffed with the king, East discarding another heart. The queen of trumps was led next, East taking his ace.

From here in, the defenders took no more tricks, for South was able to discard his losing club on the board's queen of hearts. And so, with a little bit of luck, declarer fulfilled his doubled contract.

Deal 8

In this deal the West defender has my deepest sympathy—and I hope he gets yours after you've read his sad story. He had listened closely to the North-South bidding, and as a result he came up with a thoughtful and imaginative lead. But, unfortunately for him, his opponents were not telling the truth while he was listening. If a title were required for this deal, a fitting one would be: "The Operation Was Successful—but the Patient Died."

East-West vulnerable. South deals.

```
                        NORTH
                     ♠ Q 4
                     ♥ Q 7 3 2
                     ♦ J 6 4
                     ♣ A 10 9 2
      WEST                              EAST
   ♠ A K J 10 3                      ♠ 9 7 5 2
   ♥ A                               ♥ 8 6 5
   ♦ 10 9 8                          ♦ Q 7 3 2
   ♣ 8 7 5 3                         ♣ Q 4
                        SOUTH
                     ♠ 8 6
                     ♥ K J 10 9 4
                     ♦ A K 5
                     ♣ K J 6
```

The bidding:	SOUTH	WEST	NORTH	EAST
	1 ♥	1 ♠	2 ♥	Pass
	3 ♣ (!)	Pass	4 ♣	Pass
	4 ♥	Pass	Pass	Pass

Opening lead: Eight of ♣.

If the reader is wondering why West opened the eight of clubs instead of the obvious lead of a spade, allow me to present what motivated him.

South, on his rebid, had bid three clubs, which West assumed denoted a four-card suit. When North raised to four clubs, there was no doubt whatsoever in West's mind that North possessed four clubs. That meant that East had been dealt a singleton club.

Thus, via card reading (*sic!*), West *knew* that East would be able to ruff a second club lead, and West also knew (for sure) that he would have to obtain the lead somewhere along the line with his trump ace. He would then be able to lead a second club for East to trump.

On West's opening club lead dummy's ten was put up, covered by East's queen, and captured by South's king. A trump lead was then made and taken by West's ace. After cashing his king and ace of spades, West then confidently led a second club and, much to his surprise (and anguish), East followed suit as declarer took the trick with his jack.

Declarer then picked up East's trumps, after which he cashed the board's two top clubs, discarding his five of diamonds on the second of the club leads. The rest of the tricks belonged to him.

Had West paid no attention to the North-South bidding, he would have opened the king of spades (according to custom) and followed up by leading the spade ace. He would then have cashed the ace of trumps, after which he would have exited with the ten of diamonds. The success of declarer's contract would now depend on guessing which way to finesse for the queen of clubs. As to whether he would have guessed that East possessed this card will, of course, never be known.

If one judges by results, West's club opening was a poor lead. Personally, I don't think it was. But, then, I am prejudiced—I was the West defender.

12

The Defenders
Fail to Card-Read

In virtually all of the preceding deals presented in this book either the declarer or the defenders did a top-notch job of card reading which resulted in the downfall of the adversaries.

In this chapter and in Chapter 13 the reverse is true: that is, a defender or the declarer either failed to do the requisite card reading which would have turned defeat into victory, or his card reading didn't go far enough, resulting in his being a loser instead of a winner.

It is my hope that the reader will profit from the understanding of the card-reading errors of neglect or omission that were committed by the various players involved.

Deal 1
Normally, against no-trump contracts, in the absence of a bid from partner, the defender on lead leads "the fourth from the highest in his longest and strongest suit." But there are times when one's judgment, grounded to his sense of hearing, dictates that the book lead is not called for. Such was the case in this deal —but our South defender either wasn't paying attention to what was being said or he just wasn't listening at all.

Neither side vulnerable. North deals.

```
                        NORTH
                    ♠ K Q 10 7
                    ♥ A K 3
                    ♦ A J 10
                    ♣ K 7 3
        WEST                                EAST
    ♠ 6 5 3                             ♠ A 9 2
    ♥ 8 4                               ♥ J 10 9 6
    ♦ 9 8 5                             ♦ K 7 3 2
    ♣ A Q 10 5 4                        ♣ 9 8
                        SOUTH
                    ♠ J 8 4
                    ♥ Q 7 5 2
                    ♦ Q 6 4
                    ♣ J 6 2
```

The bidding:

NORTH	EAST	SOUTH	WEST
1 ♠	Pass	1 NT	Pass
3 NT	Pass	Pass	Pass

Opening lead: Five of ♣.

The three of clubs was played from dummy on West's opening lead of the club five, and East's eight was taken by South's jack. A low spade was then led, the board's king being taken by East's ace. It mattered not what East now returned. If it was a club, then dummy's king would become declarer's ninth trick. If, instead, he played back, say, a heart, declarer would make his ninth trick either by establishing dummy's king of clubs or by taking the diamond finesse, thus creating a second winner in diamonds. Once West had led his fourth-highest club at trick one, the defenders were doomed to defeat. And West made a mistake when he opened the club five. Let us see why.

South's one-no-trump response was purely a negative bid, promising absolutely nothing in the way of stoppers in the unbid suits. Therefore when North bid three no-trump, he rated to have a 19 to 21-point hand *with protection in each of the unbid suits*. Thus, as West looked at his hand, he should have realized that North almost surely possessed the king of clubs. Where the jack was, West of course didn't have the slightest idea.

West's opening lead should have been the queen of clubs, putting *North* in the position of winning the trick with the king. If South happened to possess the jack of clubs (if it was East, it would be even better), then West would retain the A 10 of clubs behind South's jack. And if East obtained the lead, a club return by him would entrap South's jack.

In the actual setup, assuming that North's king of clubs won the opening lead, declarer would now attack the spade suit, recognizing that unless he established this suit, he could not fulfill his contract. East would take the ace and return his remaining club. South's doubleton J 6 would now be entrapped by West's A 10 5 4, and West would make four club tricks.

Of course, if on the lead of the club queen, declarer did not put up dummy's king, it would be a different story. In this case, the defenders could not make more than two club tricks, one spade, and one diamond, for while West could establish his suit by continuing it at trick two, he had no outside entry subsequently to obtain the lead for the cashing of his clubs.

However, the point of the deal is not whether declarer would have been gifted enough not to put up the club king on the queen. The point is, simply, that it had to be wrong for West to have led his fourth-from-the-highest club instead of the queen.

Deal 2

In most of the deals that come up during the course of any afternoon's or evening's play, the sole clue as to what one's opening lead should be is not based merely on one's sense of sight (that is, by looking at his own hand), but by interpreting the bidding of the opponents and/or his partner. After all, when the opponents have purchased the contract, the defender on lead will usually not have something like the A K Q J in some suit.

In this deal our West defender was confronted with a bidding situation that does not arise too frequently, but nevertheless arises often enough to justify its presentation and analysis.

North-South vulnerable. South deals.

NORTH
♠ K J 9 3
♥ J 6 2
♦ 8 3
♣ 9 6 4 2

WEST
♠ A Q 10 8 7 5
♥ K 3
♦ 9 5
♣ K 10 5

EAST
♠ 4
♥ Q 10 9 8 7 5 4
♦ 6 2
♣ 8 7 3

SOUTH
♠ 6 2
♥ A
♦ A K Q J 10 7 4
♣ A Q J

The bidding:

SOUTH	WEST	NORTH	EAST
2 ♦	2 ♠	Double	3 ♥
5 ♦	Pass	Pass	Pass

Opening lead: King of ♥.

In justification of South's bid of five diamonds, all one can say
is that he didn't want to lose his 150 in honors. If there were no
such thing as honors, he surely would have bid three no-trump,
since he had nine guaranteed tricks in his own hand, and partner,
for his penalty double of West's two-spade overcall, certainly had
a stopper in spades.

However, his five-diamond call turned out to be a profitable
venture. After he had won the opening lead with his ace, he picked
up the outstanding trumps in two rounds. He then led a spade,
and West took his ace. Eventually West made his king of clubs,
and declarer scored a winning rubber, including the 150 in
honors. And I trust that he thanked West for his assistance, since
West could (and should) have defeated the five-diamond contract.

It is accepted procedure (at least among the better players) that
when partner makes an overcall at the one or two level and gets
doubled for penalties, the overcaller's partner does not flee to

another suit if he possesses *two or more cards* in the overcaller's suit—and especially does this hold true when the "rescuer's flight" takes him to the next-higher level. Over North's double of *two* spades, East did run to *three* hearts.

If West had been aware of this bit of philosophy, he would not have opened the king of hearts at trick one, for he would have recognized that East rated to have either one spade or no spades whatsoever. If he had opened the ace of spades and then followed up by leading a second spade, East would have ruffed the latter lead.

As is evident, declarer would eventually have had to lose another trick to West's king of clubs and thus incur a one-trick set. His only solace would have been that he would get credit for his 150 in honors and thus secure a plus score of 50 points on the deal.

But, again, West failed to attach the proper significance to East's retreat to three hearts.

Deal 3

In this deal we have a recurring type of situation in which a couple of "uncard-reading" defenders played automatically, without having paid the slightest attention to the bidding of partner. The consequence, in situations such as these, is almost always the same: declarer ends up with a profit instead of taking a loss. This deal is a case in point.

Neither side vulnerable. North deals.

NORTH
♠ A K Q 9
♥ 9 7 4 3
♦ 9 5 4
♣ 8 3

WEST
♠ 8 6 5 2
♥ —
♦ Q J 8 3
♣ K J 9 6 4

EAST
♠ 7 4
♥ A 6
♦ A K 10 7 2
♣ Q 10 5 2

SOUTH
♠ J 10 3
♥ K Q J 10 8 5 2
♦ 6
♣ A 7

The bidding:

NORTH	EAST	SOUTH	WEST
Pass	1 ♦	1 ♥	3 ♦
3 ♥	4 ♦	4 ♥	5 ♦
5 ♥	Pass	Pass	Pass

Opening lead: Queen of ♦.

After West's queen of diamonds had won the opening lead (East playing the two-spot), he continued with the diamond three. East put up his king and South ruffed.

Declarer next led the king of trumps, and East took the trick with his ace. East then led the two of clubs, upon which South promptly put up his ace. It was now a routine matter for declarer to pick up East's remaining trump, after which he cashed four spade tricks, discarding his losing seven of clubs on dummy's fourth spade. Thus his only two losers were a trump and a diamond.

It is apparent that if West had shifted to a club at trick two, declarer would have gone down, for he would have been unable to avoid the loss of a club trick. And West should be faulted for his failure to lead a club at trick two. After all, East had rebid the diamond suit at the four level, and he surely rated to have five cards in that suit. Hence West should have figured out that South had no more diamonds. And even if West had given his card-reading judgment a rest for a moment, his sense of sight should have told him that a club lead was called for at trick two: East had played the deuce of diamonds at trick one, thereby denoting no interest in the continuation of the suit he had bid twice.

But, in my opinion, East was more at fault than West. Surely West, for his jump to three diamonds, held at least four diamonds, and possibly five. Hence, as East should have viewed the setup, South possessed a *maximum* of one diamond.

East, therefore, should have overtaken West's queen of diamonds with his ace, in order to lead a club. Had he done so, the defenders would have established a club trick before East's ace of trumps was driven out. Declarer would now have been compelled to lose three tricks, and his contract.

Deal 4

The theme of this deal is virtually identical with the theme of the preceding one—only the cards and the characters have been changed. As will be observed, East and West were both guilty in permitting declarer to fulfill his slam contract. West was at fault for ignoring his partner's signal, and East was at fault for giving the signal instead of taking more positive action. At the conclusion of play each screamed at the other for being stupid. And each of them was right.

North-South vulnerable. East deals.

NORTH
♠ 9 4
♥ K 10 2
♦ 8 6 5
♣ K J 9 8 2

WEST
♠ Q 10 7 5 2
♥ J 8 6 4
♦ K Q 3
♣ 5

EAST
♠ A K J 8 3
♥ —
♦ A J 10 9 7 2
♣ 6 4

SOUTH
♠ 6
♥ A Q 9 7 5 3
♦ 4
♣ A Q 10 7 3

The bidding:

EAST	SOUTH	WEST	NORTH
1 ♦	1 ♥	Pass	Pass
1 ♠	2 ♣	3 ♠	4 ♣
4 ♠	5 ♣	Pass	Pass
5 ♠	6 ♣	Double	Pass
Pass	Pass		

Opening lead: King of ♦.

On West's opening lead of the diamond king, East followed suit
with the discouraging deuce. Ignoring East's "no interest" signal,
West nevertheless persisted in the diamond suit, laying down the
queen at trick two. South ruffed this lead, after which the king
and ace of trumps gathered in the three outstanding pieces.

When declarer next cashed the ace of hearts, East discarded a
diamond. It now became a routine matter to lead a low heart and
finesse dummy's ten-spot, with the assurance that it would win the
trick. Then followed the king of hearts, after which declarer returned to the South hand via the trump ten.

The queen of hearts now felled West's jack, and on his two remaining hearts dummy's two spades were discarded. After he next
trumped his only spade, South claimed his slam contract.

West made the initial mistake when, at trick two, he led the queen of diamonds. On the opening lead of the king, East had played the most discouraging diamond in the deck, the deuce. Certainly, if East, who had opened the bidding with one diamond, had wanted diamonds to be continued, he would have gotten his fingers on some diamond other than the deuce. Hence, whether West shifted to a spade or to a heart at trick two, he certainly could not have been accused of stupidity.

Actually, of course, East wanted West to lead a heart at trick two, since East could trump that lead. Had an expert been sitting in the West seat, he might have come up with the heart lead, since South, who had made an overcall in hearts on a suit that was lacking both the king and the jack, certainly rated to have at least five hearts, and possibly six. So it would have been a distinct possibility (in the mind of an expert West) that East might well be void of hearts. But, in the actual setup, East knew that West was not of expert caliber—and East should have realized that the chances of West's leading a heart at trick two were virtually nil (unless West happened to possess *five* hearts, in which case he *might* have figured out that East was void of hearts) .

In my opinion, based in part on the foregoing, East was unquestionably the guiltier of the two defenders. I believe that it is accepted practice that when the opponents are in a doubled slam contract, and you are just about certain that you can beat them one trick, you *never* try to beat them two tricks if in so trying you might be giving them a chance to fulfill the slam.

From East's position, his card-reading sense should have told him that South's bidding had indicated that the latter possessed a two-suited hand in hearts and clubs, and that there existed the real danger that South might fulfill the slam contract if a diamond was continued at trick two.

To avoid the possibility of this happening, East certainly should have taken the initiative and not simply made a negative signal by playing the deuce of diamonds. Instead, he should have overtaken his partner's king with his ace. He would then have laid down the spade king, to defeat the slam contract.

It may be argued by some that the overtaking of West's king with the ace, in order to cash the spade king, could have been the wrong play if South had held, for example:

        ♠ —
        ♥ A Q x x x x
        ♦ x x
        ♣ A Q x x x

True, in this setup it would have been the wrong play. But if South had held this hand, then West would have possessed six spades consisting of the Q 10 7 6 5 2, plus the diamond king which West had led at trick one, plus *at least* four hearts (which a good card-reading East would have known that West possessed, since South rated to have a maximum of six hearts in his hand). With this hand, containing six trumps within an unbalanced hand, surely West, having passed initially, would have bid four spades (not vulnerable against vulnerable opponents) instead of the three-spade call he actually did make. Hence South assuredly held at least one spade in his hand.

Deal 5

The first four deals in this chapter have been concerned with the play to trick one. In these deals either the illogical lead was made or the partner of the leader erred in not applying card reading and/or judgment to the specific situation at hand.

In this deal we have another illustration of card misreading made by East, the partner of the opening leader. Before presenting what did happen at the table, allow me to put you into the East seat, to see whether you can work out correctly the problem that confronted our actual defender.

The bidding has proceeded:

SOUTH	WEST	NORTH	EAST
2 ♠	Pass	3 ♥	Pass
3 ♠	Pass	4 ♠	Pass
4 NT	Pass	5 ♦	Pass
6 ♠	Pass	Pass	Pass

Your partner, West, opens the three of diamonds, and you find yourself looking at:

NORTH

♠ Q 5
♥ A Q 6 2
♦ 8 6 5 4 2
♣ J 9

EAST

♠ 7
♥ J 10 8 3
♦ A J 10 9
♣ A Q 8 4

The diamond deuce is played from the dummy, you put up your ace, and South follows suit with the diamond king.

You then promptly reach for the ace of clubs, are about to play it for the setting trick, when a little voice (Miss Card Reading) whispers in your ear: "STOP! THINK!" So you stop, begin to think —and to do some card reading.

En route to his slam, South has employed the Blackwood Slam Convention, and has learned that North possesses one ace. South then has bid the slam. Is it really conceivable that South would have bid the slam with a singleton king of diamonds *and* a singleton club? With these two minor-suit losers staring him in the face, would not South have stopped at five spades, especially when he was certain, on the given bidding, that West figured to lead a diamond or a club at trick one?

Continuing your card reading, as you look at your hand and dummy, you see three aces. Thus you know that South has bid the slam knowing that his partnership is lacking two aces. Is it not correct to come to the conclusion that South must be void of clubs, and that South has assumed that the ace which his partner has is the heart ace, the suit which the latter bid? Surely South would not have bid the slam with a void in hearts, for North's presumed heart ace would, in this case, be worthless to South, since the defenders would have it in their power to cash the first two tricks. So you arrive at the conclusion that if you play the ace of clubs at trick two, that card will be ruffed by South.

You now reflect on the significance of partner's opening lead of the three of diamonds, and the fall of South's king. What is the diamond setup around the table?

Well, on the face of it, it looks as if partner had opened his third-highest diamond, from the Q 7 3. He could not have had the doubleton 7 3 (which would give South the doubleton K Q at the outset), for with this holding West would have led the seven-spot, the top card of a worthless doubleton. So West's lead of the three must be from either the tripleton Q 7 3, or . . . ?

The only other plausible construction that can be placed on partner's three-spot is that it is a singleton—and that declarer has falsecarded with the king from an original holding of K Q 7. Admittedly, this is wishful thinking on your part, but it is a possibility. And the more you reflect, the more this possibility becomes a reality, for what other hope do you have of defeating South's slam contract? As we agreed, surely not with a club lead. By observation of your own hand and dummy, surely not with a heart lead. A trump lead is, obviously, hopeless. By a process of elimination, therefore, you indulge in the wishful thinking that South was not telling the truth when he played the king of diamonds on the opening lead.

Thus it comes to pass that you place the jack of diamonds on the table at trick two. These were the four hands:

NORTH
♠ Q 5
♥ A Q 6 2
♦ 8 6 5 4 2
♣ J 9

WEST
♠ 9 3
♥ 9 7 5
♦ 3
♣ K 10 7 6 5 3 2

EAST
♠ 7
♥ J 10 8 3
♦ A J 10 9
♣ A Q 8 4

SOUTH
♠ A K J 10 8 6 4 2
♥ K 4
♦ K Q 7
♣ —

As is evident, when South covers your jack with the queen, your partner ruffs, for the setting trick.

As is equally evident, had you attempted to cash your club ace at trick two, declarer would have ruffed. He would then have drawn trumps, after which he would have cashed the king, ace, and queen of hearts. On the latter lead, he would have discarded his losing seven of diamonds. And it is my sad duty to report that when the deal arose in actual combat, our East defender, upon winning the opening lead with his ace of diamonds, immediately plunked the ace of clubs on the table. He got what he deserved, no more and no less. But I do feel sorry for his partner, who had to pay half of the losses.

The discussion of this deal would not be complete without saying a few words about South's excellent false-card of the diamond king. Had he mechanically followed suit with the seven-spot, he would have had no chance for survival. In this case, East (despite his obvious inadequacy at card reading) would have known that West was not leading the diamond three from a holding of K 3, Q 3, or K Q 3. Hence the only possible interpretation that East could have placed on West's lead would be that it had to be a singleton—and East would promptly have returned a diamond.

Of course South's false-card of the diamond king was based on card reading. From his position, looking at eight diamonds in the North-South hands, declarer was fully aware that West's three of diamonds figured to be a singleton. It couldn't be the top of a worthless doubleton, since the diamond deuce was reposing in dummy. Hence declarer recognized that his sole hope was to deceive the East defender. As was observed, he accomplished his objective.

From South's position, the false-card of the diamond king could never be a losing play, since South was cognizant of the fact that he could always discard his seven of diamonds on dummy's queen of hearts. Actually, of course, he did so.

At this point I believe that a few words on deceptive tactics are in order. It goes without saying that the primary reason that the experts are such consistent winners is that they possess great technical skill in both bidding and play. But the fact remains that the possession and application of all the relevant technical knowledge is not in itself sufficient to make one a really good player. One simply cannot become top-notch until he has learned how to deceive.

After all, if one reflects on it (and thinks of the deal just presented) , situations continually arise where skillful play—and even perfect intuition—are not enough to fulfill a given contract. And when observation reveals that one is destined to accept the bitter pangs of defeat if the opponents play correctly, his only salvation lies in the hope that he can trick them into playing incorrectly. So deceptive tactics must be employed not merely for self-protection on any given deal but, in the long run, for self-preservation.

This deceit is, of course, available to both the declarer and the defenders. In practice, declarer gets greater mileage out of his deceptive tactics than do the defenders, for the declarer has an advantage in this area; he has no thinking partner he can fool, for his partner is the passive dummy. Thus declarer has more freedom of action, and more worry-free opportunities, for utilizing deceptive tactics.

The defenders, on the other hand, must be much more selective in picking their spots to employ deception, for a deceptive play made by a defender to deceive declarer may boomerang; it may easily mislead partner as to the true state of affairs and cause him to misdefend in the ensuing play. To deceive partner is not deception—it is sabotage.

Thus, appreciating the position that in virtually all deals declarer is quite apt to indulge in chicanery, when one is a defender he must always be on the lookout for a "dishonest" declarer. And a defender must cultivate the habit of never automatically accepting a declarer's play at face value, since the declarer will always be trying to create an erroneous impression in the minds of the defenders.

As an example of a successful bit of trickery by a declarer, observe the deal that follows. The hand arose in a tournament held in New York City in 1971. In retrospect, the deception should not have succeeded. The fact of the matter, however, is that it did.

Deal 6

In this deal there is featured a classic type of deception, in which psychology forms the foundation. It is an accepted psychological fact that when a declarer immediately attacks some suit, the defenders, when they obtain the lead, will shy away from leading that suit. After all, if the declarer appears to have a very positive interest in developing a suit, the defenders certainly are not going to help him. The appreciation of this point enabled our South declarer to capitalize on it.

North-South vulnerable. North deals.

```
                      NORTH
                    ♠ K Q J 4
                    ♥ A 5 3
                    ♦ J 7 4
                    ♣ A 10 6
      WEST                                   EAST
   ♠ 10 8 7 2                             ♠ 9 6
   ♥ 8                                    ♥ J 10 9 6 2
   ♦ Q 8 3                                ♦ A K 9 2
   ♣ 7 5 4 3 2                            ♣ K 8
                      SOUTH
                    ♠ A 5 3
                    ♥ K Q 7 4
                    ♦ 10 6 5
                    ♣ Q J 9
```

The bidding:

NORTH	EAST	SOUTH	WEST
1 ♣	1 ♥	2 NT	Pass
3 NT	Pass	Pass	Pass

Opening lead: Eight of ♥.

Upon viewing dummy after West had opened the eight of hearts, declarer perceived that he had just eight tricks. He realized also that the club finesse figured to lose, since East, for his overcall on a jack-high suit, rated to have the club king. And if East obtained the lead with this card, he might well shift to a diamond.

So South, hoping to prevent the shift to diamonds, which would be disastrous to him, captured the opening lead with dummy's ace of hearts—and promptly led the jack of diamonds! East, upon winning the trick with his king, never gave even a passing thought to returning a diamond, for it surely appeared that South was trying to create winners in this suit.

At trick three East played back the jack of hearts, hoping in time to establish two heart winners for himself. South took this trick with his king, after which he led the queen of clubs. After taking his king, East came back with the ten of hearts—and South had his contracted-for nine tricks: four spades, three hearts, and two clubs.

South's deception was well conceived. If he had won the opening heart lead with his king or queen and then had taken the club finesse, he almost surely would have gone down. After capturing the trick with his king, East, glancing at the dummy, would have recognized that if declarer had any weak spot it was in diamonds. A shift to a diamond by East would now have enabled the defenders to have cashed four tricks in this suit.

Without taking anything away from declarer's timely trickery, the fact nevertheless remains that the defenders should have defeated the contract. Specifically, it was East who was responsible for declarer's success.

Certainly East cannot be faulted for having failed to lead a diamond at trick three (after he had captured dummy's jack of diamonds with his king). But when South, after winning trick three with the king of hearts, then led a club and took the finesse, East, upon winning with the king, should have asked himself, Why isn't South continuing his attack on the diamond suit?

I think that if this question had been asked, the answer would have suggested itself: South must be weak in diamonds and must be trying to create the impression that he isn't. A shift to a diamond is now in order.

Deal 7

In the average bridge game a fair assumption for each player to make would be that his opponents are not the most brilliant players in the world. Conversely, it is an equally fair assumption for each player, in this hypothetical average game, to appreciate that neither of his opponents is a downright stupid player (unless previous occasions have demonstrated quite clearly that this is a fact).

In this deal both East and South were slightly better-than-average players—and each of them should have known this, since they had played together on numerous previous occasions. But somehow, during the early stages of play, the East defender suddenly assumed that either South was just plain stupid, that he had lost control of his senses temporarily, or that he had committed a flagrant, unbelievable error. And once East made this assumption, he just became a loser.

Both sides vulnerable. South deals.

NORTH
♠ 8 4 3
♥ K J 9 8 5
♦ 9 7 2
♣ A 7

WEST
♠ J 9 7 5 2
♥ 6 3
♦ Q 8 4
♣ 6 4 2

EAST
♠ Q 10 6
♥ A 7 4 2
♦ K 5 3
♣ K 9 5

SOUTH
♠ A K
♥ Q 10
♦ A J 10 6
♣ Q J 10 8 3

The bidding:

SOUTH	WEST	NORTH	EAST
1 ♣	Pass	1 ♥	Pass
2 NT	Pass	3 NT	Pass
Pass	Pass		

Opening lead: Five of ♠.

After South's king of spades had captured East's queen on the opening lead, he led the queen of hearts, which won the trick. He then played the ten of hearts, dummy following suit with the eight-spot. Once again East declined to take his ace.

South now heaved a sigh of relief. He next led a club to the board's ace, after which he returned a club. East played low and South's queen captured the trick. The jack of clubs was led next,

East's king winning. When play had ended, South had his contracted-for nine tricks: two spades, two hearts, one diamond, and
four clubs.

Had East taken his ace of hearts on either the first or second
lead of that suit, and returned a spade, thereby establishing West's
spade suit, declarer would have incurred a one-trick set. In this
case, he would have made two spade tricks, four hearts, one diamond, and just one club.

The guilt for the failure to defeat South's contract must be
placed squarely on East's shoulders. His "technical" error came
when he refused to take his ace of hearts on South's second lead
of that suit. His reason for not taking his ace is a simple one to
understand—but not to justify.

When West had followed suit to the second heart lead, as did
dummy with the eight-spot, basic, elementary counting told East
that South had no more hearts (dummy had five hearts originally,
East had four, and both South and West had each followed suit to
the first two heart leads). Therefore, East said to himself, if he
declined to win South's second heart lead, he would automatically
prevent the establishing *and* cashing of dummy's heart suit. This
had to be, since dummy had but one outside entry, the club ace.
And if declarer used that card to get to dummy to lead another
heart, driving out East's ace, never again could he return there to
cash the remaining hearts.

As was stated, East must have assumed that South was stupid, or
that he had made an error when he failed to overtake his own ten
with the board's jack of hearts. East was, of course, very wrong,
primarily because he knew from past experiences that South was
not stupid. Surely if South were interested in developing dummy's
heart suit, he would, *at no cost,* have overtaken his ten with
dummy's jack in order to continue playing the suit to create four
winners. His failure to do so had to mean just one thing: that
South was hoping that his ten-spot would be permitted to win the
second heart lead.

So, very simply, South tried to create the impression that he had
pulled a boner—and East fell for it, hook, line, and sinker.

One final statement regarding the area of card reading. From a
purely technical point of view, card reading is defined as "drawing the correct inferences about the nature of an opponent's high-

card holding and/or distribution, said inferences being obtained from either the bidding, the fall of the cards, or both." But merely "drawing the correct inferences" is an academic concept, for these inferences are not sufficient to yield the optimum result unless they are put to practical, intelligent use. And this our East defender did not do in the above deal.

Deal 8

In this final "dereliction of card-reading duty by a defender" deal, our East defender found himself in a perfect position to do some practical card reading at trick one. But, judging from his unhesitating and automatic play at trick two, he failed to indulge in any card reading whatsoever. The result was a "normal" one under such circumstances: South fulfilled a contract that should have been defeated.

Once again, allow me to put you into the East seat and to confront you with the situation that faced our actual East defender. With neither side vulnerable, the bidding has proceeded:

SOUTH	WEST	NORTH	EAST
2 NT	Pass	3 ♥	Pass
3 NT	Pass	Pass	Pass

```
              NORTH
          ♠ 6
          ♥ Q J 8 5 2
          ♦ 7 5 4
          ♣ J 9 6 3
                          EAST
                      ♠ A 4 2
                      ♥ K 10 3
                      ♦ Q 10 8 2
                      ♣ 8 7 4
```

Opening lead: Three of ♠.

Your partner, West, opens the three of spades, the six is played from dummy, and you capture the trick with your ace as South follows suit with the spade five. Let us assemble the facts which you have in your possession at this moment.

First, the dummy has four high-card points, and you have nine in your own hand. That adds up to 13. South, for his two-no-trump opening bid, has promised 22 to 24 high-card points. Thus, this subtotal comes to 35 to 37 high-card points in the North, East, and South hands. That means that your partner, West, possesses 3 to 5 high-card points.

Second, your partner has opened the three of spades, as his fourth-from-the-highest spade. You possess the deuce. Therefore your partner started with *exactly* four spades—*and declarer was dealt five spades.*

The above, then, are the basic facts. Where do you go from here?

Well, if your partner's five points (his theoretical maximum) consist of the king and queen of spades, then a spade return by you would enable your side to win three spade tricks immediately. But this wouldn't do you much good (if your objective is to defeat declarer's contract) , since declarer, who had five spades originally, would now have his fourth and fifth spades as winners. And, frankly, if your partner happens to have the king and queen of spades, then declarer has the jack of spades, the ace of hearts, the A K J of diamonds, and the A K Q of clubs, which, combined with what you see in dummy, is more than enough to give declarer his contract. And if you hope that perhaps your partner has the K Q 10 3 of spades, forget it. If he had this combination, he would have led the king originally, not the three-spot. As you sit in the East seat, pondering over what to return at trick two, you should indulge in the hope that partner doesn't have the king and queen of spades. If he does, your side was predestined to defeat.

Going further, in terms of card reading through the application of judgment and imagination, you do feel in your heart that partner, who has 3 to 5 high-card points, doesn't really figure to have, specifically, the king and queen of spades. If he has, let us say, the K x x x or the Q x x x, a spade return by you at trick two will develop a spade trick for partner, but simultaneously *it will create three spade winners for declarer.*

Thus, if you play back a spade, either you will establish three spade winners for declarer immediately, or you will assist him in the development of three spade tricks. So you do not return part-

ner's spade suit at trick two, since you are in business for yourself
and not for declarer.

Looking at dummy, you recognize the futility of leading either
a heart or a club, for no matter what declarer or partner has (or
rates to have) in these suits, you will be helping declarer. By a
process of elimination, you lead a diamond—and things work out
beautifully. These were the four hands:

NORTH

- ♠ 6
- ♥ Q J 8 5 2
- ♦ 7 5 4
- ♣ J 9 6 3

WEST

- ♠ K 9 7 3
- ♥ 9 7 4
- ♦ J 9 6 3
- ♣ K 5

EAST

- ♠ A 4 2
- ♥ K 10 3
- ♦ Q 10 8 2
- ♣ 8 7 4

SOUTH

- ♠ Q J 10 8 5
- ♥ A 6
- ♦ A K
- ♣ A Q 10 2

With your diamond return, declarer is now en route to defeat.
He wins the trick with his king, and leads the queen of spades.
West takes this with his king, and continues his attack on the diamond suit, driving out South's ace. Declarer's cause is now lost,
since he must lose (as a minimum) two spades, two diamonds,
and a club to West's king.

It is my unhappy duty to report that when this deal was actually
played, our East defender had no problem whatsoever. He captured
the opening lead with his ace of spades and, quick as a flash, he
returned a spade, South's queen being taken by West's king. When
West next played back the spade seven, South took the trick with
his eight. Now followed the ace of clubs and then the queen of
clubs, West taking his king.

Later on, declarer entered dummy via the club jack, and took
the heart finesse successfully. At the conclusion of play, he had

made ten tricks: three spades, two hearts, two diamonds, and three clubs.

If the reader will look back at the South hand, he will observe that South did not possess the 22 to 24 high-card points normally associated with an opening bid of two no-trump. All he had were 20 high-card points. Such misbids will, of course, happen on occasion (or more often).

Nevertheless, when you are defending a hand, you should always assume that declarer has a hand consistent with his bidding, and base your thinking and subsequent action on this premise. At times you will misdiagnose the true situation, since you will be applying logical reasoning in interpreting what happened to be an illogical bid. But far more often than not you will be a winner thereby, for declarer will have what he was supposed to have had (and what his partner *expected him to have*).

13

The Declarer
Fails to Card-Read

In each of the deals that constitute this chapter, our South declarer went down to defeat at a game or slam contract. In each case, he was solely responsible for his demise—it was not a case of "circumstances beyond his control," or a matter of being "wrecked on the rocks of distribution," or any other excuse. And in each deal his defeat could be attributed directly to either (1) his failure to do any card reading, (2) his failure to card-read intelligently, or (3) his inability to "create" the conditions via which success could be assured. The latter situation is the theme of this first deal.

Deal 1

This deal is the toughest one contained in this chapter, and 99 percent of our nation's players, had they been in the South seat, would have been excused for having failed to fulfill the contract. But our actual declarer happened to be a fairly good bridge player, and his major crime in the play would not be that (in my opinion) he failed to give an all-out effort, but rather that, at the completion of trick three, he made a statement that no player should ever make during the first few tricks: "I'm down one." He then faced his remaining cards on the table. The opponents accepted his settlement of 100 points.

The fact that he could have fulfilled his contract is, for the moment, a secondary issue. Even if he felt that he had no chance of making his contract, he nevertheless should have played on. After all, there are times when the opponents can commit unbelievable blunders, and there are days when they do things such as revoking. And, at the risk of sounding naïve, games and slams made because the opponents erred or blundered (or revoked) count exactly as much as games or slams brought home safely through brilliant technical execution.

As was stated, this deal is a tough one. Would you like to try your hand at playing it?

You are sitting South, vulnerable, and the bidding has proceeded:

NORTH	EAST	SOUTH	WEST
Pass	Pass	1 ♠	Pass
3 ♠	Pass	4 NT	Pass
5 ♥	Pass	6 ♠	Pass
Pass	Pass		

West opens the jack of diamonds, and you find yourself looking at:

NORTH
♠ J 6 5 3
♥ Q 7 4
♦ A 9 5
♣ A 7 3

Opening lead: Jack of ♦.

SOUTH
♠ A K 7 4 2
♥ A K 10
♦ K 7
♣ K 6 5

West's jack of diamonds lead is taken by your king, after which you cash the ace and king of trumps. When West discards a low club on the second trump lead, you have just become the recipient of the discouraging news that East has a sure trump winner in his queen.

As you survey your combined assets, your club loser stands out like a sore thumb. Also, observation reveals that there is simply no place where you can park it, for there is absolutely nothing in dummy that can be built up as a winner, and the law forbids you to dispose of it by throwing it on the floor.

It was at this point that our actual South declarer put his hand face up on the table and stated: "I'm down one."

Admittedly, as you view the setup confronting you, there is nothing to stand up and cheer about. However, there is a ray of hope, a hope which would be found by the expert player. Can you isolate this hope and put it to practical use?

This was the actual setup:

NORTH
♠ J 6 5 3
♥ Q 7 4
♦ A 9 5
♣ A 7 3

WEST
♠ 9
♥ 8 6 3
♦ J 10 8 4
♣ Q 10 9 8 2

EAST
♠ Q 10 8
♥ J 9 5 2
♦ Q 6 3 2
♣ J 4

SOUTH
♠ A K 7 4 2
♥ A K 10
♦ K 7
♣ K 6 5

To review, you have won the opening diamond lead with your king, after which you have cashed your two top trumps, leaving East with the high queen. You next cash the queen, king, and ace of hearts, noting with satisfaction that East follows suit to all three leads. Then comes the ace of diamonds, and this is followed by dummy's remaining diamond, which you ruff. You next lead a club to dummy's ace, after which you return a club to your king, leaving this position:

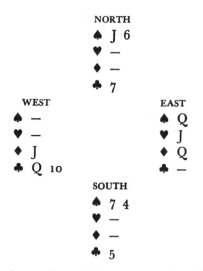

NORTH
♠ J 6
♥ —
♦ —
♣ 7

WEST
♠ —
♥ —
♦ J
♣ Q 10

EAST
♠ Q
♥ J
♦ Q
♣ —

SOUTH
♠ 7 4
♥ —
♦ —
♣ 5

You now lead your four of trumps, putting East into the lead. As is apparent, East has no option but to lead either the jack of hearts or the queen of diamonds. Whichever he leads, you are home, for you will discard your losing five of clubs as you simultaneously ruff the trick with the board's remaining trump.

Unquestionably, you were lucky to fulfill your contract. If East had had a third club to lead, the defenders would have made a club trick. But what alternative did you have except to indulge in the wishful thinking that East had been dealt no more than two clubs—and then to proceed to play the hand on the assumption that your hope was a reality?

Deal 2

This deal features a simple but recurring type of card-reading situation in which a defender tries to outwit a declarer by attempting to create a certain impression in the latter's mind. Usually this attempt to deceive is accomplished via a false-card, and it is up to declarer to diagnose whether the false-card is truly a false-card or whether it was an honest play.

As you observe declarer's seduction in this deal, it should be appreciated that the participants were below-average players. In these circumstances, South should not be censured too severely for his soon-to-be-observed naïveté.

Both sides vulnerable. North deals.

NORTH
♠ A K Q
♥ A K 6 4
♦ Q J 4
♣ K J 7

WEST		EAST
♠ 9 7 5 3		♠ 10 8 2
♥ Q J 10 8		♥ 9 7 3
♦ 7 2		♦ 6 5
♣ A 8 3		♣ Q 10 9 6 2

SOUTH
♠ J 6 4
♥ 5 2
♦ A K 10 9 8 3
♣ 5 4

The bidding:

NORTH	EAST	SOUTH	WEST
2 NT	Pass	6 ♦	Pass
Pass	Pass		

Opening lead: Queen of ♥.

West's queen of hearts was captured by dummy's king, after which declarer cashed the queen and ace of trumps. He then led a heart to dummy's ace, and he followed up by ruffing a heart. Next came a spade to dummy's queen, after which the king and ace of spades were cashed.

The board's remaining heart was now ruffed. On this lead East discarded the *nine of clubs*. South then led the four of clubs out of his own hand, and when West followed suit with the three, declarer promptly put up dummy's jack. East took this with his queen and made haste to return a club to West's ace. Of course, if dummy's king of clubs had been put up on the initial club lead, that card would have won the trick; and it would have given declarer his slam.

In theory, declarer was confronted with a pure guess in the club suit. If West possessed the club queen, then the play of dummy's jack would be the winning one. If West had the club ace, then the play of the board's king would give declarer his twelfth trick (and, of course, if *East* had the ace and queen, then declarer would automatically lose two tricks in clubs) .

In my opinion, declarer was influenced unduly by East's come-on discard of the nine of clubs on the lead of dummy's fourth heart. I know this to be a fact because he told me so. Actually, he should have paid no attention whatsoever to East's discard, for it was a meaningless one.

After declarer had drawn trumps and ruffed the third heart lead, it was perfectly obvious to everyone at the table that the success of South's contract was going to depend on how he guessed to play the club suit, and that East, if he elected to discard a club somewhere along the line, would toss away a low club whether he possessed the ace *or* queen. Therefore the fact that East had elected to go out of his way to get fancy by discarding the club nine should possibly have tipped off declarer that East did not have the ace, for if he had had it, he would just have sat back and minded his own business, thereby leaving South with an outright 50–50 guess to make.

I have dwelt on the rather obvious situation presented above for just one reason: at the conclusion of play, when I asked South why he had put up the jack of clubs so promptly, he answered: "Because of East's discard of the club nine. I thought East had the ace." Therefore, by his own admission, South was guilty of a failure to indulge in logical card reading.

Deal 3

In this deal, our South declarer overlooked (or forgot) a telltale clue that he had obtained in the early stages of play, and, instead, accepted as fact an inference that he had secured from a defender's play in the middle stages of the game. And I hope that nobody will shed any tears for South, for he committed the unpardonable error: he jeopardized his game contract in order to try for an overtrick.

Both sides vulnerable. North deals.

<pre>
                        NORTH
                     ♠ A 3
                     ♥ A 10 6 4
                     ♦ A Q 4
                     ♣ A Q J 2
        WEST   EAST
     ♠ K J 7 2   ♠ Q 10 4
     ♥ 9 7 3   ♥ 8 5 2
     ♦ 7 6 2   ♦ K 9 5 3
     ♣ 8 6 3   ♣ K 7 5
                        SOUTH
                     ♠ 9 8 6 5
                     ♥ K Q J
                     ♦ J 10 8
                     ♣ 10 9 4
</pre>

The bidding:

NORTH	EAST	SOUTH	WEST
1 ♥	Pass	1 NT	Pass
3 NT	Pass	Pass	Pass

Opening lead: Two of ♠.

The three of spades was played from dummy on West's opening lead of the deuce, and East captured the trick with his queen. East returned the ten of spades, the trick being won perforce by dummy's ace.

Declarer came to his own hand via the heart king, after which he took the club finesse, his ten losing to East's king. East now made what turned out to be the killing play: he made the safe return of a club, the trick being won by dummy's jack.

East's reason for the return of a club was an excellent one. He knew that his partner had started with exactly four spades, since the latter had led the deuce (as his fourth highest) originally. East felt (correctly, as can be observed) that the defenders' prospects of defeating the contract were slim, since South, who was known to have no high cards in clubs and diamonds (at most the jack in diamonds), rated to have the K Q or the K Q x of hearts. From East's position, it looked as if the defenders might get just three spades and their already won king of clubs, since declarer, in all probability, would make four heart tricks. Actually, of course, East had no guarantee that declarer would make four heart tricks (it would not have been the case if declarer had started with the doubleton K Q of hearts), but East's thinking was nevertheless in the right direction.

In making the safe or neutral lead of a club, East's purpose was to create in declarer's mind the belief that East had no more spades, the suit that West had led originally. And if East was able to convince declarer that the former had no more spades, then declarer might well take the diamond finesse, enabling East to make his king. Now East would return his remaining spade—and hope that West would be able to make two spade tricks.

Declarer fell for the bait. He concluded that East's failure to play back a spade (after winning his club king) indicated East's inability to do so. And since East had no more spades, South said to himself, then it must be safe to take the diamond finesse, for even if it lost, it would lose to the nondangerous East defender.

So declarer won East's club return at trick five with the board's jack, after which he reentered his own hand via the heart queen. He then led the jack of diamonds, and finessed against West's hoped-for king. Upon taking this trick with his king, East produced his "hidden" four of spades, and West now cashed his jack and king. Thus declarer went down, losing three spades, a club, and a diamond.

As was stated, declarer committed an unpardonable sin when he took the diamond finesse, for upon winning East's neutral return of a club, declarer had nine guaranteed tricks: one spade, four hearts, one diamond, and three clubs.

Declarer's other major error was in making the assumption that East had no more spades and, hence, that it was safe for him to take the diamond finesse.

Evidently declarer had failed to notice (or had ignored) West's opening lead of the *deuce* of spades (East didn't forget). Assuming that West was making an honest fourth-from-the-highest lead, the deuce announced that West had exactly four spades. Hence East had to have been dealt three spades—and East's failure to play back a spade at trick five indicated not that East had no more spades, but rather that East had an ulterior motive in playing back a club instead.

Deal 4

On most deals that arise during one's lifetime, declarer finds that he has a choice of optional methods of play. In many of these hands, the percentage in favor of one particular line of play, rather than another, is very slight. If one happens to be a good guesser or is lucky, he will bring home his contract.

But in quite a few of these deals where alternative methods of play present themselves, proper analysis (grounded in card reading) must be substituted for guesswork and luck. Here is one of those deals.

Both sides vulnerable. West deals.

```
                        NORTH
                    ♠ Q 10 8
                    ♥ Q 8
                    ♦ K 5
                    ♣ K J 10 9 6 4
        WEST                              EAST
    ♠ A 7 5 4 2                       ♠ 6 3
    ♥ K 6 3                           ♥ 7 4 2
    ♦ Q 7 2                           ♦ J 10 6 4 3
    ♣ A 8                             ♣ Q 7 2
                        SOUTH
                    ♠ K J 9
                    ♥ A J 10 9 5
                    ♦ A 9 8
                    ♣ 5 3
```

The bidding:	WEST	NORTH	EAST	SOUTH
	1 ♠	2 ♣	Pass	3 NT
	Pass	Pass	Pass	

Opening lead: Four of ♠.

When this deal arose in actual combat, declarer won the opening lead with the board's ten of spades, after which he led the queen of hearts and finessed. Upon capturing the trick with his king, West laid down the ace of spades, and followed up by leading another spade to South's king, East discarding a heart. All declarer now had were eight tricks: two spades, four hearts, and two diamonds—and he couldn't develop his ninth trick in clubs, for when he tried this, West took the club ace and cashed his two established spades.

Had South reflected on the bidding *before* playing to the first trick, he would have fulfilled his contract. For his first position opening bid, West figured to have the two outstanding aces and the heart king. And West certainly rated to have a five-card spade suit, since in this day and age (circa 1972) one rarely opens the bidding on a four-card spade suit consisting of the A x x x (declarer was looking at the K Q J 10 9 8 in his hand and dummy).

Based on the foregoing, South should have realized that the heart finesse would lose and that West would then persist in spades (as he did), thereby establishing his suit, with the club ace serving as a future entry for the cashing of the spades. As South played the hand, then, he figured to go down.

By making the sound assumption that West figured to be the possessor of the two black aces and the heart king, plus a five-card spade suit, a good South player would have fulfilled the contract. He would have won the opening spade lead with his jack, and would have led a low club. Assuming that West played low, the board's king would be put up. With the king winning, declarer would now lead the queen of hearts and finesse. West would win the trick with the king—and declarer would end up with nine tricks: two spades, four hearts, two diamonds, and one club.

If, when declarer led a club at trick two, West were to take his club ace, the result would be the same. He would clear the spade suit by cashing the ace and then leading a third round of spades. South, upon winning with his king, would now play his remaining club and take the finesse against the queen, secure in the knowledge that if East won the trick (as he would have), East would have no spade to return, and there would be no way to put West into the lead for the latter to cash his two remaining spades. And, again, declarer would have his contract made: two spades, one heart, two diamonds, and four clubs.

Deal 5

The key to the winning line of play in this deal lay in coming up with the correct answer to the question: "Why was East capturing a deuce with an ace when there appeared to be no valid reason for his so doing?" Although I cannot be absolutely certain of it, I'd bet dollars to doughnuts that our South declarer never even thought of the question. In all fairness to South, however, this is a tough hand to play properly.

Both sides vulnerable. South deals.

```
                    NORTH
                 ♠ Q 8 7 2
                 ♥ 9 6 3
                 ♦ 8 4 3 2
                 ♣ A K
      WEST                        EAST
   ♠ 9 6 4 3                   ♠ A J
   ♥ 7 5 4                     ♥ J 10 8 2
   ♦ K 10                      ♦ Q 9 7 6
   ♣ Q 10 8 2                  ♣ 6 5 3
                    SOUTH
                 ♠ K 10 5
                 ♥ A K Q
                 ♦ A J 5
                 ♣ J 9 7 4
```

The bidding:

SOUTH	WEST	NORTH	EAST
1 ♣	Pass	1 ♠	Pass
2 NT	Pass	3 NT	Pass
Pass	Pass		

Opening lead: Two of ♣.

After capturing the opening club lead with the board's king, South led the deuce of spades off dummy. East won this trick with his ace as South followed suit with the five-spot. East returned a club, driving out dummy's ace.

The seven of spades was now led, covered by East's jack, and taken by declarer's king. The ten of spades was cashed next. As is evident, dummy's high queen of spades was unreachable. When play had ended, declarer had but eight tricks, one short of his contract.

When declarer led the deuce of spades off dummy at trick two, and East rose with his ace, declarer should have asked himself the question, Why is East capturing the deuce with his ace? Two logical possibilities would have suggested themselves: (1) East has a singleton ace, in which case he has no choice in his play, or (2) East has the doubleton A J, and he doesn't want to waste the jack.

If the assumption is made that East possesses the doubleton A J, then declarer's winning play is to drop the ten-spot on East's ace. In this presumed setup, when South subsequently leads a spade to the king, he will fell East's jack. He could then lead his remaining five of spades and finesse the board's eight-spot, knowing that West possesses the nine. Declarer will now have three spade tricks and a fulfilled contract.

Actually, the dropping of South's ten of spades on East's ace could never be a losing play. If it turned out that East's ace of spades was a singleton (which would be revealed on South's next spade lead to his king), then all South could ever make in spades would be two tricks. That is, if he didn't drop the ten (leaving himself with the doubleton K 10), after he cashed the king and led the ten, West would cover with the jack (from a theoretical holding of J 9 6 4 3) and dummy's queen would win the trick. West's nine-spot would now be the top spade in the deck.

So, in retrospect, by applying card reading, South's play of the spade ten on East's ace stood to gain everything—and to lose nothing.

Deal 6

In 1951 the team of Sam Stayman, George Rapee, B. J. Becker, and John Crawford won the Vanderbilt Cup Championships. This is one of the deals that contributed to their victory. In it, both East defenders came up with two identical excellent plays. At the table where Stayman held the South hand, he was able—via card reading and perhaps a bit of luck—to parry East's thrust. But when the board was replayed with Crawford holding the East cards, the South declarer failed to indulge in the sort of card reading that is necessary to win championships.

Both sides vulnerable. East deals.

NORTH

♠ Q 7 3
♥ 5 2
♦ A Q J 10 7
♣ A J 5

WEST		EAST
♠ 2		♠ K J 5
♥ 10 9 7		♥ A K Q J 8 3
♦ 8 6 5 4		♦ 2
♣ 8 7 4 3 2		♣ Q 10 9

SOUTH

♠ A 10 9 8 6 4
♥ 6 4
♦ K 9 3
♣ K 6

The bidding:

EAST	SOUTH	WEST	NORTH
1 ♥	1 ♠	Pass	4 ♠
Pass	Pass	Pass

Opening lead: Ten of ♥.

The bidding sequence presented above was the same at both tables, as was the play to the first three tricks. West's opening lead of the heart ten was overtaken by East's jack. The deuce of diamonds was returned, dummy's ten-spot winning. It was rather obvious to all that East's deuce was a singleton.

Against Crawford, declarer now led the queen of spades, which was covered by the king, and taken by South's ace. A trump was then played back, Crawford winning the trick with his jack. He then made the (perhaps gambling) underlead of the heart three, the trick being captured by West's seven. West promptly returned a diamond, which Crawford ruffed, for the setting trick.

When Stayman held the South cards, he also won. East's diamond return at trick two with dummy's ten-spot, and led the queen of spades, which was covered by East's king and taken by South's ace. But at this point he did not lead another trump, for he saw the handwriting on the wall. His worry, of course, was that West would obtain the lead, to play back a diamond for East to ruff.

What Stayman now did was based on years of experience at the bridge table: he led the king of clubs and followed up by leading his remaining club to dummy's ace. Next came the jack of clubs —and when East put up his queen, Stayman simply discarded his remaining heart.

The East-West line of communication was now broken, for East could not get West into the lead to play a diamond. Actually, East did make the fine return of a low heart, but to no avail. South ruffed, and then led the spade ten to East's jack. When Stayman regained the lead, he picked up East's last trump and claimed his contract.

Thus Stayman carried his card reading to the nth degree and worked out the winning counterattack to East's singleton diamond lead at trick two, whereas our other declarer failed to unearth the counterattack.

In conclusion, the reader might ask the question: "But what if West had held the club queen, instead of East?" The answer to this is simple: both declarers would have gone down at their four-spade contracts.

Deal 7

In this final deal, which technically would be classified under "failure to card-read intelligently," I owe an apology (for offending him) to any South declarer who was not an expert, since card reading was applied intelligently—up to a point.

However, our actual declarer was an expert, and his card-reading horizons were longer and broader than those of the nonexpert. And being an expert, after having been presented with what appeared to be a perfect clue by a defender's play, he should not have terminated his card reading at that point and said to himself, "I'm all set. Here I go." Instead, he should have proceeded further and attempted to analyze the motivation behind the defender's play. Had he done so, he would probably have changed his original conclusion—and would have become the victor instead of the vanquished. His card-reading error might be called one of omission, rather than one of commission.

Both sides vulnerable. South deals.

NORTH
- ♠ A 10 9 6
- ♥ J 5
- ♦ A J 7 2
- ♣ K 9 4

WEST
- ♠ Q 8 4 2
- ♥ Q 8 3 2
- ♦ 10 4 3
- ♣ J 6

EAST
- ♠ —
- ♥ 10 9 7 6 4
- ♦ 9 8 6 5
- ♣ A Q 10 3

SOUTH
- ♠ K J 7 5 3
- ♥ A K
- ♦ K Q
- ♣ 8 7 5 2

The bidding:

SOUTH	WEST	NORTH	EAST
1 ♠	Pass	3 ♠	Pass
4 ♠	Pass	Pass	Pass

Opening lead: Jack of ♣.

West made an inspired opening when he led the jack of clubs. This was covered by dummy's king and taken by East's ace. Next came the queen of clubs, followed by the high ten of clubs. Although the ten of clubs would have won the trick, West ruffed the ten-spot with the trump deuce! To trick four, West led a low heart, which South captured with his king.

From declarer's point of view, it appeared that West's (needless) trumping of his partner's high ten of clubs denoted a lack of interest in spades—and presumably he would not have ruffed if he was concerned with the protection of the queen of trumps. It was therefore not illogical to assume that West had no interest in spades, which, in turn, surely implied that West did not have the spade queen (Q x, Q x x, Q x x x).

Thus, when declarer captured West's heart return at trick four, he led a spade to dummy's ace, intending next to finesse against East for the spade queen. When East discarded a heart on this lead, West's queen of spades had become a winner, and the setting trick.

West's voluntary (and deliberate) ruffing of the third club lead was of course an excellent play, and was designed to create the impression that his trump holding was worthless. Had South been left to his own resources, and had not been steered in the wrong direction, he might still have gone down (normally) by misguessing the location of the trump queen. In all probability, however, he would have guessed right, on the assumption that West, who had two clubs, rather than East, who had four clubs, figured to be the possessor of the trump queen (the player with the greater number of unknown cards rates to have any specific outstanding key card).

But now let us turn our attention to declarer's play of the trump suit. There is no question but that West's "unnecessary" trumping of his partner's ten of clubs seemed to indicate that West was not the possessor of the trump queen. But why, declarer should have asked himself, was an expert West defender trumping this trick? To shift to a heart? Certainly the latter could not be the case, for if East had been permitted to win the third club lead, wouldn't he, by looking at the dummy, shift to a heart (or, if East had the heart ace, wouldn't he take it at trick four, for the setting trick)?

The only rational answer to West's *seemingly irrational* trumping of his partner's trick would have to be that West was trying to throw dust into South's eyes, to create a mirage. I firmly believe that our expert South declarer should have arrived at this conclusion. Thus, assuming that West's seemingly irrational play was rational, West's justification for having made it would have to be that West possessed the queen of trumps.

At trick five, had declarer come to the above conclusion, he would have cashed his king of trumps. With East failing to follow suit, the true state of affairs would now be an open book, and it would become a simple matter to finesse against West for the queen of spades, thereby avoiding the loss of a trump trick.

14

The Rule of Eleven

If one thinks of card reading as exclusively a spur-of-the-moment judgment applied to the specific situation at hand, then this chapter on the Rule of Eleven would be considered as being out of context. However, card reading does not come into being out of thin air. It is always based on the interpretation of the facts evidenced during the bidding and/or play. These facts are not necessarily current ones, and they may well have been experienced earlier in one's career and stored in one's mind for future reference and practical application.

It is in the above light that the Rule of Eleven is being introduced and expounded upon, for the knowledge of the operation of this rule is frequently a must if card reading is to accomplish the desired objective of obtaining the optimum result. Throughout this text, we have had illustrations of this rule in operation— as, for example, when a defender led the deuce of spades against a declarer's three-no-trump contract, it was known by both the leader's partner and the declarer that the lead was the "fourth highest"; hence, that the leader had, in this case, *exactly* three cards higher than the deuce.

Let us now look into the workings of this Rule of Eleven and observe how the practical knowledge of it can serve as the foundation upon which card reading is superimposed.

The conventional, standard lead of the fourth highest card of a long suit goes back many centuries, to the days of whist, the great-grandparent of contract bridge. This lead is still being observed diligently and applied by virtually all defenders, especially against no-trump contract, since the logical lead against no-trump is in one's longest suit.

The use of the fourth-highest lead makes possible the application of the Rule of Eleven, which was discovered in 1889 by R. F. Foster. This rule is a kind of magical arithmetical gadget designed to interpret the opening lead. It is a tool available to both declarer and the defenders, and is an extremely valuable one to know, for many problems that develop during the play can be solved through the use of this rule. Whenever the fourth-highest card of a suit is led, the rule is infallible.

It should be emphasized that the Rule of Eleven is not a sometimes workable, sometimes unworkable instrument. It is an exact mathematical equation. Here is the way it works:

Whenever the card led is the leader's fourth highest of a suit, subtract the denomination (number) of that card from the number 11. The result will be the total number of cards, higher than the card led, held by the other three players.

For example, if West should open the *seven* of clubs (as his fourth-highest) against South's three-no-trump contract, by subtracting the denomination of that card (7) from the number *11*, it becomes a fact that North, East, and South possess exactly *four* cards higher than the seven-spot. From the viewpoint of the partner of the opening leader, it is a routine matter to determine how many of these four higher cards are possessed by the declarer, for the leader's partner sees his own hand and the dummy, and whichever of the four higher cards in circulation are not in evidence must be in declarer's hand. And, conversely, declarer can utilize the Rule of Eleven in precisely the same way as the leader's partner does: by subtracting the denomination of the card led (7) from the number 11, declarer knows that the dummy, the leader's partner, and declarer himself, have exactly four cards higher than the seven-spot. Since declarer sees his own hand and the dummy, whichever of the four higher cards are not in evidence must be in the hand of the leader's partner. Here is the foregoing in diagram form:

From the leader's partner's seat:

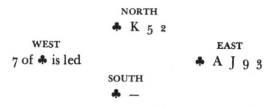

NORTH
♣ K 5 2

WEST
7 of ♣ is led

EAST
♣ A J 9 3

SOUTH
♣ —

On the lead of the club seven against South's three-no-trump contract, the deuce is played from dummy. By subtracting 7 from 11, East knows that the North, East, and South hands have four cards higher than the seven-spot. Since the king is in dummy, and East is looking at the ace, jack, and nine, all four higher cards have been accounted for. Therefore South can have no card higher than the seven. And so, on the play of the deuce from dummy, East follows with the three-spot, knowing that West's seven of clubs will win the trick.

Actually, of course, East could have come to the same conclusion by counting on his fingertips: West must have started with the Q 10 8 7 for the seven-spot to have been the fourth highest (of course, West might also have had the 6 and/or 4 of clubs). But isn't it simpler—and much more polite—to subtract 7 from 11 than to count on your fingertips in public?

From the declarer's seat:

NORTH
♠ Q 9 2

7 of ♠ is led.

SOUTH
♠ A 10 3

On the lead of the spade seven against South's three-no-trump contract, South knows that dummy, East, and South have four cards higher than the seven. Since South (declarer) is looking at the queen and nine in dummy, and the ace and ten in his own hand, he knows that East can have no card higher than the seven. So South finds himself in the catbird's seat if he wants the lead in the North hand, he simply puts up dummy's nine-spot, which will win the trick, or, if he wants the lead in his own hand, he can let the seven ride around to his ten.

Again, declarer could have figured it out on his fingertips: for the seven to be the fourth-highest spade, West had to have the K J 8 7. But there will be days when your fingernails are a bit dirty and you're reluctant to show them in public. Certainly, in this situation, the application of the Rule of Eleven will save you embarrassment.

For those who are interested in *why* the "magic" number 11 is used, here is how it is worked out:

Assign the proper numerals to the unnumbered cards, according to their rank:

> Jack ...... is No. 11
> Queen .... is No. 12
> King ..... is No. 13
> Ace ...... is No. 14

Hence, each suit, if all the cards were thus numbered, would be designated as follows:

$$2–3–4–5–6–7–8–9–10–11–12–13–14$$

Assume that the leader opens the *6*, his fourth-highest card of a suit. There are obviously eight cards outstanding higher than the 6. Since the *6* is, by definition, his fourth-highest card in the suit, *the leader must automatically hold 3 of the 8 higher cards.* That leaves exactly *5* outstanding higher cards in the hands of the other three players at the table (11 minus 6 equals 5).

There are in circulation in each suit:

> 12 cards higher than the 2.
> 11 cards higher than the 3.
> 10 cards higher than the 4.
> 9 cards higher than the 5.
> 8 cards higher than the 6.
> 7 cards higher than the 7.
> 6 cards higher than the 8.
> 5 cards higher than the 9.
> 4 cards higher than the 10.
> 3 cards higher than the 11 (jack).
> 2 cards higher than the 12 (queen).
> 1 card higher than the 13 (king).
> 0 cards higher than the 14 (ace).

To repeat, when opener leads his fourth-highest in a suit, quite obviously he therefore has *exactly 3 cards higher* than the one he has led.

Hence:

If opener leads the *2*, there are *9* cards higher in the other three hands.

If opener leads the *3*, there are *8* higher cards in the other three hands.

If opener leads the *4*, there are *7* higher cards in the other three hands.

If opener leads the *5*, there are *6* higher cards in the other three hands.

If opener leads the *6*, there are *5* higher cards in the other three hands.

If opener leads the *7*, there are *4* higher cards in the other three hands.

If opener leads the *8*, there are *3* higher cards in the other three hands.

If opener leads the *9*, there are *2* higher cards in the other three hands.

If opener leads the *10*, there is one higher card in the other three hands.

If opener leads the *11* (jack), there are *0* higher cards in the other three hands.

NOTE: *The italicized figures on each line always total 11.*

Of course, if opener leads the 12, 13, or 14 (queen, king, ace, respectively), the lead cannot be the fourth-highest, and the Rule of Eleven is inoperative.

Thus, if you subtract the denomination of the card led from the "magic" number 11, the figure you obtain *must always* equal the number of cards (higher than the one led) that are in circulation in the three other hands.

Let us now look at some illustrations of the Rule of Eleven as they arose in actual competition. The reader will note that on some deals familiarity with the Rule of Eleven operates to the advantage of the declarer, and on other deals to the advantage of the defenders. All of the deals presented depict type situations that arise regularly in every session of bridge.

Deal 1: Defenders' Play
Both sides vulnerable. South deals.

NORTH
♠ 8 6 3
♥ A Q 10 9
♦ K 6 5
♣ K 8 3

WEST
♠ Q 10 2
♥ J 7 3
♦ Q 10 8 7
♣ J 7 5

EAST
♠ J 9 7 4
♥ K 5 2
♦ A J 9 3
♣ 9 4

SOUTH
♠ A K 5
♥ 8 6 4
♦ 4 2
♣ A Q 10 6 2

The bidding:

SOUTH	WEST	NORTH	EAST
1 ♣	Pass	1 ♥	Pass
1 NT	Pass	3 NT	Pass
Pass	Pass		

Opening lead: Seven of ♦.

If the bidding could have been maneuvered somehow so that
North became the declarer at three no-trump, this contract would
have been fulfilled with ease. If East elected to lead a diamond
initially, North's king would become declarer's game-going trick.
If East opened a spade instead, the ninth trick would be made in
the heart suit.

But it is difficult to conceive of a correct sequence of bids
whereby North could have become the declarer, except if South
elected to bid his three-card spade suit over North's one-heart
response.

On West's opening lead of the diamond seven against South's
three-no-trump contract, the five was played from dummy. Without the application of the Rule of Eleven, the normal play for
East would be to put up the jack, which would win the trick if

West were leading from the queen. Had he played the jack, declarer would have made his contract by eventually creating his ninth trick in hearts.

But East was familiar with the Rule of Eleven, and he applied it. By subtracting the denomination of West's card (seven) from the number 11, East arrived at the number 4. That meant that in the North, East, and South hands there were four diamonds higher than the seven-spot.

Dummy had one of these four cards, the king. And East himself had the other three. That meant that South had no diamond higher than the seven. So East played the diamond three, and West's seven won the trick.

A diamond continuation by West now enabled the defenders to cash three more diamond tricks, for the defenders' book. In time, East took his heart king, for the setting trick.

Deal 2: Defenders' Play
Neither side vulnerable. North deals.

```
                        NORTH
                    ♠ J 8 3
                    ♥ K 7 5
                    ♦ A K 10
                    ♣ A K Q 6
        WEST                            EAST
    ♠ Q 10 6 5 2                    ♠ K 9 7
    ♥ Q 10 8 2                      ♥ 6 4
    ♦ 9                             ♦ 7 6 4 3 2
    ♣ 7 5 3                         ♣ 9 8 4
                        SOUTH
                    ♠ A 4
                    ♥ A J 9 3
                    ♦ Q J 8 5
                    ♣ J 10 2
```

The bidding:

NORTH	EAST	SOUTH	WEST
1 ♣	Pass	2 NT	Pass
6 NT	Pass	Pass	Pass

Opening lead: Five of ♠.

The bidding was more or less routine, South's response of two no-trump showing 13 to 15 high-card points. North, counting to an assured minimum of 33 high-card points, promptly contracted for the small slam.

On West's five-of-spades opening lead, the eight was played from dummy—and East made the proper play of the nine-spot. South won this trick with his ace. After cashing his diamonds and clubs, declarer led a heart to dummy's king, after which he returned a heart and finessed his jack. As is evident, he went down when the finesse lost to West's queen.

Had East put up the spade king (third hand high!) on the opening spade lead, declarer almost surely would have fulfilled his contract. He would have captured the trick with his ace, and would have returned a spade, on the sound hypothesis that if East had held both the king and queen of spades, he would have played the queen, the lower of adjacent honors. Dummy's jack would now have become declarer's twelfth trick.

To one accustomed to employing the Rule of Eleven, East's play of the spade nine (instead of the king) was routine. When West opened the five of spades, by subtracting the number 5 from the number 11, it showed that there were 6 cards higher than the five-spot in the North, East, and South hands. Dummy had two cards higher than the five, and East held three higher cards. Hence declarer had only one card that was higher than West's five-spot. Surely that card was the ace, for no West defender, on the given bidding, would have underled the ace against South's slam contract.

Deal 3: Defenders' Play
Neither side vulnerable. North deals.

```
                        NORTH
                        ♠ A J 8
                        ♥ 4
                        ♦ A Q J 9 3
                        ♣ Q 9 8 5
        WEST                                    EAST
        ♠ K 10 6 5 2                            ♠ Q 9 7
        ♥ A Q 10                                ♥ J 9 6 5 3 2
        ♦ 10 6 4                                ♦ K 8 2
        ♣ 4 2                                   ♣ 7
                        SOUTH
                        ♠ 4 3
                        ♥ K 8 7
                        ♦ 7 5
                        ♣ A K J 10 6 3
```

The bidding:

NORTH	EAST	SOUTH	WEST
1 ♦	Pass	2 ♣	Pass
4 ♣	Pass	5 ♣	Pass
Pass	Pass		

Opening lead: Five of ♠.

The eight of spades was played from dummy on the opening lead. Had East erroneously put up the queen, declarer would have had available to him a spade finesse against West's king. If he took this finesse, rather than the diamond finesse, he would have been able to discard his losing diamond on the board's ace of spades.

But East, familiar with the Rule of Eleven, and interpreting his partner's lead of the spade five as being West's fourth-from-the-highest, knew that South had no spade that could beat the nine that East played on dummy's eight (5 from 11 leaves 6). Since dummy had three spades higher than the five, and East himself had three spades higher, the setup was an open book to East.

Upon winning the trick with his nine of spades, East returned the spade queen, dummy's ace winning. On this trick West played the *deuce of spades,* a most meaningful play, as will be observed in a moment.

After cashing the queen and king of trumps, declarer next led a low diamond and finessed dummy's queen, East capturing the trick with his king. East now had a problem as to whether to play back a spade, hoping that declarer had started with three low spades, rather than two, or to return a heart, hoping his partner had the ace.

The resolution of his problem was simple. With the five of spades being accepted as West's fourth-from-the-highest spade, West's play of the spade deuce specifically announced that West had started with five spades (since the deuce is below the five-spot in rank). Therefore it became a fact that declarer had been dealt exactly two spades—and had none remaining.

So, logically, after taking his king of diamonds, East led a heart, and West's ace took the setting trick. Naïvely, if East had returned a spade instead, declarer would have fulfilled his contract by discarding his three hearts on the board's third, fourth, and fifth diamonds.

Deal 4: Defenders' Play

In this final Rule of Eleven deal from the defenders' point of view, there is presented a recurring type of situation, in which a defender misdefends because he does not possess a working knowledge of the rule.

Actually, when the deal arose in a low-level rubber-bridge game, our East defender was (evidently) not familiar with the Rule of Eleven. The result was that declarer fulfilled a contract that should have been defeated.

Both sides vulnerable. South deals.

NORTH
♠ K 7 3
♥ K 4 2
♦ A 8 4 2
♣ K 7 5

WEST
♠ A 10 8 6 5
♥ 9 5
♦ 6 3
♣ J 9 6 4

EAST
♠ Q J 4
♥ 8 7
♦ K J 10 9 5
♣ A 10 2

SOUTH
♠ 9 2
♥ A Q J 10 6 3
♦ Q 7
♣ Q 8 3

The bidding:

SOUTH	WEST	NORTH	EAST
1 ♥	Pass	2 NT	Pass
3 ♥	Pass	4 ♥	Pass
Pass	Pass		

Opening lead: Four of ♣.

When the deal was played, the five of clubs was put up from dummy on West's opening club lead, and East captured the trick with his ace. Declarer now had no trouble in fulfilling his contract, his only subsequent losers being a spade and a diamond. I think we will all agree that East got what he deserved for his play, but let us see why it was wrong, and why it was right to put up the ten instead.

First, South was known to possess at least two clubs. The reason is an obvious one. Accepting West's lead of the club four as his fourth-from-the-highest club, West had to have either four or five clubs, since East was looking at the deuce in his own hand. Thus, if West happened to have the three-spot, then he had five clubs to start with. If he didn't have the three, then West had precisely four clubs.

Applying the Rule of Eleven, East subtracts the number 4 (West's lead) from the number 11. That leaves seven cards in the North, East, and South hands that are higher than the four. Dummy has three cards higher. East himself has two cards higher. That means that South has *two cards* higher than the four-spot. What these two are, East of course does not know—but he does know that by declining to play the ace at trick one, he will not lose it, since he can always win a club trick when clubs are led next.

Going further, East knows that if he puts up the club ace at trick one, not only does he surely make a winner out of dummy's king, but if South happens to have the club queen (as he did), the play of the ace gives declarer two club tricks. Therefore the initial play of the club ace can never be the winning play—and it can very easily be the losing play.

Had East played the club ten on the opening lead, declarer would have gone down. He would have captured the trick with his queen, after which he would have drawn trumps. When West obtained the lead later via his spade ace, the lead of the club jack would have entrapped dummy's king; and the defenders would have made two club tricks. No matter how brilliantly declarer played from here in, he would not have been able to avoid losing a diamond trick to East's king. But East spoiled everything by putting up the club ace.

In the four preceding deals the use of the Rule of Eleven was presented from the defenders' point of view. Now let us take a look at this rule from the viewpoint of declarer.

Deal 5: Declarer's Play
East-West vulnerable. North deals.

NORTH
♠ K J 4
♥ 8 5
♦ 5 2
♣ Q J 10 9 8 6

WEST
♠ Q 10 7 5 2
♥ Q 9 7 4
♦ J
♣ 7 3 2

EAST
♠ 8 3
♥ K J 6
♦ Q 10 9 8 3
♣ A 5 4

SOUTH
♠ A 9 6
♥ A 10 3 2
♦ A K 7 6 4
♣ K

The bidding:

NORTH	EAST	SOUTH	WEST
3 ♣	Pass	3 NT	Pass
Pass	Pass		

Opening lead: Five of ♠.

The four of spades was played from dummy, East put up the eight-spot, and South promptly won the trick, not with his nine, but with the ace!

The king of clubs was then laid down, and East allowed the king to win. The six of spades was played next, and dummy's jack was finessed successfully. The queen of clubs now drove out East's ace, and that was that. Thus South made three spade tricks, one heart, two diamonds, and five clubs.

How different the result would have been if South had been a firm believer in "economy at all costs" and had won the opening spade lead with his nine-spot. Had he done so, he would have been able to get to dummy only once, since he would have the doubleton A 6 remaining. Thus he would have been unable *both* to establish *and* to cash dummy's club suit.

South's reason for winning the opening lead with the spade ace was, of course, based on his knowledge of the Rule of Eleven. West's lead of the spade five, as his fourth-highest, stated that

North, East, and South had six spades higher than the five-spot
(by subtracting the number 5 from the number 11). Dummy had
two of these higher cards. South had three, and East had one (the
eight-spot which East had played to trick one). Therefore West
had to have the spade queen; and, consequently, it had to be right
for South to have captured the opening lead with the ace, not with
the nine, thus *guaranteeing* that the board's king and jack of
spades could be utilized as two entries to dummy.

Deal 6: Declarer's Play

It is my opinion that 99 percent of our nation's players, had
they been occupying the South seat in this deal, would have mis-
played their game contract of three no-trump. It is a tough deal to
play correctly. However, if one has a practical knowledge of the
Rule of Eleven, the winning line of play is not too difficult to find.

Neither side vulnerable. North deals.

```
                            NORTH
                            ♠ K 8 4
                            ♥ A J 2
                            ♦ J 10 9 5
                            ♣ A 8 6
        WEST                                    EAST
        ♠ Q 7 2                                 ♠ 10 6 5 3
        ♥ 9 5 4                                 ♥ 10 8 7 3
        ♦ A 6                                   ♦ K 4 2
        ♣ K 9 7 5 3                             ♣ J 4
                            SOUTH
                            ♠ A J 9
                            ♥ K Q 6
                            ♦ Q 8 7 3
                            ♣ Q 10 2
```

The bidding:

NORTH	EAST	SOUTH	WEST
1 ♦	Pass	2 NT	Pass
3 NT	Pass	Pass	Pass

Opening lead: Five of ♣.

Dummy's six of clubs was played on the opening lead, East put up the jack—and South played the deuce, allowing the jack to win! East returned the club four, South followed with the ten, and West's king was captured by the board's ace.

The diamond jack was now led, both East and South played low, and West won the trick with the ace. West played back a club, South's queen winning as East discarded a heart. Another diamond was led next, driving out East's king. Declarer now had his contract—for nine tricks: two spades, three hearts, two diamonds, and two clubs.

The "normal" play on the hand would have been to capture East's jack of clubs with the queen at trick one. Had South done this, the defenders would have had it in their power to defeat the contract.

Assuming South next led a diamond, East would take the trick with his king. He would then return his remaining club, South playing low (it mattered not whether he played low or put up the ten, for West had South covered), West would insert his nine-spot, and if declarer didn't take his ace, another club lead by West would force dummy's ace.

West would now have two established clubs in his hand. And when he obtained the lead either with the ace of diamonds or queen of spades, he would cash those two clubs, to hand declarer a one-trick set.

South's refusal to win the opening club lead with his queen was based, first, on the appreciation that he had to establish his diamond suit. The danger to the hand was, of course, that when the diamond suit became established (by driving out the defenders' ace and king), the West defender might cash sufficient clubs to defeat the contract. Thus South's play of the hand had to be geared toward preventing (or minimizing) the possibility of West's cashing his to-be-established club suit.

By employing the Rule of Eleven, South accomplished his objective, which, incidentally, was based on the realistic assumption that one defender had the ace of diamonds and the other defender the king of diamonds. West's opening lead of the club five had indicated that North, East, and South possessed six clubs higher than the five (11 minus 5 equals 6). Dummy had three higher cards, South had two higher cards—and East's jack had to be the only card he had that was higher than the five-spot. Hence West had to have the king of clubs.

By not capturing the opening club lead, declarer preserved his Q 10 holding (in combination with dummy's A x) and thereby left himself in the position where he could always make two club tricks by finessing against West's known king. Simultaneously, his play had the effect of eliminating clubs from the East hand, so that when East obtained the lead with one of the top diamonds (in theory), he would be unable to return a club. Thus South would now have the time to establish and cash his diamond suit before West got around both to establishing and to cashing his club suit. As has been observed, this is exactly what happened.

Deal 7: Declarer's Play

This final deal, in my opinion, embodies much of what is encompassed in the field of card reading and counting. Starting on the foundation of the factual significance of West's opening lead, declarer was able to create a false impression in the leader's partner's mind. In so doing, he virtually forced the leader's partner to make a natural card-reading error.

Before presenting what actually did happen when this deal arose, once again I would like to put you into the South seat and confront you with the situation that faced our South declarer. With neither side vulnerable, the bidding has proceeded:

SOUTH	WEST	NORTH	EAST
1 NT	Pass	2 ♣ *	Pass
2 ♦	Pass	2 NT	Pass
3 NT	Pass	Pass	Pass

* The Stayman Convention, asking opener to name a four-card, or longer, major suit if the opener possesses one. South's two-diamond response denies the possession of four or more cards in either of the major suits.

NORTH
♠ K 10 9 4
♥ K J 6 3
♦ 7 5 2
♣ J 9

SOUTH
♠ A Q J
♥ A 7 2
♦ A 4
♣ Q 10 8 3 2

Opening lead: Four of ♣.

After West opens the club four against your three-no-trump contract, and the dummy comes into view, you pause to take stock. You know one thing for sure: that West has *exactly four clubs,* no more and no less. This is a guaranteed fact, since you are looking at the two and the three in your own hand, and West assuredly is making the standard lead of the fourth from the highest in his longest suit.

It is quite likely that East has either the ace or king of clubs and that he will capture the opening lead. You are scared to death that he might not return a club, and, instead, will shift to a diamond. If he does, your ace will be driven out before you have a chance to create a couple of club winners. And if the opponents establish their diamond suit before you establish your club suit, you will be sunk. How can you encourage East to return a club at trick two?

In retrospect, the winning play is a simple one: after East captures the opening lead with his king of clubs, you follow suit with your eight-spot! Let us now pick up the action as it developed at the table.

NORTH
♠ K 10 9 4
♥ K J 6 3
♦ 7 5 2
♣ J 9

WEST
♠ 8 6 5 2
♥ 9 4
♦ Q 10 8
♣ A 7 6 4

EAST
♠ 7 3
♥ Q 10 8 5
♦ K J 9 6 3
♣ K 5

SOUTH
♠ A Q J
♥ A 7 2
♦ A 4
♣ Q 10 8 3 2

Upon winning with his king of clubs, and perceiving the fall of South's eight-spot, East now paused for reflection. Assuming honesty on South's part, the eight of clubs was South's lowest card in that suit. Hence, reasoned East, West was the possessor of both the two and three of clubs. Since the four of clubs was West's fourth-highest, West therefore had a six-card club suit at the outset.

So, at trick two, East returned his remaining club—as South followed with the deuce. West won this lead with the ace, and South was now home with ten tricks: three clubs, one diamond, two hearts, and four spades.

It cannot be predicted what East might have led to trick two if South had played the club deuce on the opening lead. In this case, as East would have viewed the situation, West had no more than five clubs, and possibly just four if South also possessed the three of clubs. With the club deuce being played on the opening lead, East would have known that South had either four or five clubs.

Had South not falsecarded on the opening lead, it is quite conceivable that East might have returned a club anyway, or he might have shifted to a diamond. But, regardless of what might have been, South's false-card made it more or less automatic for East to have returned partner's club suit.

15

The Proper Use of "Sight," Hearing, and Judgment

In this book I have been focusing on what is unquestionably one of the most important—if not *the* most important—elements of play, namely, card reading. This subject includes an essential component—namely, counting out a hand. The latter is based primarily on one's sense of sight (observation), while card reading necessitates not only the application of one's sense of sight, but also his sense of hearing; that is, listening to the bidding of the opponents and interpreting it.

The employment of these two physical senses in gathering in the vital data (clues, intimations, hints) relevant to the opponents' holdings does not constitute an end in itself. When it has been collected, it has to be assembled and analyzed—and this requires the application of a nonphysical sense—namely, *judgment*. The latter task might be categorized as "skilled labor," whereas the collection of the data through the senses of seeing and hearing might be described as "unskilled," or, perhaps, "semiskilled" labor. In many of the deals in this book it was either impossible to count out a hand, or to indulge in card reading, or it was possible to obtain only a partial count or to make an inference about the nature of an opponent's holdings—an inference which offered no guarantees. In these cases, the "unskilled" senses of sight and hearing took a back seat temporarily—and "skilled" judgment rose to the fore. And thus it will always be: judgment must forever be the prime mover if the optimum result is to be obtained.

In the deal that follows, we have an example of the two physical senses (sight and hearing) and the nonphysical sense (judgment) all coming into play. In addition, we have the perhaps paradoxical occurrence of a blind player applying not only her sense of hearing but also her sense of "sight." The blind player was Dr. Lois Wiley of Chicago. She is one of our nation's top-ranking players.

The deal came up in the National Championships of 1964. Dr. Wiley, in her counting out, had the assistance of Braille cards, which are marked by symbols on the corners to denote the suit and rank of each card. Thus Dr. Wiley was compelled to apply still another sense: the sense of touch. It should be mentioned that whenever a hand is being played, a blind player may at any time ask that the remaining cards in dummy be called out to him.

During the play of this deal, the lights in the playing area went out. There was much hubbub. Dr. Wiley, when told what had happened, exclaimed: "Hurrah! Now we're all even."

Actually, Dr. Wiley didn't need any advantage. During the play not once did she ask that the remaining cards in dummy be read out to her. She "saw" all of the cards from the commencement to the termination. Dr. Wiley was sitting in the South seat.

East-West vulnerable. East deals.

NORTH
♠ Q 3 2
♥ Q 8 7 4
♦ A 7 2
♣ A 7 3

WEST
♠ 5
♥ K 9 5 3 2
♦ 9 6 4
♣ Q J 8 6

EAST
♠ A 9 6 4
♥ A J 10 6
♦ K J 3
♣ 10 2

SOUTH
♠ K J 10 8 7
♥ —
♦ Q 10 8 5
♣ K 9 5 4

The bidding:

EAST	SOUTH	WEST	NORTH
1 ♦	1 ♠	Pass	3 ♠
Pass	Pass	Pass	

Opening lead: Four of ♦.

East's opening bid of one diamond on a three-card suit was mandatory in the system East-West were employing, for East was not allowed to open the bidding in a four-card major suit in either first or second position.

On West's four of diamonds opening lead, a low diamond was played from dummy, East's king capturing the trick. East returned a low diamond, South's ten winning.

Dr. Wiley next led the spade jack to East's ace, after which East returned a diamond, dummy's ace taking the trick. Now came the ace of clubs, the king of clubs, and a third round of clubs, West's jack winning as East discarded a heart. The club queen was played next by West, dummy ruffing with the queen as East discarded another heart.

East's distribution was now an open book to Dr. Wiley: he had been revealed as the possessor of exactly two clubs, and exactly three diamonds. If he had held five hearts originally, he would have opened the bidding with one heart instead of one diamond on a three-card suit. Hence East had to have started with four hearts and four spades.

Dr. Wiley now led dummy's remaining trump. When East followed with the six-spot, she inserted her seven, finessing successfully against East's nine. The king and ten of trumps then picked up East's two remaining pieces. Thus with her remaining trump and the good queen of diamonds she made an overtrick, so vital in a duplicate game.

I have often wondered how many bridge players are gifted with such a sense of "sight" as displayed by Dr. Wiley.

A CATALOG OF SELECTED
DOVER BOOKS
IN ALL FIELDS OF INTEREST

A CATALOG OF SELECTED DOVER
BOOKS IN ALL FIELDS OF INTEREST

CONCERNING THE SPIRITUAL IN ART, Wassily Kandinsky. Pioneering work by father of abstract art. Thoughts on color theory, nature of art. Analysis of earlier masters. 12 illustrations. 80pp. of text. 5⅜ x 8½. 23411-8 Pa. $4.95

ANIMALS: 1,419 Copyright-Free Illustrations of Mammals, Birds, Fish, Insects, etc., Jim Harter (ed.). Clear wood engravings present, in extremely lifelike poses, over 1,000 species of animals. One of the most extensive pictorial sourcebooks of its kind. Captions. Index. 284pp. 9 x 12. 23766-4 Pa. $14.95

CELTIC ART: The Methods of Construction, George Bain. Simple geometric techniques for making Celtic interlacements, spirals, Kells-type initials, animals, humans, etc. Over 500 illustrations. 160pp. 9 x 12. (USO) 22923-8 Pa. $9.95

AN ATLAS OF ANATOMY FOR ARTISTS, Fritz Schider. Most thorough reference work on art anatomy in the world. Hundreds of illustrations, including selections from works by Vesalius, Leonardo, Goya, Ingres, Michelangelo, others. 593 illustrations. 192pp. 7⅛ x 10¼. 20241-0 Pa. $9.95

CELTIC HAND STROKE-BY-STROKE (Irish Half-Uncial from "The Book of Kells"): An Arthur Baker Calligraphy Manual, Arthur Baker. Complete guide to creating each letter of the alphabet in distinctive Celtic manner. Covers hand position, strokes, pens, inks, paper, more. Illustrated. 48pp. 8¼ x 11. 24336-2 Pa. $3.95

EASY ORIGAMI, John Montroll. Charming collection of 32 projects (hat, cup, pelican, piano, swan, many more) specially designed for the novice origami hobbyist. Clearly illustrated easy-to-follow instructions insure that even beginning papercrafters will achieve successful results. 48pp. 8¼ x 11. 27298-2 Pa. $3.50

THE COMPLETE BOOK OF BIRDHOUSE CONSTRUCTION FOR WOODWORKERS, Scott D. Campbell. Detailed instructions, illustrations, tables. Also data on bird habitat and instinct patterns. Bibliography. 3 tables. 63 illustrations in 15 figures. 48pp. 5¼ x 8½. 24407-5 Pa. $2.50

BLOOMINGDALE'S ILLUSTRATED 1886 CATALOG: Fashions, Dry Goods and Housewares, Bloomingdale Brothers. Famed merchants' extremely rare catalog depicting about 1,700 products: clothing, housewares, firearms, dry goods, jewelry, more. Invaluable for dating, identifying vintage items. Also, copyright-free graphics for artists, designers. Co-published with Henry Ford Museum & Greenfield Village. 160pp. 8¼ x 11. 25780-0 Pa. $10.95

HISTORIC COSTUME IN PICTURES, Braun & Schneider. Over 1,450 costumed figures in clearly detailed engravings–from dawn of civilization to end of 19th century. Captions. Many folk costumes. 256pp. 8⅜ x 11¾. 23150-X Pa. $12.95

STICKLEY CRAFTSMAN FURNITURE CATALOGS, Gustav Stickley and L. & J. G. Stickley. Beautiful, functional furniture in two authentic catalogs from 1910. 594 illustrations, including 277 photos, show settles, rockers, armchairs, reclining chairs, bookcases, desks, tables. 183pp. 6½ x 9¼. 23838-5 Pa. $11.95

AMERICAN LOCOMOTIVES IN HISTORIC PHOTOGRAPHS: 1858 to 1949, Ron Ziel (ed.). A rare collection of 126 meticulously detailed official photographs, called "builder portraits," of American locomotives that majestically chronicle the rise of steam locomotive power in America. Introduction. Detailed captions. xi + 129pp. 9 x 12. 27393-8 Pa. $13.95

AMERICA'S LIGHTHOUSES: An Illustrated History, Francis Ross Holland, Jr. Delightfully written, profusely illustrated fact-filled survey of over 200 American light-houses since 1716. History, anecdotes, technological advances, more. 240pp. 8 x 10¾. 25576-X Pa. $12.95

TOWARDS A NEW ARCHITECTURE, Le Corbusier. Pioneering manifesto by founder of "International School." Technical and aesthetic theories, views of indus-try, economics, relation of form to function, "mass-production split" and much more. Profusely illustrated. 320pp. 6⅛ x 9¼. (USO) 25023-7 Pa. $9.95

HOW THE OTHER HALF LIVES, Jacob Riis. Famous journalistic record, expos-ing poverty and degradation of New York slums around 1900, by major social reformer. 100 striking and influential photographs. 233pp. 10 x 7⅞. 22012-5 Pa. $11.95

FRUIT KEY AND TWIG KEY TO TREES AND SHRUBS, William M. Harlow. One of the handiest and most widely used identification aids. Fruit key covers 120 deciduous and evergreen species; twig key 160 deciduous species. Easily used. Over 300 photographs. 126pp. 5⅜ x 8½. 20511-8 Pa. $3.95

COMMON BIRD SONGS, Dr. Donald J. Borror. Songs of 60 most common U.S. birds: robins, sparrows, cardinals, bluejays, finches, more—arranged in order of increasing complexity. Up to 9 variations of songs of each species. Cassette and manual 99911-4 $8.95

ORCHIDS AS HOUSE PLANTS, Rebecca Tyson Northen. Grow cattleyas and many other kinds of orchids—in a window, in a case, or under artificial light. 63 illus-trations. 148pp. 5⅜ x 8½. 23261-1 Pa. $5.95

MONSTER MAZES, Dave Phillips. Masterful mazes at four levels of difficulty. Avoid deadly perils and evil creatures to find magical treasures. Solutions for all 32 exciting illustrated puzzles. 48pp. 8¼ x 11. 26005-4 Pa. $2.95

MOZART'S DON GIOVANNI (DOVER OPERA LIBRETTO SERIES), Wolfgang Amadeus Mozart. Introduced and translated by Ellen H. Bleiler. Standard Italian libretto, with complete English translation. Convenient and thoroughly portable—an ideal companion for reading along with a recording or the performance itself. Introduction. List of characters. Plot summary. 121pp. 5¼ x 8½. 24944-1 Pa. $3.95

TECHNICAL MANUAL AND DICTIONARY OF CLASSICAL BALLET, Gail Grant. Defines, explains, comments on steps, movements, poses and concepts. 15-page pictorial section. Basic book for student, viewer. 127pp. 5⅜ x 8½. 21843-0 Pa. $4.95

BRASS INSTRUMENTS: Their History and Development, Anthony Baines. Authoritative, updated survey of the evolution of trumpets, trombones, bugles, cornets, French horns, tubas and other brass wind instruments. Over 140 illustrations and 48 music examples. Corrected and updated by author. New preface. Bibliography. 320pp. 5⅜ x 8½. 27574-4 Pa. $9.95

HOLLYWOOD GLAMOR PORTRAITS, John Kobal (ed.). 145 photos from 1926-49. Harlow, Gable, Bogart, Bacall; 94 stars in all. Full background on photographers, technical aspects. 160pp. 8⅜ x 11¼. 23352-9 Pa. $12.95

MAX AND MORITZ, Wilhelm Busch. Great humor classic in both German and English. Also 10 other works: "Cat and Mouse," "Plisch and Plumm," etc. 216pp. 5⅜ x 8½. 20181-3 Pa. $6.95

THE RAVEN AND OTHER FAVORITE POEMS, Edgar Allan Poe. Over 40 of the author's most memorable poems: "The Bells," "Ulalume," "Israfel," "To Helen," "The Conqueror Worm," "Eldorado," "Annabel Lee," many more. Alphabetic lists of titles and first lines. 64pp. 5³⁄₁₆ x 8¼. 26685-0 Pa. $1.00

PERSONAL MEMOIRS OF U. S. GRANT, Ulysses Simpson Grant. Intelligent, deeply moving firsthand account of Civil War campaigns, considered by many the finest military memoirs ever written. Includes letters, historic photographs, maps and more. 528pp. 6⅛ x 9¼. 28587-1 Pa. $12.95

AMULETS AND SUPERSTITIONS, E. A. Wallis Budge. Comprehensive discourse on origin, powers of amulets in many ancient cultures: Arab, Persian Babylonian, Assyrian, Egyptian, Gnostic, Hebrew, Phoenician, Syriac, etc. Covers cross, swastika, crucifix, seals, rings, stones, etc. 584pp. 5⅜ x 8½. 23573-4 Pa. $15.95

RUSSIAN STORIES/PYCCKNE PACCKA3bl: A Dual-Language Book, edited by Gleb Struve. Twelve tales by such masters as Chekhov, Tolstoy, Dostoevsky, Pushkin, others. Excellent word-for-word English translations on facing pages, plus teaching and study aids, Russian/English vocabulary, biographical/critical introductions, more. 416pp. 5⅜ x 8½. 26244-8 Pa. $9.95

PHILADELPHIA THEN AND NOW: 60 Sites Photographed in the Past and Present, Kenneth Finkel and Susan Oyama. Rare photographs of City Hall, Logan Square, Independence Hall, Betsy Ross House, other landmarks juxtaposed with contemporary views. Captures changing face of historic city. Introduction. Captions. 128pp. 8¼ x 11. 25790-8 Pa. $9.95

AIA ARCHITECTURAL GUIDE TO NASSAU AND SUFFOLK COUNTIES, LONG ISLAND, The American Institute of Architects, Long Island Chapter, and the Society for the Preservation of Long Island Antiquities. Comprehensive, well-researched and generously illustrated volume brings to life over three centuries of Long Island's great architectural heritage. More than 240 photographs with authoritative, extensively detailed captions. 176pp. 8¼ x 11. 26946-9 Pa. $14.95

NORTH AMERICAN INDIAN LIFE: Customs and Traditions of 23 Tribes, Elsie Clews Parsons (ed.). 27 fictionalized essays by noted anthropologists examine religion, customs, government, additional facets of life among the Winnebago, Crow, Zuni, Eskimo, other tribes. 480pp. 6⅛ x 9¼. 27377-6 Pa. $10.95

FRANK LLOYD WRIGHT'S HOLLYHOCK HOUSE, Donald Hoffmann. Lavishly illustrated, carefully documented study of one of Wright's most controversial residential designs. Over 120 photographs, floor plans, elevations, etc. Detailed perceptive text by noted Wright scholar. Index. 128pp. 9¼ x 10¾. 27133-1 Pa. $11.95

THE MALE AND FEMALE FIGURE IN MOTION: 60 Classic Photographic Sequences, Eadweard Muybridge. 60 true-action photographs of men and women walking, running, climbing, bending, turning, etc., reproduced from rare 19th-century masterpiece. vi + 121pp. 9 x 12. 24745-7 Pa. $10.95

1001 QUESTIONS ANSWERED ABOUT THE SEASHORE, N. J. Berrill and Jacquelyn Berrill. Queries answered about dolphins, sea snails, sponges, starfish, fishes, shore birds, many others. Covers appearance, breeding, growth, feeding, much more. 305pp. 5¼ x 8¼. 23366-9 Pa. $9.95

GUIDE TO OWL WATCHING IN NORTH AMERICA, Donald S. Heintzelman. Superb guide offers complete data and descriptions of 19 species: barn owl, screech owl, snowy owl, many more. Expert coverage of owl-watching equipment, conservation, migrations and invasions, etc. Guide to observing sites. 84 illustrations. xiii + 193pp. 5⅜ x 8½. 27344-X Pa. $8.95

MEDICINAL AND OTHER USES OF NORTH AMERICAN PLANTS: A Historical Survey with Special Reference to the Eastern Indian Tribes, Charlotte Erichsen-Brown. Chronological historical citations document 500 years of usage of plants, trees, shrubs native to eastern Canada, northeastern U.S. Also complete identifying information. 343 illustrations. 544pp. 6½ x 9¼. 25951-X Pa. $12.95

STORYBOOK MAZES, Dave Phillips. 23 stories and mazes on two-page spreads: Wizard of Oz, Treasure Island, Robin Hood, etc. Solutions. 64pp. 8¼ x 11. 23628-5 Pa. $2.95

NEGRO FOLK MUSIC, U.S.A., Harold Courlander. Noted folklorist's scholarly yet readable analysis of rich and varied musical tradition. Includes authentic versions of over 40 folk songs. Valuable bibliography and discography. xi + 324pp. 5⅜ x 8½. 27350-4 Pa. $9.95

MOVIE-STAR PORTRAITS OF THE FORTIES, John Kobal (ed.). 163 glamor, studio photos of 106 stars of the 1940s: Rita Hayworth, Ava Gardner, Marlon Brando, Clark Gable, many more. 176pp. 8⅜ x 11¼. 23546-7 Pa. $14.95

BENCHLEY LOST AND FOUND, Robert Benchley. Finest humor from early 30s, about pet peeves, child psychologists, post office and others. Mostly unavailable elsewhere. 73 illustrations by Peter Arno and others. 183pp. 5⅜ x 8½. 22410-4 Pa. $6.95

YEKL and THE IMPORTED BRIDEGROOM AND OTHER STORIES OF YIDDISH NEW YORK, Abraham Cahan. Film Hester Street based on Yekl (1896). Novel, other stories among first about Jewish immigrants on N.Y.'s East Side. 240pp. 5⅜ x 8½. 22427-9 Pa. $6.95

SELECTED POEMS, Walt Whitman. Generous sampling from *Leaves of Grass.* Twenty-four poems include "I Hear America Singing," "Song of the Open Road," "I Sing the Body Electric," "When Lilacs Last in the Dooryard Bloom'd," "O Captain! My Captain!"–all reprinted from an authoritative edition. Lists of titles and first lines. 128pp. 5³⁄₁₆ x 8¼. 26878-0 Pa. $1.00

THE BEST TALES OF HOFFMANN, E. T. A. Hoffmann. 10 of Hoffmann's most important stories: "Nutcracker and the King of Mice," "The Golden Flowerpot," etc. 458pp. 5⅜ x 8½. 21793-0 Pa. $9.95

FROM FETISH TO GOD IN ANCIENT EGYPT, E. A. Wallis Budge. Rich detailed survey of Egyptian conception of "God" and gods, magic, cult of animals, Osiris, more. Also, superb English translations of hymns and legends. 240 illustrations. 545pp. 5⅜ x 8½. 25803-3 Pa. $13.95

FRENCH STORIES/CONTES FRANÇAIS: A Dual-Language Book, Wallace Fowlie. Ten stories by French masters, Voltaire to Camus: "Micromegas" by Voltaire; "The Atheist's Mass" by Balzac; "Minuet" by de Maupassant; "The Guest" by Camus, six more. Excellent English translations on facing pages. Also French-English vocabulary list, exercises, more. 352pp. 5⅜ x 8½. 26443-2 Pa. $9.95

CHICAGO AT THE TURN OF THE CENTURY IN PHOTOGRAPHS: 122 Historic Views from the Collections of the Chicago Historical Society, Larry A. Viskochil. Rare large-format prints offer detailed views of City Hall, State Street, the Loop, Hull House, Union Station, many other landmarks, circa 1904-1913. Introduction. Captions. Maps. 144pp. 9⅜ x 12¼. 24656-6 Pa. $12.95

OLD BROOKLYN IN EARLY PHOTOGRAPHS, 1865-1929, William Lee Younger. Luna Park, Gravesend race track, construction of Grand Army Plaza, moving of Hotel Brighton, etc. 157 previously unpublished photographs. 165pp. 8⅞ x 11¾. 23587-4 Pa. $13.95

THE MYTHS OF THE NORTH AMERICAN INDIANS, Lewis Spence. Rich anthology of the myths and legends of the Algonquins, Iroquois, Pawnees and Sioux, prefaced by an extensive historical and ethnological commentary. 36 illustrations. 480pp. 5⅜ x 8½. 25967-6 Pa. $10.95

AN ENCYCLOPEDIA OF BATTLES: Accounts of Over 1,560 Battles from 1479 B.C. to the Present, David Eggenberger. Essential details of every major battle in recorded history from the first battle of Megiddo in 1479 B.C. to Grenada in 1984. List of Battle Maps. New Appendix covering the years 1967-1984. Index. 99 illustrations. 544pp. 6½ x 9¼. 24913-1 Pa. $16.95

SAILING ALONE AROUND THE WORLD, Captain Joshua Slocum. First man to sail around the world, alone, in small boat. One of great feats of seamanship told in delightful manner. 67 illustrations. 294pp. 5⅜ x 8½. 20326-3 Pa. $6.95

ANARCHISM AND OTHER ESSAYS, Emma Goldman. Powerful, penetrating, prophetic essays on direct action, role of minorities, prison reform, puritan hypocrisy, violence, etc. 271pp. 5⅜ x 8½. 22484-8 Pa. $7.95

MYTHS OF THE HINDUS AND BUDDHISTS, Ananda K. Coomaraswamy and Sister Nivedita. Great stories of the epics; deeds of Krishna, Shiva, taken from puranas, Vedas, folk tales; etc. 32 illustrations. 400pp. 5⅜ x 8½. 21759-0 Pa. $12.95

BEYOND PSYCHOLOGY, Otto Rank. Fear of death, desire of immortality, nature of sexuality, social organization, creativity, according to Rankian system. 291pp. 5⅜ x 8½. 20485-5 Pa. $8.95

A THEOLOGICO-POLITICAL TREATISE, Benedict Spinoza. Also contains unfinished Political Treatise. Great classic on religious liberty, theory of government on common consent. R. Elwes translation. Total of 421pp. 5⅜ x 8½. 20249-6 Pa. $9.95

EARLY NINETEENTH-CENTURY CRAFTS AND TRADES, Peter Stockham (ed.). Extremely rare 1807 volume describes to youngsters the crafts and trades of the day: brickmaker, weaver, dressmaker, bookbinder, ropemaker, saddler, many more. Quaint prose, charming illustrations for each craft. 20 black-and-white line illustrations. 192pp. 4⅝ x 6. 27293-1 Pa. $4.95

VICTORIAN FASHIONS AND COSTUMES FROM HARPER'S BAZAR, 1867–1898, Stella Blum (ed.). Day costumes, evening wear, sports clothes, shoes, hats, other accessories in over 1,000 detailed engravings. 320pp. 9⅜ x 12¼. 22990-4 Pa. $15.95

GUSTAV STICKLEY, THE CRAFTSMAN, Mary Ann Smith. Superb study surveys broad scope of Stickley's achievement, especially in architecture. Design philosophy, rise and fall of the Craftsman empire, descriptions and floor plans for many Craftsman houses, more. 86 black-and-white halftones. 31 line illustrations. Introduction 208pp. 6½ x 9¼. 27210-9 Pa. $9.95

THE LONG ISLAND RAIL ROAD IN EARLY PHOTOGRAPHS, Ron Ziel. Over 220 rare photos, informative text document origin (1844) and development of rail service on Long Island. Vintage views of early trains, locomotives, stations, passengers, crews, much more. Captions. 8⅞ x 11¾. 26301-0 Pa. $13.95

THE BOOK OF OLD SHIPS: From Egyptian Galleys to Clipper Ships, Henry B. Culver. Superb, authoritative history of sailing vessels, with 80 magnificent line illustrations. Galley, bark, caravel, longship, whaler, many more. Detailed, informative text on each vessel by noted naval historian. Introduction. 256pp. 5⅜ x 8½. 27332-6 Pa. $7.95

TEN BOOKS ON ARCHITECTURE, Vitruvius. The most important book ever written on architecture. Early Roman aesthetics, technology, classical orders, site selection, all other aspects. Morgan translation. 331pp. 5⅜ x 8½. 20645-9 Pa. $8.95

THE HUMAN FIGURE IN MOTION, Eadweard Muybridge. More than 4,500 stopped-action photos, in action series, showing undraped men, women, children jumping, lying down, throwing, sitting, wrestling, carrying, etc. 390pp. 7⅞ x 10⅝. 20204-6 Clothbd. $27.95

TREES OF THE EASTERN AND CENTRAL UNITED STATES AND CANADA, William M. Harlow. Best one-volume guide to 140 trees. Full descriptions, woodlore, range, etc. Over 600 illustrations. Handy size. 288pp. 4½ x 6⅜. 20395-6 Pa. $6.95

SONGS OF WESTERN BIRDS, Dr. Donald J. Borror. Complete song and call repertoire of 60 western species, including flycatchers, juncoes, cactus wrens, many more–includes fully illustrated booklet. Cassette and manual 99913-0 $8.95

GROWING AND USING HERBS AND SPICES, Milo Miloradovich. Versatile handbook provides all the information needed for cultivation and use of all the herbs and spices available in North America. 4 illustrations. Index. Glossary. 236pp. 5⅜ x 8½. 25058-X Pa. $7.95

BIG BOOK OF MAZES AND LABYRINTHS, Walter Shepherd. 50 mazes and labyrinths in all–classical, solid, ripple, and more–in one great volume. Perfect inexpensive puzzler for clever youngsters. Full solutions. 112pp. 8⅛ x 11. 22951-3 Pa. $4.95

PIANO TUNING, J. Cree Fischer. Clearest, best book for beginner, amateur. Simple repairs, raising dropped notes, tuning by easy method of flattened fifths. No previous skills needed. 4 illustrations. 201pp. 5⅜ x 8½. 23267-0 Pa. $6.95

A SOURCE BOOK IN THEATRICAL HISTORY, A. M. Nagler. Contemporary observers on acting, directing, make-up, costuming, stage props, machinery, scene design, from Ancient Greece to Chekhov. 611pp. 5⅜ x 8½. 20515-0 Pa. $12.95

THE COMPLETE NONSENSE OF EDWARD LEAR, Edward Lear. All nonsense limericks, zany alphabets, Owl and Pussycat, songs, nonsense botany, etc., illustrated by Lear. Total of 320pp. 5⅜ x 8½. (USO) 20167-8 Pa. $7.95

VICTORIAN PARLOUR POETRY: An Annotated Anthology, Michael R. Turner. 117 gems by Longfellow, Tennyson, Browning, many lesser-known poets. "The Village Blacksmith," "Curfew Must Not Ring Tonight," "Only a Baby Small," dozens more, often difficult to find elsewhere. Index of poets, titles, first lines. xxiii + 325pp. 5⅝ x 8¼. 27044-0 Pa. $8.95

DUBLINERS, James Joyce. Fifteen stories offer vivid, tightly focused observations of the lives of Dublin's poorer classes. At least one, "The Dead," is considered a masterpiece. Reprinted complete and unabridged from standard edition. 160pp. 5³⁄₁₆ x 8¼. 26870-5 Pa. $1.00

THE HAUNTED MONASTERY and THE CHINESE MAZE MURDERS, Robert van Gulik. Two full novels by van Gulik, set in 7th-century China, continue adventures of Judge Dee and his companions. An evil Taoist monastery, seemingly supernatural events; overgrown topiary maze hides strange crimes. 27 illustrations. 328pp. 5⅜ x 8½. 23502-5 Pa. $8.95

THE BOOK OF THE SACRED MAGIC OF ABRAMELIN THE MAGE, translated by S. MacGregor Mathers. Medieval manuscript of ceremonial magic. Basic document in Aleister Crowley, Golden Dawn groups. 268pp. 5⅜ x 8½. 23211-5 Pa. $9.95

NEW RUSSIAN-ENGLISH AND ENGLISH-RUSSIAN DICTIONARY, M. A. O'Brien. This is a remarkably handy Russian dictionary, containing a surprising amount of information, including over 70,000 entries. 366pp. 4½ x 6⅛. 20208-9 Pa. $10.95

HISTORIC HOMES OF THE AMERICAN PRESIDENTS, Second, Revised Edition, Irvin Haas. A traveler's guide to American Presidential homes, most open to the public, depicting and describing homes occupied by every American President from George Washington to George Bush. With visiting hours, admission charges, travel routes. 175 photographs. Index. 160pp. 8¼ x 11. 26751-2 Pa. $11.95

NEW YORK IN THE FORTIES, Andreas Feininger. 162 brilliant photographs by the well-known photographer, formerly with *Life* magazine. Commuters, shoppers, Times Square at night, much else from city at its peak. Captions by John von Hartz. 181pp. 9¼ x 10¾. 23585-8 Pa. $13.95

INDIAN SIGN LANGUAGE, William Tomkins. Over 525 signs developed by Sioux and other tribes. Written instructions and diagrams. Also 290 pictographs. 111pp. 6⅛ x 9¼. 22029-X Pa. $3.95

ANATOMY: A Complete Guide for Artists, Joseph Sheppard. A master of figure drawing shows artists how to render human anatomy convincingly. Over 460 illustrations. 224pp. 8⅜ x 11¼. 27279-6 Pa. $11.95

MEDIEVAL CALLIGRAPHY: Its History and Technique, Marc Drogin. Spirited history, comprehensive instruction manual covers 13 styles (ca. 4th century thru 15th). Excellent photographs; directions for duplicating medieval techniques with modern tools. 224pp. 8⅜ x 11¼. 26142-5 Pa. $12.95

DRIED FLOWERS: How to Prepare Them, Sarah Whitlock and Martha Rankin. Complete instructions on how to use silica gel, meal and borax, perlite aggregate, sand and borax, glycerine and water to create attractive permanent flower arrangements. 12 illustrations. 32pp. 5⅜ x 8½. 21802-3 Pa. $1.00

EASY-TO-MAKE BIRD FEEDERS FOR WOODWORKERS, Scott D. Campbell. Detailed, simple-to-use guide for designing, constructing, caring for and using feeders. Text, illustrations for 12 classic and contemporary designs. 96pp. 5⅜ x 8½. 25847-5 Pa. $3.95

SCOTTISH WONDER TALES FROM MYTH AND LEGEND, Donald A. Mackenzie. 16 lively tales tell of giants rumbling down mountainsides, of a magic wand that turns stone pillars into warriors, of gods and goddesses, evil hags, powerful forces and more. 240pp. 5⅜ x 8½. 29677-6 Pa. $6.95

THE HISTORY OF UNDERCLOTHES, C. Willett Cunnington and Phyllis Cunnington. Fascinating, well-documented survey covering six centuries of English undergarments, enhanced with over 100 illustrations: 12th-century laced-up bodice, footed long drawers (1795), 19th-century bustles, 19th-century corsets for men, Victorian "bust improvers," much more. 272pp. 5⅜ x 8¼. 27124-2 Pa. $9.95

ARTS AND CRAFTS FURNITURE: The Complete Brooks Catalog of 1912, Brooks Manufacturing Co. Photos and detailed descriptions of more than 150 now very collectible furniture designs from the Arts and Crafts movement depict davenports, settees, buffets, desks, tables, chairs, bedsteads, dressers and more, all built of solid, quarter-sawed oak. Invaluable for students and enthusiasts of antiques, Americana and the decorative arts. 80pp. 6½ x 9¼. 27471-3 Pa. $8.95

HOW WE INVENTED THE AIRPLANE: An Illustrated History, Orville Wright. Fascinating firsthand account covers early experiments, construction of planes and motors, first flights, much more. Introduction and commentary by Fred C. Kelly. 76 photographs. 96pp. 8¼ x 11. 25662-6 Pa. $8.95

THE ARTS OF THE SAILOR: Knotting, Splicing and Ropework, Hervey Garrett Smith. Indispensable shipboard reference covers tools, basic knots and useful hitches; handsewing and canvas work, more. Over 100 illustrations. Delightful reading for sea lovers. 256pp. 5⅜ x 8½. 26440-8 Pa. $8.95

FRANK LLOYD WRIGHT'S FALLINGWATER: The House and Its History, Second, Revised Edition, Donald Hoffmann. A total revision—both in text and illustrations—of the standard document on Fallingwater, the boldest, most personal architectural statement of Wright's mature years, updated with valuable new material from the recently opened Frank Lloyd Wright Archives. "Fascinating"—*The New York Times*. 116 illustrations. 128pp. 9¼ x 10¾. 27430-6 Pa. $12.95

AUTOBIOGRAPHY: The Story of My Experiments with Truth, Mohandas K. Gandhi. Boyhood, legal studies, purification, the growth of the Satyagraha (nonviolent protest) movement. Critical, inspiring work of the man responsible for the freedom of India. 480pp. 5⅜ x 8½. (USO) 24593-4 Pa. $8.95

CELTIC MYTHS AND LEGENDS, T. W. Rolleston. Masterful retelling of Irish and Welsh stories and tales. Cuchulain, King Arthur, Deirdre, the Grail, many more. First paperback edition. 58 full-page illustrations. 512pp. 5⅜ x 8½. 26507-2 Pa. $9.95

THE PRINCIPLES OF PSYCHOLOGY, William James. Famous long course complete, unabridged. Stream of thought, time perception, memory, experimental methods; great work decades ahead of its time. 94 figures. 1,391pp. 5⅜ x 8½. 2-vol. set.
Vol. I: 20381-6 Pa. $13.95
Vol. II: 20382-4 Pa. $14.95

THE WORLD AS WILL AND REPRESENTATION, Arthur Schopenhauer. Definitive English translation of Schopenhauer's life work, correcting more than 1,000 errors, omissions in earlier translations. Translated by E. F. J. Payne. Total of 1,269pp. 5⅜ x 8½. 2-vol. set.
Vol. 1: 21761-2 Pa. $12.95
Vol. 2: 21762-0 Pa. $12.95

MAGIC AND MYSTERY IN TIBET, Madame Alexandra David-Neel. Experiences among lamas, magicians, sages, sorcerers, Bonpa wizards. A true psychic discovery. 32 illustrations. 321pp. 5⅜ x 8½. (USO) 22682-4 Pa. $9.95

THE EGYPTIAN BOOK OF THE DEAD, E. A. Wallis Budge. Complete reproduction of Ani's papyrus, finest ever found. Full hieroglyphic text, interlinear transliteration, word-for-word translation, smooth translation. 533pp. 6½ x 9¼.
21866-X Pa. $11.95

MATHEMATICS FOR THE NONMATHEMATICIAN, Morris Kline. Detailed, college-level treatment of mathematics in cultural and historical context, with numerous exercises. Recommended Reading Lists. Tables. Numerous figures. 641pp. 5⅜ x 8½.
24823-2 Pa. $11.95

THEORY OF WING SECTIONS: Including a Summary of Airfoil Data, Ira H. Abbott and A. E. von Doenhoff. Concise compilation of subsonic aerodynamic characteristics of NACA wing sections, plus description of theory. 350pp. of tables. 693pp. 5⅜ x 8½. 60586-8 Pa. $14.95

THE RIME OF THE ANCIENT MARINER, Gustave Doré, S. T. Coleridge. Doré's finest work; 34 plates capture moods, subtleties of poem. Flawless full-size reproductions printed on facing pages with authoritative text of poem. "Beautiful. Simply beautiful."–Publisher's Weekly. 77pp. 9¼ x 12. 22305-1 Pa. $7.95

NORTH AMERICAN INDIAN DESIGNS FOR ARTISTS AND CRAFTSPEOPLE, Eva Wilson. Over 360 authentic copyright-free designs adapted from Navajo blankets, Hopi pottery, Sioux buffalo hides, more. Geometrics, symbolic figures, plant and animal motifs, etc. 128pp. 8⅜ x 11. (EUK) 25341-4 Pa. $8.95

SCULPTURE: Principles and Practice, Louis Slobodkin. Step-by-step approach to clay, plaster, metals, stone; classical and modern. 253 drawings, photos. 255pp. 8⅛ x 11.
22960-2 Pa. $11.95

THE INFLUENCE OF SEA POWER UPON HISTORY, 1660–1783, A. T. Mahan. Influential classic of naval history and tactics still used as text in war colleges. First paperback edition. 4 maps. 24 battle plans. 640pp. 5⅜ x 8½. 25509-3 Pa. $14.95

THE STORY OF THE TITANIC AS TOLD BY ITS SURVIVORS, Jack Winocour (ed.). What it was really like. Panic, despair, shocking inefficiency, and a little heroism. More thrilling than any fictional account. 26 illustrations. 320pp. 5⅜ x 8½. 20610-6 Pa. $8.95

FAIRY AND FOLK TALES OF THE IRISH PEASANTRY, William Butler Yeats (ed.). Treasury of 64 tales from the twilight world of Celtic myth and legend: "The Soul Cages," "The Kildare Pooka," "King O'Toole and his Goose," many more. Introduction and Notes by W. B. Yeats. 352pp. 5⅜ x 8½. 26941-8 Pa. $8.95

BUDDHIST MAHAYANA TEXTS, E. B. Cowell and Others (eds.). Superb, accurate translations of basic documents in Mahayana Buddhism, highly important in history of religions. The Buddha-karita of Asvaghosha, Larger Sukhavativyuha, more. 448pp. 5⅜ x 8½. 25552-2 Pa. $12.95

ONE TWO THREE . . . INFINITY: Facts and Speculations of Science, George Gamow. Great physicist's fascinating, readable overview of contemporary science: number theory, relativity, fourth dimension, entropy, genes, atomic structure, much more. 128 illustrations. Index. 352pp. 5⅜ x 8½. 25664-2 Pa. $8.95

ENGINEERING IN HISTORY, Richard Shelton Kirby, et al. Broad, nontechnical survey of history's major technological advances: birth of Greek science, industrial revolution, electricity and applied science, 20th-century automation, much more. 181 illustrations. ". . . excellent . . ."–*Isis.* Bibliography. vii + 530pp. 5⅜ x 8¼. 26412-2 Pa. $14.95

DALÍ ON MODERN ART: The Cuckolds of Antiquated Modern Art, Salvador Dalí. Influential painter skewers modern art and its practitioners. Outrageous evaluations of Picasso, Cézanne, Turner, more. 15 renderings of paintings discussed. 44 calligraphic decorations by Dalí. 96pp. 5⅜ x 8½. (USO) 29220-7 Pa. $4.95

ANTIQUE PLAYING CARDS: A Pictorial History, Henry René D'Allemagne. Over 900 elaborate, decorative images from rare playing cards (14th–20th centuries): Bacchus, death, dancing dogs, hunting scenes, royal coats of arms, players cheating, much more. 96pp. 9¼ x 12¼. 29265-7 Pa. $12.95

MAKING FURNITURE MASTERPIECES: 30 Projects with Measured Drawings, Franklin H. Gottshall. Step-by-step instructions, illustrations for constructing handsome, useful pieces, among them a Sheraton desk, Chippendale chair, Spanish desk, Queen Anne table and a William and Mary dressing mirror. 224pp. 8⅛ x 11¼. 29338-6 Pa. $13.95

THE FOSSIL BOOK: A Record of Prehistoric Life, Patricia V. Rich et al. Profusely illustrated definitive guide covers everything from single-celled organisms and dinosaurs to birds and mammals and the interplay between climate and man. Over 1,500 illustrations. 760pp. 7½ x 10⅛. 29371-8 Pa. $29.95

Prices subject to change without notice.

Available at your book dealer or write for free catalog to Dept. GI, Dover Publications, Inc., 31 East 2nd St., Mineola, N.Y. 11501. Dover publishes more than 500 books each year on science, elementary and advanced mathematics, biology, music, art, literary history, social sciences and other areas.